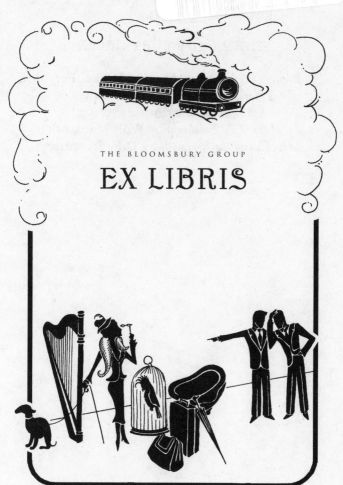

THE BLOOMSBURY GROUP

EX LIBRIS

THE BLOOMSBURY GROUP

A NOTE ON THE AUTHOR

FRANK BAKER was born in Hornsey, London in 1908 and was educated at Winchester Cathedral School. A keen musician, Baker enjoyed singing in choir and playing the piano. After moving to Cornwall he made a living as an organist, earning £1 per week. There he wrote his first novel, *The Twisted Tree* (1935).

In 1939 his most successful novel, *Miss Hargreaves*, was published. It was consequently reprinted several times and was adapted for the stage in 1952 at the Royal Court Theatre Club in London, with Dame Margaret Rutherford in the leading role. The novel has also been adapted for the radio.

Baker then became a professional actor and toured during the Second World War. He later worked at the Old Vic and was an accompanist at the Players Theatre in London. After moving to Cardiff, Baker worked as a script editor and playwright for the BBC and continued to write more novels and several short stories. Over the course of his lifetime he published fifteen novels, including *The Birds* (1936), and three works of non-fiction, of which his final book was *The Call of Cornwall* (1976). He was also a contributor to the *Guardian* and the *Radio Times*.

Frank Baker died in 1983 at the family home in Cornwall.

All papers used by Bloomsbury USA are natural, recyclable products made
from wood grown in well-managed forests. The manufacturing processes
conform to the environmental regulations of the country of origin.

LIBRARY OF CONGRESS CATALOGING-IN-PUBLICATION DATA HAS BEEN
APPLIED FOR.

ISBN 978-1-60819-051-5

First published in 1940 by Eyre and Spottiswoode
This paperback edition published in 2010 by Bloomsbury USA

10 9 8 7 6 5 4 3

Typeset by Macmillan Publishing Solutions
Printed in the United States of America by Quad/Graphics Fairfield

Miss Hargreaves

A Novel

Frank Baker

NEW YORK · BERLIN · LONDON

To
Jimmy
without whom it could not have happened

NOTE

The correct pronunciation of her name is, of course, 'Hargrayves'. Astonishing as it must seem, there exist people who refer to her as Miss 'Hargreeves'. Doubtless they belong to the ranks of those who 'Macleen' their teeth.

F.B.

'Creative thought creates . . .'

(FROM THE POSTCARD
BY A.F.W.)

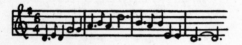

Over the sea to Skye . . .

PROLOGUE

'MISS HARGREAVES - ' I murmured. 'Miss Hargreaves - ?'
I leant over the rail and looked into the darkness
of the Irish Sea. It was night. The lights of our boat were
the only lights upon the black water. No answer came from
the sea as I murmured that name. And yet, it seemed to me
that very faintly in the cold December air, in the wind,
I could hear the sighing of my own name. 'Norman -
Norman - Norman - '

* * *

Nine years have passed since that night, the night which
saw the end of a great adventure. I wrote an account of it
all and kept it locked up, showing it to nobody but Henry,
Marjorie and my father. In those days I was a lay-clerk in
the choir of Cornford Cathedral, and I used to study the
organ under Dr Carless. I was, and I dare say I still am, in
every way but one, a perfectly ordinary sort of a fellow. You
want to know in what particular way I differ from other
people? You must read this book to find that out. Were you
to look at me, you'd say there was nothing exceptional
about me; merely Norman Huntley, who used to live at 38
London Road, Cornford, with his parents and his sister Jim.
Thirty-two I am now, and possibly a little wiser than the
youth who leant over the rail of the Belfast boat that
December night, murmuring a lost name upon the wind.

A lost name . . . a lost name. But, maybe, you are one of
those who remember? I don't live in Cornford now. I run

a bookshop in the West of England. I'm not going to be more definite than that: I went there to get away from publicity and I don't want any more of it. Marjorie, my wife, often hears from her parents, and my mother also writes to give me the Cornford news. I have her last letter before me:

' . . . people still talk about Miss Hargreaves and some of them are silly enough to believe she must have been something to do with the I.R.A. What an extraordinary business it all was and how I do wish, dear boy, you would tell us what you *really* know. A shadow comes over me whenever I think of her. I can never quite get over your having to leave the town as you did - though, as you know, dear, nothing would even make me begin to believe the wicked things they said about you. I happened to meet the Dean in the shop the other day and he asked quite kindly about you. Think he would really like you to come back. Why don't you write to him? It all happened so long ago now . . . '

Go back? Back to Cornford? Yes, I want to go back to that lovely cathedral, back to the Thames meadows where Henry and I went fishing as boys. But can I bear, even now, to face it?

I remember the last occasion I was in Cornford Cathedral. The Dean had most politely suggested it would be better for me to resign - meaning it would be better for the Cathedral and him. Too much was being said about me, and although the police could never prove a thing (there was no body, of course) suspicion fastened on me as closely as lichen to an old apple tree.

My bags were all packed; I was glad to go. On my last morning, before breakfast, as had been my habit, I went to the Cathedral, there for the last time to play the organ. I went through the Bach B Minor Fantasia, but it sounded empty to me. Stricken by a sense of the unrecoverable past, I played a movement of a Mendelssohn sonata, increasing my registration to full organ at the end. Raising my hands from the keys sharply, I listened to the sound chasing itself in and out of the nave; I half hoped that, as the sound died away, I should hear a voice crying from below, 'Bravo! Oh, bravo, Norman!'

But there was no voice. I came down from the loft, went along the nave, unlocked the west door to the roof and climbed up, hardly knowing what I wanted to do. Slowly I traced my steps over the narrow plankway. Like great beeskeps the domes over the nave arches rose up in a long chain before me. It was cold. Everything shrouded in a green, gloomy light. I stood there for a few minutes, half afraid. I wanted to call her name. But my tongue was dry; I could make no sound.

That day I left Cornford and came to live in the West. The town of my youth, of my birth, had become unbearable to me; in all these years I have never once revisited it.

Perhaps I shall go back now. Her name is dying to a legend. Soon, for memory is fickle, she will be forgotten.

Forgotten? But that, too, is unbearable. Shall it be said of her, 'but some there be that have no memorial'? Not while I am alive.

So I offer the reader this account of a mystery which he may remember if he reads his newspapers. It was written years ago, part of it in Ulster, and reading through it now I see no reason to alter much of it. I offer these pages solely as a memorial to a person I loved. Let the reader call me a liar; let him examine my family history for signs of queer-ness; I am prepared for that.

All that I ask of him is this: that if I chance to meet him in any house where toasts are drunk, he will raise his glass with me and say:

'God bless Miss Hargreaves!'

WHEN I wrote essays at school I was always told to begin at the beginning and end at the end. I'm not at all sure that this story *has* an end. As for a beginning - well, in my opinion it really begins - as I began - with my father. Anyway that's where I'm going to start.

Let me introduce you to him. Cornelius Huntley, rather a speciality of Cornford in every way. He runs a bookshop in the town. If you know the place you're almost certain to know number 17 Wells Street, the little street branching off from the old market hall in Disraeli Square.

Huntley's bookshop is as well known as the Cathedral. Most days I work there with father, except when I'm studying music. We sell everything, modern and old, any language you like. Though I say it myself, Cornelius Huntley knows a good deal more about books than you'd imagine from his rather muddled talk.

At this point I think Henry comes in. Henry Beddow is my oldest friend; at school together, and so on. He's my age, but he's much more of a lad than I am. Dark hair and eyes, fine teeth, and a swaggering sort of style that could get him into Buckingham Palace. A fine footballer and swimmer. I never was any good at football. I once made a phenomenal effort and scored a goal; unfortunately it was at the wrong end of the field. Rather embarrassing.

The real link between Henry and me is that we both have a pretty fanciful imagination. We like to use it, too. I'll tell you a story about that, which seems to me to have a bearing on the future, though I don't want to turn this book into an autobiography.

When we were kids, Henry and I were sent off to Cathedral together on Sunday mornings. Our parents used to go in the evenings. Well, after a bit we got tired of spending this hour and a half in Cathedral on fine summer mornings. One Sunday - they were doing the Litany - we cut, and spent the time fishing for eels. While we fished we made up the sermon, knowing we should be asked what it was about, as we always were.

'So long as we've got a good text,' remarked Henry, 'they won't bother much about the rest. They always want to know the text.'

I thought. Then suddenly I said, 'What about "They also serve who only stand and wait"?'

'Spiffing!' said Henry.

'I don't know where it comes from,' I said.

'Say Isaiah,' suggested Henry. 'All the bits people remember come from Isaiah.'

Well, apart from father suggesting it was queer to choose a text from Wordsworth, it went down like a lozenge. The queer thing is this. The following Sunday we went to Matins because it was raining and there didn't seem anything else much to do. Believe me or not, but Canon Mercer - who was rather what they'd call a Modernist - did actually preach a sermon on that text. I don't know which was the worse shock: hearing our yarn actually come true or realizing we'd credited the Bible with a line of Milton's.

Later, partly because I wanted to point out that he'd been wrong about Wordsworth, I owned up to father. He said a very queer thing. 'Always be careful, my boy, what you make up. Life's more full of things made up on the Spur of the Moment than most people realize. Beware of the Spur of the Moment. It may turn and rend you.'

I often think father's warning only spurred me on to fresh and more daring inventions. At any rate I got into the habit of making up stories, sometimes inventing people I'd never met or heard of, simply for the fun of doing it. Henry was generally my accomplice; he lacked initiative himself but he was always very good at developing my themes. One occasion I made up an ancestor called Dr Philip Hayes; he was, I said, the fattest organist at Oxford University who wrote anthems and kept does. Later on they did an anthem of his at the Cathedral. Funny thing is, I really can't remember now whether the old boy is an ancestor of mine or not.

Call me a raging liar if you like, although it's an actual fact that I've never lied in order to get *out* of things so much as to get *into* things. Sometimes I think all those books in father's shop led me astray. Books *do* lead you on. I mean, look at father. If any man revels in the intoxication of the Spur more than he does, I should like to meet him. I shouldn't like to say how many times I've heard him talking to customers about places he's never visited, and he's developed a really amazing flair for finding out first whether *they've* been there. I've heard him talking expansively about the West Indies, Mount Everest (*not* the top; he was careful to halt at about 15,000 feet), Finland, the Amazon and the Eiffel Tower. Actually, he was born in Cornford and never went farther east than London (I think he climbed the Monument), south than the Channel Islands, west than Plymouth. He never went north at all.

That's father, and I suppose I inherit something from him.

*   *   *

Like me, Henry works in his father's business, a big garage and motor mechanic in the High Street. He's learning the business from the bottom, his father being a believer in not missing out any rungs in the ladder, and so on. 'No royal road to success,' he's always saying.

Last August Henry asked me if I'd like to go to Ulster with him. A cousin of his had offered to lend him his house and car for a month.

'There's an old witch who keeps house for him, and of course it's topping country, mountains and things. What do you say? The bus is a Hillman.'

Of course I said yes. We went.

Lusk, where Cousin Bill lives, is only a street, very wide, like most of those Irish villages, two rows of houses, four shops, a church and a pub - not open on Sundays unless you know the local password. We were really miles from anywhere.

The house lay in a valley with a river quite near and corn-fields all round. There were white turkeys, a monkey-puzzle tree and quite a lot of gravel in the garden. Not much furniture in the house; it smelt rather of oil-lamps and dogs. Cousin Bill's housekeeper had a room in the back some-where; in bed when we arrived and didn't seem to know who we were for some time. She was very old, with teeth that strayed about, and a high-pitched, fluty sort of voice. There was no food in the house except mustard-coloured bread, home-made, which tasted sour.

I'm not going to tell you much about the holiday except to say it was a grand month and we enjoyed every bit of it even though it rained much of the time. We went miles in the car, swam in the river, messed about in an old tub of a boat belonging to a farmer; and we spent a good many evenings in the hotel at Dungannon, drinking Irish whiskey and flirting with a cheeky girl Henry rather fell for. We climbed the Mourne Mountains and sang the right song on the top, though we couldn't remember the words.

For some reason we hardly ever stopped to look at Lusk itself. Henry had dismissed it in a minute, 'A one-eyed place.' I must say, it did seem to look at you sideways. But on our last evening we suddenly decided we'd treated it rather unfairly.

For once, instead of using the car, we'd been walking all day. About seven in the evening we turned back into Lusk on our way home. We were just passing the church, an ugly flint building with a savage-looking square tower, when Henry said:

'I think we ought to look into the church. There might be some brasses worth seeing.'

'I hate brasses,' I said, 'but still, I see your point.'

'We ought just to see what it's like.'

'I can see,' I said.

'There might be something interesting inside,' said Henry obstinately.

The sky had blackened over and it was beginning to rain.

'We might as well shelter there as anywhere else,' added Henry. 'Come on. Don't look so gloomy.'

'I hate Lusk,' I complained. 'I feel it's got its knife into us somehow.'

And really, you know, I couldn't help feeling it was haunted by something, particularly just then, with that great black cloud hanging over it, not one single person in the senselessly wide street, rows of slaty houses, a butcher's shop with only a chopper in the window, and an immense oak tree bang in the middle of the road, penned in by iron railings as though to prevent it from straying. I couldn't see what business it had there at all.

Well, before we could say any more, the rain began to pour down, so I ran after Henry up the gravel drive to the west porch.

'Damn,' said Henry. 'Place is locked.'

'Oh, well,' I said happily, 'that settles that.' I don't know why, but I was growing more and more reluctant to go into the church. 'Let's wait here,' I suggested, 'till the rain stops, then go home, take the car to Dungannon and have a last binge at the County Hotel.'

Here Henry's obstinacy comes in.

'One of the other doors might be open,' he said. He darted round the tower and I heard him rattling the handle of the north door. 'No good,' he complained when he came back. 'I reckon they ought to be ashamed of themselves, locking churches.'

'Why shouldn't they lock them?'

'Well, look how inconvenient it is for people wanting to shelter from the rain. Besides, it's bad for religion, definitely bad.'

Actually, the rain was easing off a bit by now.

'Come on,' I said, 'we'd better get back before another shower.'

'No,' said Henry. 'I don't see why they should lock us out of this horrible building, I'm damned if I do.'

'It's not *your* church,' I argued.

'It's everybody's church,' maintained Henry.

'No,' I said, 'it's Ireland's church. It says so on the board.'

'Well, we're in Ireland, aren't we? I'm going to see if I can get the key.'

CHAPTER ONE

We were just brewing up to a proper row when a man came round the corner with a broom and a wheelbarrow. He looked disappointed, but perhaps it was only his squint. You felt he craved for admiration; very lonely face it was. He was wearing a green baize apron and he had a grave-digging manner. I mean, he gazed at you obviously relating you to the earth and wondering how you'd fit.

'Are you the sexton?' asked Henry.

Yes, he was. Did the gentlemen wish to see the church? There was a pleading quality in his voice. I don't suppose that once in a century anybody had ever wanted to see anything more of Lusk church than they could see from the street.

'That's exactly what we are wanting,' said Henry.

'Speak for yourself,' I muttered, looking gloomily at the dead leaves in the barrow. I felt disconsolate. There was a woebegone air over everything; end-of-holiday feeling.

'My friend,' remarked Henry, with disgusting brightness, 'is very interested in old churches.'

It was amazing how quickly that sexton cheered up, smiling hideously at me as though he had discovered an old friend.

'You have come,' he said, 'to the right place. For this is a *very* old church, dedicated by the Bishop of Armagh in 1863. Before I was born.'

From somewhere about him, under the apron, he produced a colossal key. Unlocking the door, he threw it open with a flourish of triumph. Inside the porch he almost feverishly dragged apart some heavy red curtains, alive with dust and sooty fleurs-de-lis. Hurling himself on an inner door, he flung out an arm and, like a conjurer producing a rabbit, invited our inspection and admiration.

We went inside.

'My God!' I said.

'Kindly remember where you are, Norman,' said Henry.

I will say this about Lusk church: it was bad enough to be reasonably funny, which was something.

Squint, before we could turn back, seized our arms and dragged us down the nave, rapturously commenting upon the treasures of which he was guardian.

'We are very proud of our beautiful pews, very handsome pieces of wood, I will say.'

I touched one and shivered. They were made of fumed oak and they had doors with rusty bolts to them. Very tall they were; you felt there ought to be hay in them. I looked up to the galleries. Apart from the usual cleaner's brooms and pails the only curiosity was a stack of card-tables piled in one corner. I turned to the chancel, hoping to find something - however slight - that I could praise. But it was worse up there. Seaweed-green altar frontal; dead flowers; lichenous-looking brass candlesticks; pitch-pine organ with a pyramid of dumb pipes soaring over a candle-greased console; 'Sanctus, Sanctus, Sanctus', splashed in chrome Gothic lettering over the choir walls; mural cherubim reminding you of cottonwool chicks from Easter eggs; very stained glass; tattered hymn-books, tattered hassocks - it was a horrible church. But there were, mercifully, two redeeming features: those were the dust-sheets spread over lectern and pulpit. Somehow you felt a little safer with those dust-sheets.

Meanwhile, Squint was rhapsodizing.

'I beg you to observe the beautiful lettering and decoration on the chancel wall. "I saw the Lord sitting upon a Throne." You like it?'

He had a habit of hissing like a goose, particularly when he was eager about something.

'Very pretty indeed,' I said.

'Original,' said Henry.

'*Unusual*, in a sense.'

'Full of feeling.'

'Filthy,' I said.

'The font,' said Henry hurriedly, glaring at me, 'is superb.'

'The choir screen,' I added, 'is definitely in a class by itself.'

'We think,' said Squint simply, folding his hands and looking modestly at the ground, 'we think that the whole church is in a class by itself.'

We proceeded step by step up the nave towards the lectern. It grew darker; we could hear the rain pattering on the roof. My spirits sank. There was something so unutterably depressing about the place. The sexton was standing by the draped lectern, one hand on the corner of the sheet, waiting for us to approach so that he might unveil what I knew could only be a fresh horror.

'Here,' whispered Henry, 'this place is awful. Let's get out quickly.'

'All very well for you to talk like that,' I muttered, 'but you started it. We've got to go through with it now.'

Patiently, Squint waited by the lectern. It's hard to explain the awful sinking feeling that had come over Henry and me. 'A day we shall never forget,' I told myself. And as I said it, I thought, 'Well, you might as well make it really memorable. Get some fun out of this while you're about it.'

Some *fun*. Oh, God! If I had only *known*!

Suddenly the sexton whipped aside the dust-sheet and disclosed the lectern, obviously a favourite of his. We saw an avaricious-looking brass fowl with one eye cocked sideways as though it feared somebody were going to bag the Bible - or perhaps as though it hoped somebody were going to. You couldn't quite tell; it had an ambiguous expression.

'Now this,' said Squint, 'this most distinctive lectern was presented by members of the congregation in memory of the late Reverend Mr Archer, vicar here for forty years who died in 1925.' He hissed and glared at us. 'You will be kind enough to read the inscription. Mr Archer was a good man.'

'Dear Mr Archer,' I said.

No more. Said it without thinking much. Didn't even realize that I had sown the seed.

'Dear Mr Archer.' Like that. Nothing more. Queer how those three simple words affected the sexton.

'You,' he teethed eagerly, 'were a friend of the late very beloved Reverend Mr Archer?'

I was cautious.

'By no means,' I said. 'But I have heard a lot about him. Haven't I, Henry?'

'You bet we have,' said Henry cheerily. He was always very quick in this way.

'Oh, but, indeed,' screamed the sexton in a frenzy of delight, whipping off the dust-sheet from the pulpit - 'a friend of Mr Archer's is a friend of Lusk.'

I fondled the tail-feathers of the bird half absently.

'I wish to emphasize,' I said, 'that I never knew Mr Archer *personally*. But I have a great friend who knew him well in his' - I peered at the brass plate - 'in his Cambridge days,' I added.

'Oxford,' said Henry, annoyingly going off on his own track.

'I said Cambridge,' I remarked acidly, 'and Cambridge I meant.'

The sexton seemed not to hear us. 'Mr Archer was our best-beloved pastor,' he said, speaking in a dreamy hiss, through his nose like a Welsh *hwyl*. 'There was not a man more respected. He was a darling man, most free with his money. And his daughters - ah! They were the lovely creatures and all!'

CHAPTER ONE

'Let me see,' I said, biting my lip reminiscently and looking at the roof, 'there were four, weren't there?'

'Three,' said the sexton.

I frowned. 'Surely - four?' It was annoying to be contradicted.

'Yes, you are right, sir,' cried the sexton. 'Four it is - four beautiful creatures. There was Miss Emily, there was Miss Angela, Miss Dorothea, and - and - ' He paused and looked at me suspiciously. 'There were only three!' he snapped suddenly.

'Surely,' I corrected gently, 'you are forgetting Miss Seraphica?'

'Miss Seraphica,' said Henry gravely, 'was - alas! - always overlooked.'

'Consistently overlooked. She died,' I reminded him, 'in *complete* obscurity.'

'Maybe I forget,' sighed Squint. 'My poor memory is not so good as once it was.'

Thanking God for his poor memory, I asked him what had become of Mr Archer's surviving daughters.

'Miss Emily,' he said, 'teaches in Belfast. Every Christmas she writes to me, the darling lady. Miss Angela married an army gentleman called - called - '

Henry quickly took advantage of the poor memory.

'Major Road?' he suggested, 'M.C.'

'Possibly,' said the sexton. 'And Miss Dorothea went to live in America with an aunt. She was the most beautiful one. Gone!' He waved his arm mournfully.

'Baltimore?' I murmured.

'That is so,' said the sexton.

I sighed. 'Dear, dear! For so long I have looked forward to seeing Mr Archer's church. And now - here we are! Something very moving about it, isn't there, Henry?'

Henry touched his eye with his handkerchief and declared that he had never been so moved.

'If I had been told,' said the sexton, 'that two gentlemen would come into this church this evening who knew Mr Archer, I would not have believed it. No, I would not! Holy God - no!'

I reminded him again that I had never known Mr Archer personally. But he ignored this and went on to talk about the Communion plate.

'It is,' he said, 'of the very finest beaten gold, studded with onyx, opals and agate. You will please to follow and I will show you. It was Mr Archer's gift to the church. Holy God, it is beautiful plate!'

We followed him to the vestry, feeling much less depressed. While we examined the plate I spun a few more fancies concerning Mr Archer. He had edited, I suggested, a hymn-book and been fond of fishing. The sexton, after a little encouragement, readily agreed.

About twenty minutes later we came to the west door, still talking enthusiastically of the late vicar. Henry stood a little apart from us, uneasily smothering laughter into a handkerchief. He's like that, I'm afraid; not completely reliable.

'And now,' said Squint, 'you will please to give me your name so that I may tell Miss Angela when I next write that a friend of her darling reverend father has - '

'I did *not* know Mr Archer myself,' I snapped.

Immediately the sexton's happy smile vanished and an angry flush came over his face.

'You did not know Mr Archer,' he hissed, 'and, Holy God, there was I showing you the Communion plate!'

'My friend,' I explained, 'she knew him.'

His face brightened. 'Ah. Your friend! And what is his name?'

'A *lady*,' I corrected sharply. For one second I paused. Then, 'Miss Hargreaves,' I said. 'Miss - *Connie* Hargreaves,' I added.

It seemed to me there was a sort of stirring of air in the church, like - like what? Rather like someone opening a very old umbrella. I looked round sharply, but couldn't see anything unusual. A ray of feeble sun had broken through the dark clouds and was shining down on the dust in the galleries. I realized I was trembling. Sweating too. No doubt about it. I was precariously poised on the Spur of the Moment. Father's ancient warning came back to me. No good now. When you're on the Spur you can't go back. I wiped my brow with my handkerchief and smiled at the sexton. I knew I was powerless to move except in one direction.

'Miss Connie Hargreaves,' echoed Henry.

'Miss Connie Hargreaves,' re-echoed the sexton.

'Who lives in Rutlandshire,' I added.

'And knew Mr Archer many, many years ago,' said Henry; 'long before daylight saving and such things.'

'Childhood friends,' I continued happily. I could feel I was getting into my stride. 'They had never once met since those happy far-off days. Many are the stories - many, many are the stories - delightful and otherwise - that Miss Hargreaves has told me about Mr Archer.'

'And this lady, this Miss Hargreaves, she is still alive?'

'Ten minutes old, precisely,' said Henry.

I trod on his toe brutally.

'The soul of youth,' I said. 'She is a poet,' I added dreamily.

'She would be an old lady,' said Squint. 'Over eighty.'

'Nearer ninety,' said Henry.

'A touch of rheumatoid arthritis,' I said, 'but no more than a touch.'

We began to wander out of the church at last.

'You must give me your friend's address,' said the sexton, 'so that I may tell Miss Angela. The darling lady likes to keep in touch with the Reverend's old connections.'

I took out my pocket-book and wrote.

'Henry,' I said, 'is it 28 or 29 Dawsington Road, Oakham?'

'Oh,' he said easily, 'she's too well known to bother about the number. In any case, the name of the house - Sable Lodge - is more than sufficient.'

'Of course,' I murmured. I wrote on the paper: 'Miss Constance Hargreaves, Sable Lodge, Oakham, Rutlandshire,' and handed it to the sexton.

'This is a happy day,' he said as we walked slowly away down the drive.

'A niece of the Duke of Grosvenor,' remarked Henry.

'And writes poetry,' I emphasized.

* * *

'Oh, bravo, Norman!' said Henry when we'd finished laughing. 'I already feel as though I've known her all my life.'

I was modest. 'I can't take the entire credit for her,' I said. 'Your bits helped enormously.'

'I suppose you agree to her connection with Grosvenor?'

'Oh, definitely! That was first class. Full marks.'

'Still, she's entirely your creation.'

'Yes. I'm afraid she is,' I said.

'Why afraid?'

'Oh, I don't know.'

A beggarman wandered up the street, playing 'Over the sea to Skye' on a melancholy penny whistle. I gave him sixpence and caught Henry's arm. 'Let's get on to Dungannon,' I said.

* * *

CHAPTER ONE

The rest of that evening we spent at Dungannon. Miss Hargreaves was the topic of conversation all the time. We found, after several glasses of sherry, that she was a far more widely travelled and more accomplished lady than we had originally supposed.

'Of course,' said Henry, 'she always winters in the South of France.'

'Wonderful,' I said, 'how she takes her cockatoo about. It's gone with her everywhere.'

'You mean Hector?'

'Dr Pepusch,' I corrected. 'Hector, you remember, died of psittacosis.'

Henry wrinkled his brow. 'Dr Pepusch?'

'M'm,' I said. 'Dr Pepusch, you remember - who wrote the *Beggar's Opera* - had a parrot who used to sing an air from one of Handel's operas. Miss Hargreaves named her bird after him. She's a keen musician.'

'I should like to know who this dame is you two keep talking about,' said the girl behind the bar.

'No dame about her,' said Henry. 'This is a niece of the Duke of Grosvenor. So kindly be careful what you say.'

The girl seemed rather impressed.

Henry drained his glass. 'Horsy?' he murmured.

'No. Doggy,' I said. 'She keeps a Bedlington; a lady Bedlington by the name of Sarah. Don't you remember how she forgot herself in one of the Duke's grandfather clocks?'

'What beautiful little water-colours those were that she used to paint,' mused Henry, tipping his glass up and holding it out to the girl to be filled.

'She is more of a poet than a painter,' I reminded him. 'Some of her lyrics - do you remember *Wayside Bundle?* - bid fair to rival the immortal Ella.'

'You mean Wheeler W.?'

'Just so. Another sherry, please, miss.'

'She has more than a mere taste for music, eh?'

'Oh, yes! A born musician. It occurs to me, incidentally,' I added, 'that it was perhaps a mistake to give the sexton her home address.'

'Oh? Is she away from home, then?'

'Undoubtedly. She will just have left for the Three Choirs Festival. She has never been known to miss it.'

'How stupid of me to forget!'

Henry asked the girl to fetch him an A.A. Guide.

'Where is the Festival being held this year?' he asked me.

'Hereford.'

I turned over the pages of the guide, then snapped it to with an air of finality.

'I suppose, as usual,' I remarked, 'she will be staying at the Manor Court Hotel?'

'Oh, it's almost a second home to her,' he agreed. 'Any mention made, by the way, of charges for dogs?'

'M'm. Two-and-six a day.'

'How many stars?'

'Five.'

'Pity. Ought to be six. Cockatoos mentioned?'

'Not mentioned. But of course she has had a special arrangement with the management for a great many years.'

We were silent for a little while. I think we were impressed with ourselves and each other; but most especially we were impressed by Miss Hargreaves.

'I suppose,' I mused, 'she will go on to Bath as usual?'

'I see nothing to prevent her,' said Henry.

Neither did I.

*   *   *

CHAPTER ONE

Just as I was drawing the sheets over my head, feeling a bit hazy, Henry - who never can leave a good joke where it is - poked his head round the door.

'You ought to write to her,' he said, 'and tell her we've at last seen Mr Archer's church. She'd be so pleased.'

'Of course,' I murmured. 'I'll do it to-morrow.'

*   *   *

'As from 38 London Road, Cornford, Bucks.

September 2nd

'DEAR MISS HARGREAVES,

'I'm afraid it is some time since I wrote you, but now that I am on the point of returning from a holiday in Northern Ireland, I feel that I must send you a line from a place so intimately bound up with memories of your old friend Mr Archer. You have told me so much about him that I almost felt, when I stood in Lusk church yesterday, that I had known him myself. The sexton was overjoyed to hear news of you, although he did not actually remember your name.

'What of you, my dear old friend? I am assuming that, as usual, you will be attending the Choirs Festival and I am therefore addressing this to the Manor Court Hotel at Hereford which I know you always patronize. Do let me hear from you. Will you be going to Bath as usual?

'Any time you care to come and stay with us at Cornford you will be more than welcome. My mother and father have long hoped to meet you and I need hardly say that this invitation extends also to Sarah and Dr Pepusch. Send me a card any time you feel like coming.

'With warmest regards,
'Ever most sincerely,
'NORMAN HUNTLEY.'

'You ought to put "My" dear Miss Hargreaves,' said Henry after he'd read the letter through.

'Oh, do you think so? I was inclined to think that "my dear old friend" was a bit too familiar.'

'Too familiar! My dear Norman, nothing could be too familiar for such an old friend.'

'You agree the regards ought to be warm?'

'As hot as hell.'

I sealed the letter, and addressed it to the Manor Court Hotel, Hereford. We posted it from Lusk, feeling that it ought to bear the Lusk postmark.

That evening we left Ulster. Just as we sailed out of Belfast and were leaning on the rail looking at the lights of the quay and feeling a bit sad that our holiday in Ireland was over, Henry said to me, 'I suppose that letter'll stay in the rack for months. Interesting to go there in a year's time and see if it's still there.'

I couldn't pass this.

'Why should it still be there?' I demanded. 'If Miss Hargreaves hasn't yet arrived, she will in a day or so.'

'I'm sorry,' said Henry hurriedly. 'I was assuming, just for a moment, that there wasn't such a person. Pure idle fancy, you know.'

'I call it damned disrespectful,' I said, 'and in the worst possible taste. You can only make up for it by coming below and standing me a drink on her behalf.'

We went down and ordered double gins.

'To Miss Hargreaves!' said Henry solemnly.

'Long may she live!' I cried.

We drank.

HENRY went straight back to Cornford, but I didn't. I'd promised mother I'd spend a day or so with Aunt Flossie who lives in Doncaster, a nice old thing as aunts go.

I had breakfast with Henry on Liverpool station, and saw him off on his London train.

'Well, old boy,' he said, stepping into his carriage and hurling his bag on to the rack, 'that was a grand holiday.'

'With a grand conclusion,' I said.

'Tell you what. Next time we have a holiday together we'll take Connie with us. Give her a treat, poor old dear.'

He swivelled his pipe from one side of his mouth to the other; he always does this when he's rather pleased with himself. 'Should like to take her on the tiles,' he added.

'She's better where she is,' I said. 'Safely tucked away in her creator's mind.'

'What about my mind?'

'Your mind?'

'Yes, she's in mine too. You've parted with her, you know. She's no longer your exclusive property.' The guard waved his flag. 'Anyway,' he added, 'she's probably on her way to Bath by now. So long! See you in a day or so.'

The train steamed out. Henry shouted to me:

'I should think she's the only person left who travels with her own bath, wouldn't you?'

'You mean,' I cried, 'the one given her by Mr Archer sixty years ago?'

Henry laughed and withdrew his head.

I went to find my Doncaster train, wondering just why Mr Archer should have given Miss Hargreaves a bath - I mean, of course, presented her with a bath, not bathed her; though, for all I knew, he might have bathed her. Rather extravagant. But still, if Miss Hargreaves was anything she was certainly eccentric.

No need to tell you anything about my Aunt Flossie, who doesn't come into the story at all. Two days later I travelled south, arriving at Cornford about seven. It was a superb September evening and Cornford was looking its best, full of red brick and sunset with the bells from the parish church playing 'Home, Sweet Home', as they always do on Saturday nights, when the crowd's thickest and nobody seems to want to have anything to do with home. I suppose it's a sort of warning to exuberant laddies, flung out by the Church at the most crucial moment of the week - for anyone who lives in a provincial town knows that Saturday evening is that.

Yes, it was lovely that evening; the market stalls full of dahlias, asters and Michaelmas daisies. Everybody was happy except a pinched-nosed-looking female in a stall selling political pamphlets - something about Marx, not the Brothers, but the German fellow who started all that Russian stuff. I felt sorry for the girl; she wanted a good steak and a little less hot air, you could see that. There were hordes

of chaps and girls lounging up and down, some of them
thronging round a black fellow selling medicine for the feet
in Disraeli Square. From the bars of the Swan people were
overflowing into the road, spilling their beer. Above all this
tapered the Cathedral spire, indulgent and kind, as much as
to say, 'I know all about you, my children; centuries ago you
wandered up and down on Saturday nights. You're just the
same; no different.' I was awfully glad to be back. There's
no place like home, you can say what you like, but there isn't.
In the air was a feeling of autumn; not a sad feeling, but a
mellow richness over everything. I like autumn; it doesn't
depress me. I like to think of winter evenings - evenings
when the great coke stoves will be burning in the Cathedral
and only about two people will wander in to hear the anthem.

I called into the shop, thinking I'd like to see father
before I went to number 38. We don't live over the shop,
of course. It's far too full of books.

Father was working out a chess problem in his favourite
corner. Nobody else was in the shop. It's a funny thing,
but people don't buy books on Saturday night.

'Hallo, Dad,' I said.

He didn't look up or answer for some time. I sat down
and waited, noticing how, in a month, the sun had shifted
from the theology shelves, below the staircase, to topogra-
phy, nearer the fireplace. Beautiful rich colour it was; it
made you want to look at the books.

Presently father said, 'Hallo, Norman. Have we got a
copy of the Kelmscott *Shakespeare* anywhere about?'

'I had a jolly good holiday.'

'Did you? I always liked Ireland.'

'Didn't know you'd been there.'

'Read about it. Who's that fellow - Moore, is it? Or Scott.
I know it pretty well from maps. Hand me that pawn, will

you? Do you know where the red queen's got to? I'm
having to use a clothes-peg and it's awkward.'

'Aunt Flossie was well,' I said.

'Yes? I've been playing the violin a good bit since you've
been away. And what do you think? That fool Claribel's
had kittens.'

'Go on!'

'Yes, the Kreutzer Sonata. It's fine work. I like the rondo.'

'She had five only last April.'

'But I'm damned if I can manage that tricky bit in the
slow movement. By the way, have we got a copy of the
Kelmscott *Shakespeare*?'

'Have you looked on the top floor?'

'No. Not yet. I'll put that devil Squeen on to it.'

Squeen's father's assistant. On Saturday he always goes
home early.

'Had a good holiday?' asked father.

'Oh, topping! Ireland's wonderful.'

'Henry looked in last night.' Father scratched his moustache with the white queen. 'Asked me whether I'd got a
volume of poems by - who was it? - Harton, or something;
Constance Harton. Called *Wayside Bundle*. Or was it *Puddle*?
Published in '95. I haven't had time to look for it yet.'

'Oh, Henry's pulling your leg.'

'Is he? Funny way to pull it. If I find the book I shall
charge him for it.'

'You'll never find it. Well, I'll be getting home. See you
later, I suppose?'

'So long, boy. Join me in skittles later at the Happy
Union.'

The Happy Union is a little place up Candole Street, not
far from our house. Father goes there quite a lot.

'So long, Dad,' I said.

Rather silly of Henry, I thought, as I walked down the High Street homewards. Futile to prolong jokes like the Hargreaves. Very nice in Lusk, but now - back in Cornford - no, it lacked reality. As far as I was concerned, she was dead.

I reached 38 London Road. It's an old-fashioned house, tall, with a flat, plain frontage, yellow bricks and large windows with a lot of steps up to the front door. Rather a grand house in a way; you couldn't blow it over like you can a lot of modern ones. But certainly it is plain. I thought so especially that evening, comparing it with the fine Queen Anne house, bang opposite, standing in several acres of ground, with a dense triangle of rhododendrons in the front garden, and two gates. Lessways was its name; property of the Dean and Chapter. It had been empty for a long time, and there was often talk of pulling it down. Once there'd been some diocesan offices in the lower rooms; but now they'd moved and it was empty.

Mother and my sister Jim were just sitting down to supper as I came in. They were a bit off-hand to me, I thought. There wasn't that warm welcome one expects after a month's holiday; not really wholehearted. Of course, they're both rather *casual* in a way; very brisk, too; not a bit like father. Mother's tall and stoutish with hair going grey and what you might call an eagle eye; Jim's tall and not stout; but she's got the same eagly eyes. In fact, they're both rather eaglish people. Pouncers. Nice - oh, awfully nice! But a bit too up to the mark for father and me. They're both fond of games and organizations; clubs, committees and conversations. They belong to everything, and they keep diaries crammed with appointments. Father, of course, doesn't belong to anything - except mother and the shop; he doesn't like going out very much, apart from the Happy Union. Quiet, my father is. So we're rather a divided family.

Personally, I like it that way; you don't get so bored with each other.

I had to tell them all about the holiday, of course, and I went through everything, from beginning to end. I left out Miss Hargreaves; knew they wouldn't understand that sort of joke.

'And now,' said mother, 'you'll have to settle down to some work, Norman.'

Mother's awfully fond of that phrase, 'settling down'. I don't like it much; makes me feel like a sort of powder.

'Marjorie and I have joined the Keep Fit Class,' said Jim. 'Pity you don't do something like that; keep that paunch down.'

'Don't be rude, Jim,' I said. I cut myself some cake.

'I hope this winter,' said mother, 'you'll really settle down and work for your A.R.C.O. and not spend so much time playing the piano for father's silly old violin.'

'That reminds me,' I said. 'Where are Claribel's kittens?'

'In your old tuck-box,' said Jim. 'Rather a mixed brew.'

'Henry says he can dispose of two for us,' said mother. 'By the way,' she added - I noticed she glanced at Jim - 'who's this friend of yours he keeps talking about? Somebody you met in Ireland, I suppose. What was the name, Jim?'

'Hargreaves, wasn't it?'

'Yes, that's right. Who is she, Norman?'

'Oh, she's really a friend of his.' I laughed a little uneasily. 'This is topping cake. Did Janie make it?' (Janie's our maid.)

'Henry quite clearly said *your* friend. How did the name come up, Jim?'

'Oh, we were talking about Mrs Pankhurst and votes for women, and - '

'Oh, yes, I remember. We were arguing about the date of Mrs Pankhurst's death and Henry said we'd better ask

Norman's great friend, Miss Hargreaves. He said she had known Mrs Pankhurst.'

'So *I* said,' said Jim, 'Miss Hargreaves? Never heard of her. And old Henry got quite worked up about her. Norman's guiding light, he called her.'

'We got quite curious about her, didn't we, Jim? You can't have known her very long, can you, Norman?'

I was growing a bit uncomfortable. Mother's so interested in all my friends; she's what you might call modern in that way; likes to say that she keeps an ever-open door. I wished Henry hadn't carried on the ridiculous joke. I knew it wouldn't be easy to convince mother that there wasn't such a person. They don't understand the Spur of the Moment, mother and Jim.

'Henry's been pulling your leg,' I said. 'There's no such person.' (Do you remember Mrs Gamp's fury when Betsy Prig said of Mrs Harris, 'I don't believe there's no sich a person!' Queer it was; I felt like that.)

'Of *course* he wasn't pulling our leg.' Mother sniffed contemptuously. 'Why *should* he? I always know when I'm being fooled. He spoke with great respect of her.'

'Honestly, mother,' I said, 'the whole thing was a joke. We made her up.'

Mother laughed. And when mother laughs it generally means trouble. 'If you *want* to conceal your friends from us, by all means do so. We shan't complain.'

I saw it was no use arguing about it. The best thing to do was to avoid the subject and later on get Henry to come round and bear me out.

'I can't help it if you don't believe me,' I said.

Mother looked at me oddly. 'You really don't *know* a Miss Hargreaves?'

Again I noticed a quick glance pass between her and Jim.

'See that wet,' I declaimed, 'see that dry!' I slid my finger from my tongue to my throat. 'I swear I've never met any such woman in my life.'

'Then - ' And mother has a way of making a long pause after the word 'then' which makes you tremble at the thought of what's coming. But this time she didn't say anything at all. She merely swooped something from the mantelpiece to the table.

I can only tell you this. It was one of the Graver moments of my life. All sorts of ideas about Time and Relativity and Matter and what-not floated to me as, with blurry eyes, I looked at what mother was holding out to me. It was a telegram. It was addressed to me. I read it.

'A thousand thanks for welcome invitation sent from beloved Lusk hoping arrive stay with you Monday Hargreaves.'

I read it a dozen times. It had been handed in at Hereford that morning at ten. I read it a dozen more times, held it up to the light, shook it, smelt it, and finally spilt some tea over it. Then I staggered to the window.

* * *

I felt bad. I felt rocky. I felt the sky coming down and the earth going up. Then suddenly I felt better. This was a trick of Henry's. Obviously. Sort of mad thing he would do.

Father was coming up the steps to the door. Mother and Jim were standing behind me. Deadly silence. Awful.

I swung round. 'Don't you *see*,' I cried, 'this is a trick? Henry's behind the whole thing. He never did know where to stop a joke. I'm going round to see him at once.'

Father came in. I heaved a sigh of relief. I can always cope with father. He hasn't that strict sense of orderliness that mother and Jim have.

'What's the matter?' he asked. I suppose we were all standing about in critical attitudes. 'Oh, I bought a new teapot,' he added. 'That one never would pour.' He put the new pot on the table.

'*Well*, Norman,' sighed mother with a dreadful sort of sinister gentleness, 'I shall be very glad if Henry *is* able to explain. I don't like to catch my son out in telling lies.'

'Don't you worry,' I said. 'You'll see.'

Father was pouring out the tea from the old pot into the new, then pouring it back again into the old to see how the new worked. He seemed satisfied.

'That's what I call a teapot,' he said. 'Oh - do you remember that book I was trying to find?'

'The Kelmscott *Shakespeare*?'

'Was it? Anyhow, I found it. Here it is. Jim, tea's half cold.' He pulled a slim, green, rather worn-looking volume from his pocket and flung it at me.

'That's not the Kelmscott *Shakespeare*, surely?' I said.

'No. Not *that*. The other book.'

'The other book?'

'Yes. The poems. *Wayside Spindle*, or something. Not bad, some of them. Run through the Kreutzer with me tonight?'

The little green book was lying on the floor. I had failed to catch it. I could not pick it up.

'Mother,' said father, 'did you get me a new A string?'

'Yes, I did, Cornelius.'

'Father,' I said, '*what* poems did you say?'

'Oh, don't keep bothering! Some book by a woman Henry was interested in. Friend of yours, he said.'

Mother suddenly darted down, snatched up the book, glanced at it, then shoved it before me without a word. I took it hopelessly. I shuddered. Its title was *Wayside Bundle*. Verses by Constance Hargreaves. They were dedicated to Philip Archer, M.A. 'A small craft,' declared the authoress in a foreword, 'and now for the first time launched upon the sea of criticism.'

'Holy God!' I moaned.

'And now,' said mother grimly, 'perhaps you'll be kind enough to tell us the truth about this Miss Hargreaves. Don't misunderstand me, Norman; I'm very glad to welcome any friend of yours to the house. All I expect is that we should know a little about them first.'

'Mother,' I said, and I spoke with feeling, 'if that dove flew out of that picture and fluttered about over the table, you'd be surprised, wouldn't you? You'd be bowled over?'

I pointed to a picture in a gilt frame of Greuze's girl with the dead dove.

'Yes, I certainly should be bowled over,' agreed mother.

'I've always maintained that dove *isn't* dead,' said father.

'Well,' I said, 'you couldn't be more bowled over than I am by - by this. So have a little mercy.'

'For a change,' suggested Jim, 'try telling the truth. Just try. People do. It doesn't kill them, as a rule.'

'You bitch, Jim!' I cried.

'That's enough, Norman!' snapped mother. 'I won't stand words like that - '

'Well, she is a bitch - '

'Do you hear what he is saying, Cornelius?'

'I don't know what you're all arguing about,' said father. 'Is it the new teapot? That's what I call a teapot, that is.'

He sat down and helped himself to some tongue. The volume was open in my hands. I read:

> 'O, bring me the flute and the alto bassoon,
> The mustard, the cress, and the water!
> The high and the diddle; the fiddle; for soon
> Must I go to make love to your daughter.'

It was from a poem called 'The Unwilling Suitor'.
'Father,' I said, 'where did you find this book?'
'They're rather nice little verses,' he said. 'Nice feeling. Remind me of - who is it? Christina Rossetti. She was a poet, if you like. Met her once and she - '
I laid the book on the table. Jim took it up.
'Your fancy friend must be pretty old,' she said. 'This was published in 1893. Listen to this: what on earth does it mean?'
She read another verse:

> 'My life was complete before Agatha came:
> The rosemary, dapple and fawn;
> The carraway petal, the Holloway flame,
> The gingham, the gallows, the dawn.'

'H'm. That's good,' said father. He took the book from her and read silently for a few moments. 'Yes,' he said, 'she's a poet right enough. You have to work to get at the meaning. Sure sign. That's fine, you know:

> 'Oh, why must I go with my green tender grace
> To lay all my eggs in one basket?
> If I were a mayor I could carry a mace;
> My card and address in a casket.'

'Fine!' he said.

'Sounds pure nonsense to me,' said mother.

'She's no chicken,' said Jim. 'If that book was published in 1893, she must be at least sixty.'

'Sixty!' I laughed scornfully; suddenly plunged deep into the pit. 'She's nearer ninety - that is - damn it! Hell!' I shouted. I was getting more and more tied up. 'I made her up,' I cried. 'I've never met her, I tell you!'

I really hardly knew what I was saying.

Father, taking not the slightest notice of my outburst, began to read again from the book.

'Listen,' he said. 'Here's depth. Real depth:

'All this goeth on and my mind is a blank,
  A capriciously prodigal hostage.
What *care* I when comforters tell me the Bank
  Will pay death-duties, homage and postage?'

Father walked round the room, waving the volume up and down in the air and murmuring the words 'capriciously prodigal hostage'.

'Music,' he said, 'pure music. Reminds me of Tennyson. Did I ever tell you, by the way, how I met - '

I couldn't stand much more.

'Father,' I shouted, 'where did you find this bloody book - '

'How *dare* you use language like that!' cried mother.

'On my desk,' said father. 'Just like that. Under my nose. Funny, wasn't it? Friend of yours, Henry says. You must bring her round. I like authors. This woman can write too. You might set it to music, Norman.' Again he read:

'The world is so shallow, the shoes are so tight,
  The moon is so faithful to fortune;
The cherry is ruddy, the asp is alight,
  The warrior whistleth his war-tune.'

' "Asp is alight," ' murmured father. 'H'm. True, you know. She gets to the heart of things. Realist, too. Notice how she says the warrior *whistleth* his war-tune. Observation there.'

I grabbed the book from him and went to the door.

'I can't explain all this now,' I said, 'except that I know that devil Henry's behind it.'

I opened the door and rushed into the hall.

'Glad the boy's making some nice friends,' I heard father say as I went out.

*   *   *

Henry was working late at the garage. I found him lying full length under the dismembered chassis of an old lorry.

'You've got me in a nice fix, you devil,' I said.

'Hullo! Is that you, Norman? Hand me that spanner, will you?'

I shoved a large spanner into his hand.

'What the hell do you mean, spinning all this stuff about Miss Hargreaves?'

'Miss Hargreaves? Eh? Oh, yes! Chuck over that coil of wire, will you? No - not that one, you idiot! The other one.'

'I do think the telegram, though brilliant, was going a bit too far, Henry.'

'Here, just hold the other end of this wire, will you? Look out for that oil! What telegram?'

'What utterly beats me is how you came by this book.'

'Book?'

'The poems, idiot! *Wayside Bundle.*'

Henry laughed. 'I thought you'd appreciate that. Your father took it all in; actually said he'd write to Foyle's about it - '

'I know all that. I want to know where you *got* the damn book.'

'Got the book? What do you mean? I didn't get it.'

'Come out, blast you! I can't talk to your legs.'

'Why not?' He slithered out and sat on the running-board. 'Now,' he said, 'give me a fag and don't get so worked up. Tell your Uncle Henry all about it.'

I gave him a cigarette. Then I showed him *Wayside Bundle*. 'For God's sake,' I said, 'explain this. I'm scared.'

He looked at it casually. Then he looked again. Then he grabbed it and glared at it. Then he glared at me. He seemed quite angry, for some reason.

'I always thought,' he said, 'that Miss Hargreaves was too good to come straight out of your little head. Golly, Norman, you are an old - '

I nearly wept.

'Did you, or did you not put this book on father's desk?'

'I swear I didn't. Do you mean to say - '

'He found it there. Under his nose. You *must* have.'

'Sorry, old boy, but I'm not guilty. The only thing I *did* do was to ask your old man whether he'd got the book. Thought it would be amusing.'

'Do you call this amusing?'

'I call it damned queer.'

We were silent for a bit. Then I showed him the telegram.

'Don't tell me,' I said, 'that you've got nothing to do with this. I'll forgive you anything so long as you tell me you had this telegram sent.'

He read it and looked at me half suspiciously.

'Just where did you pick up this dame?' he asked.

'Did you or did you not have it sent?' I snapped.

'Of course I didn't. A joke's a joke, but I don't believe in wasting' - he counted the words - 'one and seven-pence on it. Besides, how could I have been near Hereford?'

We were silent for a very long time. Henry said, 'I suppose you really *did* make her up, Norman? She wasn't some old trout you'd known all along? I know how partial you are to old dames.'

'Damn it all!' I cried, 'you had a good deal to do with it. Of *course* I made her up. We both did.'

'I only put in a few bits. You had all the plums.'

'I know I did most of it. But you helped.'

'Norman,' he said solemnly.

'Yes?'

'You remember that time you made up the sermon when we were kids, and - '

'Yes, of course. What's that got to do with it?'

'Nothing, I suppose. But - ' He paused. Then he slapped my knee suddenly. 'I've got it!' he cried. 'It's obvious. There just happens to be a Miss Hargreaves staying at the Manor Court Hotel. She gets your letter. She's very old, memory like a sieve, and she assumes you must be an old friend whom she's forgotten. Extraordinary coincidence. But things like that do happen.'

'Yes, and what about the book. Do things like that happen?'

'Golly, I'd overlooked that. Anyway, old boy, no good worrying too much. Send a wire and say, "Smallpox here; advise postponement of visit".'

'She's not going to be put off by smallpox,' I said. 'She's the type of female who'd rush into smallpox and never catch it.'

'Look here, I've got an idea. Phone the hotel and find out definitely whether there is a Miss Hargreaves staying there. For all you know, somebody might be playing a trick on you.'

'All right,' I said.

We went to the office and put through a trunk call. It didn't take long.

'Manor Court Hotel,' came a girl's voice.

'Oh, yes,' I said. 'Oh, yes - Manor Court Hotel - yes - I - ' I turned to Henry nervously. 'What the devil shall I say?'

'Ask if a Miss Hargreaves is staying there, you fool.'

'Have you' - I coughed and braced myself for the plunge - 'have you a Miss Hargreaves staying there?'

There was a moment's pause. Then: 'I'm afraid Miss Hargreaves has just left - this afternoon, that is.'

I turned to Henry and gave him the receiver.

'Gone,' I moaned. 'You do it, Henry. I feel faint.' Henry took the receiver.

'Do you mind telling me - eh? What? Oh, yes? Yes. Do you mind telling me if she left any address? Certainly.' (Pause. I watch three old wasps cruising round a bottle of oil. Happy creatures they seem to me.) 'Letters to be forwarded to - *where*? Yes? Oh. Yes. Thank you. Oh, one thing more. When did she arrive at your hotel? Arrive - yes. Why? Important, yes; she is wanted rather urgently. Thanks. Tuesday? About seven in the evening? Thank you. Good-bye.'

'Well?' I said. (One of the wasps had got caught in the oil, foolish creature.)

Henry looked at me and shook his head bewilderedly. 'Something very funny's going on.' He looked a bit solemn.

'Tell me everything.'

'She arrived last Tuesday evening. Keep calm, Norman; don't fidget; it won't help. Tuesday, you'll remember, was our last evening in Ulster. She's left Hereford. She asked for her post to be forwarded to - ' He paused.

'Go *on*!' I cried.

'Thirty-eight London Road, Cornford. Care of Mr Norman Huntley.'

I sat down on the high stool and stupidly looked at a map of the British Isles with a lot of flags in it.

'Where's she gone?' I asked.

'I'm - well' - Henry lit another cigarette - 'I'm rather afraid she's gone to Bath.'

* * *

I always blame Henry for plunging me deeper and deeper into this miserable business. It was at his advice that I agreed we'd tell my parents that we had actually met a Miss Hargreaves in Ireland. Henry said they'd never swallow the truth, and since she was certain not to turn up, that would probably be an end of it. The worst mistake I could have made, of course. I see now that I ought to have flatly denied all knowledge of her from the first. But there you are. Easy to be wise after, etc.

We went round to number 38 when Henry had washed and changed his clothes. Mother pounced on him at once.

'Now, Henry,' she said, 'perhaps you can tell us something about this friend of Norman's. He seems to be extraordinarily muddled by it all.'

'Oh, no muddle about it, Mrs Huntley,' he said airily. 'You see, this old trout - she's a regular trout, isn't she, Norman?'

'Schubert knew a thing or two about trouts,' said father. And he began to hum *Die Forelle*.

'Oh, definitely!' I said. I was so pleased; so certain that Henry, in his brilliant way, was dragging me out of a difficult fix.

'We ran across her in an hotel at Dungannon. Norman picked up her stick which she'd dropped.'

'She's a bit crippled,' I elaborated.

'And then she started to talk. Talk? Is there gas in a gasometer? I never heard so much gas from a woman in my life.'

'She's very eccentric,' I added.

'Eccentric? Isn't that an under-statement, Norman?'

'Well - batty, if you like.'

'Cuckoo - completely cuckoo,' continued Henry. 'Poor old dear! We were sorry for her at first. But that soon wore off. She's a horrible old horror.'

'So you see,' I said eagerly, 'just why I simply can't have her here. For one thing, she wears the most awful hats.'

'But why on earth did you ask her here?' said Jim.

'Oh, she asked herself,' explained Henry. 'Said she'd always wanted to hear the singing at the Cathedral - '

'Actually asked if I could put her up,' I added, 'Of course, I never dreamt she'd really want to come. I think I said something vague, like I'm sure you'd be welcome.'

'Plenty of beds,' said father.

'Then you *wrote* to her,' said mother. 'That was a bit silly, wasn't it, if you didn't want her to come?'

'It was in answer to a letter of hers in which she asked me a lot of questions about the Cathedral music. She haunts cathedrals, you know, like some of the old things we've got here. I never invited her to come. Wouldn't dream of it.'

'No,' said Henry. 'She asked herself. Complete with cockatoo and dog.'

'And bath,' I added.

'And bath,' agreed Henry.

'And harp,' I said rashly, in a peak moment.

'*Harp?*' said mother and Jim together.

'I like harps,' said father. 'Wrote some music for the harp once, but could never find a harpist to play it.'

'You mean she plays the harp?' said Jim.

'Definitely,' said Henry. 'Regular wizard at it.'

'She plays it last thing every night,' I threw in. 'It helps her to write her poetry. "Over the sea to Skye" is her favourite tune.'

'Parrots are intelligent birds,' said father. 'Knew one once that could recite a Shakespeare sonnet. All except the last line.'

'Oh well,' said mother, 'I certainly don't want a harp *and* a parrot in the house.'

'Of course not,' I said. 'That's why I was so upset when you showed me her wire. I never dreamt she'd want to come.'

'Did you ever hear of that parrot in the Andaman Islands?' asked father. 'A harp got washed up from a wreck. The Boston Philharmonic Orchestra had been travelling to Europe and they all went down - all except a harp and one cymbal. They never found the cymbal, but the harp got washed up, and several weeks later - who was that fellow? - some explorer, anyway, found this parrot strumming away an Andaman folk-tune on it. Unusual incident.'

'I do think you've behaved rather funnily about this absurd woman,' said mother. 'Why couldn't you tell us all this before?'

'I don't know. She muddled me somehow.'

'Well, you'd better write to her at once and put her off. We can't have a parrot and a dog in the house. Horace'd have a fit. (Horace is our cat.) Besides, you really must settle down to work after your holiday.'

'She won't turn up,' said Henry. 'Don't worry.'

'Talking about baths,' said father, 'anyone seen my loofah?'

*　　*　　*

Later that evening I sat in the Happy Union with Henry. Father was playing skittles in the handicap; a good many chaps were gathered round the board.

'Wish we hadn't made up that bit about the harp,' I said.

'Why not? It went down damn well.'

41

'Everything goes down damn well, too well. I tell you, Henry, I feel frightened of making things up.'

'Don't be such an ass. Shouldn't mind betting the girl at the hotel was pulling our legs.'

'How could she be? How could she know my address and her going on to Bath?'

'My dear ass, wasn't your address on the letter - which she might easily have opened? And didn't you mention the visit to Bath?'

That made me feel a little easier. I ordered more drinks, watched father playing skittles, and tried to put Miss Hargreaves in the back of my mind. But she didn't want to stay there.

*   *   *

Sunday passed quite normally. The boys had come back from their summer holiday and full choral services were resumed at the Cathedral. It was nice to be back there again. In the evening I went on the river with Marjorie. She's a friend. Well, she's more than a friend. I suppose she'll be my wife one day. I suppose so. I know I don't sound enthusiastic. The truth is, she let me down terribly over - well, you'll see. I don't want so say anything against Marjorie. She's a fine girl, very spirited. She's got a job in a shop where they sell superior cakes and preserves. You know the sort of place.

'Who's this Miss Hargreaves you've been taking up with?' she asked me suddenly, when we were half-way down-stream, coming round into Hedsor wharf.

'Oh, she took up with me,' I said. 'Not I with her.'

'Well, who is she, anyway?'

I leant over the side and flicked an old cigarette packet from the water into the bank.

'She's a niece of the Duke of Grosvenor,' I said. 'She writes poetry too.'

'Oh, really?' Marjorie seemed interested. She pointed up to Cliveden House, towering through the tops of the trees. 'The Grosvenors used to live there, didn't they?'

'That's right,' I said.

'How old is she?'

'About a hundred. I like that frock you're wearing, Marjorie. Suits you like a glove.'

'I suppose she's horribly rich?'

I laughed. 'Oh, yes! A hundred-pound note slips through her hand easier than a postage stamp. Shall we go down to Cookham Lock or turn back?'

'Back, I think. It's a bit cold. What's her poetry like?'

'It's funny.'

'How do you mean - funny? Comic poetry?'

'Not exactly. I can remember one verse.' I quoted:

'O, bring me the cornet, the flute, and the axe,
     The serpent, the drum and the cymbals;
  The truth has been told; I've laid bare all the facts -
  I *cannot* make bricks without thimbles.'

This seemed to puzzle Marjorie. She was silent for a bit. I began to row home. Presently she said:

'Thimbles? Don't you mean "straw"?'

'No. Thimbles.'

'I don't see what it means,' she said.

'Don't you? It is rather tricky, I agree. But the best poets always are obscure.'

I hadn't, of course, the slightest idea what the poem meant, but in a curious way I felt I had to defend it. The poems had got hold of me. I'd read them right through last night in bed, and lain awake for hours, worried about the whole funny business. As certain as I could see the old moon rising yellow over the Cathedral spire, I could see trouble rising. I fell uneasily asleep. Next night too - I fell even more uneasily asleep.

When I woke up on Monday morning it was with that sort of a 'different' feeling you have when things are either very bad or very good. I went down to breakfast - the first down for a change. On my plate was a letter; I saw it the moment I passed through the door. I approached it gingerly. The envelope was long and pea-green; not the sort of colour you want to see at breakfast-time. I picked it up between my fingers, holding it as though it were a bomb. It bore the Hereford postmark. I might have guessed.

*　　*　　*

I couldn't open it at once, but shoved it in my pocket. Breakfast stuck. I could feel the letter close to me, burning me, if you know what I mean. When I got out into the street and was on my way to the Cathedral for Matins, I ripped it open savagely, looking first at the signature.

It was signed 'CONSTANCE HARGREAVES'. She was 'Ever most affectionately'. Sent, of course, from the Manor Court Hotel.

I stopped in the road. Suddenly I was angry. A joke had no *right* to go on like this. I had a strong instinct to crumple the letter up and throw it away. A warning voice said to me, 'Norman Huntley, if you read that letter you'll open out a whole train of troublesome events. Throw it away. Get Miss Hargreaves for ever out of your mind. Behave as though she doesn't exist.'

Doesn't exist . . . doesn't exist . . . doesn't exist. I muttered the words Couély over and over again. Next minute I was reading the letter.

The writing was very broad and flowery, like a Morris wall-paper, full of twirls, and it didn't leave much room on the envelope for the stamp. In fact, I've rarely seen a stamp so crowded out. I didn't read the letter right through at first; I read random bits here and there. I don't know about you, but I'm like that with difficult letters; never can tackle them directly, but must look at them inside-out and upside-down. Then comes the moment when, having gathered its tone from stray but important words (suppose it to be a letter from a solicitor reminding me about the tailor's bill; the sort of words that inevitably stand out are - 'Unless', 'Compelled', 'Issue'), I am faced with having to wade right through it. In this case the words that caught my eye were - 'Bath', '*bath*' (observe the distinction), '*old* friends', and - 'luggage in advance to your house'.

'Oh, God!' I moaned. Then I read it properly.

'MY DEAR NORMAN,
   'Your charming letter gave me such *great* pleasure. How *clever* of you to know I should be at Hereford. But then, of course we are such *old* friends - in spite of the discrepancy of age - that you know my habits almost as well, if not better, than I know them myself.'

('*If not better*...' Why did that strike me as being so horribly sinister?)

'I have little time for a letter now, as I am about to catch my train to Bath, but this is just to tell you that I look forward greatly to seeing you and your *dear* family on Monday evening. I am curtailing my visit to Bath this year especially to be with you. My train is due to arrive at Cornford at eight-fifteen, *post* meridian. Will you kindly arrange for a cab as I have - as usual - oh, dear! - rather a lot of luggage. I have taken the liberty of having some of it sent by luggage in advance to your house.

'I am most touched by what you say of my dear old friend, Mr Archer - now, alas, "long, *long* ago at rest". One of my most precious possessions is a *bath* that he gave me years ago. That sounds strange, does it not? But there is a very simple explanation which one day I must tell you - if you do not already know.

'There has been such *exquisite* music at the Cathedral this year. Doctor Hull conducted so admirably - beautiful *Elijah* - beautiful *Messiah* - beautiful *Beethoven Choral* - *what* a heritage!

'I have just composed a triolet which I look forward to reading to you.

'Well, dear, I hope you are in good health and will be able to find time to show me something of your native town and countryside. I may be an old woman, but I still like to get about.

'Till Monday, then,

'Ever most affectionately . . . '

Futile rage possessed me. I screwed the letter up and threw it at a passing bus, next minute ran out into the road to recover it, feeling it might be useful as evidence in some way or another. What in God's name could it all mean? One thing I decided then and there: I'd tell father the whole truth. He'd understand more than mother and Jim.

* * *

Squeen, father's assistant, was there when I arrived at the shop after Matins. Squeen is naturally thin; you lose him sometimes in the dark corners of the shop. It wouldn't surprise me to find him flattened out under the *Encyclopaedia Britannica.*

'Mr Squeen's glad to see Mr Norman back,' he said. 'And did Mr Norman enjoy his visit to the passionate Celtic Isle?'

He's got an irritating habit of avoiding the use of the first and second persons in his speech.

'Ripping,' I said.

Going straight to the phone, I called up Henry. Squeen sat on a pair of steps and examined his finger-nails.

'Mr Squeen surmises,' he surmised, 'that there are more books in this shop than there are people in the Isle of Erin.'

'Shut up, Squeen,' I said. That's one thing about him; you can shut him up. Father bullies him unmercifully.

I heard Henry's voice.

'Oh, is that you, Henry? Look, I've had a letter from the old devil. It mentions the bath.'

'You mean the visit to Bath?'

'No. I don't. Small b-a-t-h. Mr Archer's bath. Henry, I think I'm going to have a nervous breakdown. She's arriving at Cornford to-night at eight-fifteen. You'll simply have to come to the station with me.'

'Can't. We're all going to the Clovertree Dance - don't you remember? You'll have to leave the old dear to herself.'

'I daren't. We *must* be there. You've got to help me.'

'I don't believe there'll be anybody there, you know.'

'I can't risk it.'

'Well, what do you intend to do if she *is* there?'

'I've thought it all out. I shall pack her off to the Swan. If she's troublesome, I shall get her certified.'

'She might get *you* certified, old boy. Have you thought of that?'

'You might be a bit more helpful.'

'Read me the letter.' I did so. 'H'm,' he said, 'I can't say I care for that bit about luggage in advance.'

'No. Neither do I.'

'All right,' said Henry. 'I'll come with you. We can go on to the dance afterwards. The girls won't mind if we're a bit late.'

'What do you think it all means, Henry?'

'Black magic, it sounds like. Why don't you try making a wax image of her and sticking pins into it? Use drawing-pins. They stay in easier.'

He rang off and father came down, balancing a set of Tolstoy against his chest.

'Too much of Tolstoy,' he muttered, 'nothing but Tolstoy upstairs.' He shouted suddenly to Squeen. 'Squeen, make a set-to to-day and rout out that Kelmscott *Shakes.* And sort out all that Tolstoy.'

'Father,' I said, 'I want to have a serious talk with you. I'm very worried.'

'Sit down, boy. Have a cigarette. Woman?'

I nodded. My father nodded too and jabbed his cigarette-holder in and out of his moustache. It's a big moustache, rather fine. The holder's a long one; amber.

'Women,' said my father, 'have never really been my cup of tea. They do not understand major issues, and their passion for realism is something I have never felt agreeable to. Nevertheless, the race, *as* a race, would crumble without them. Squeen, you devil - where are my slippers?'

Squeen brought him his velvet slippers and father, slipping his feet into them, stretched himself out in his revolving desk-chair. It's in a corner of the shop, at the back, away from all the windows, very hard to find, hemmed in by all the dullest books to stop customers wandering there. Often you'd go into the shop and never realize father was there. He likes to play chess in his corner or paste photographs in his albums.

'This is not what you think,' I said. 'I'm not in love or anything like that. I wish it was as simple.'

'Get if off your chest, boy. I may not listen, but I shall gather the trend of it. You'll excuse me going on with this chess problem, won't you? Squeen, shut the door and put the "back-in-ten-minutes" up. Now we can have a little peace.'

'It's this Miss Hargreaves,' I said.

'A fine woman from the sound of her. Plays the oboe, don't she? Now the oboe's a funny instrument one way and another - '

'You remember that time you warned me never to make things up? Well - '

'Old Bach understood the oboe better than any man before or after. You might say old Bach made the oboe.'

'I made her up, see? On the Spur of the Moment. Henry had a finger in it; but only a little finger.'

'Here - this won't do. I'm one pawn short. Squeen, look for a black pawn, will you? Or bring a pen-nib or something. Go on, my boy. Don't let me rush you. Plenty of time.'

'She just came into my head, Dad. But she won't stay there. Everything that I made up about her is coming true. I had a letter from her this morning.'

'Now look here, my boy; be frank with your father. Have you put yourself into a compromising situation, or not? Everything turns on that; it always does.'

'You don't understand. I've never even met her.'

'Yes, I heard you say you'd made her up. What I want to know is - have you made up a compromising situation?'

'No. Not yet.'

'Well, be careful.'

'You do believe me, then?'

'Just you tell me all about it.'

I did so. I gave him the whole story, from our visit to Lusk church onwards.

'This Archer cove,' he said. 'Did you make him up too?'

'No. I told you. He's real. He's dead.'

'Why don't you make her have a railway accident on the way here?'

'It might involve a lot of other people.'

'True.' He lit another cigarette and moved two knights slowly. 'It's alchemy,' he said, 'that's what it is. A sort of alchemy. I've got a book on it somewhere.' He glanced through a row of books on his desk. 'Can't lay may hands on it now. An old book. It's quite possible. It was done in the Middle Ages, or was it the Dark ones? Who was that fellow? Gilles de Retz or Cardinal Mazarin or somebody. It's purely a matter of faith. I suppose you had faith when you started in on this job?'

'Well, certainly, the more I talked about Miss - '

'Don't keep mentioning her name,' he advised. 'It's dangerous. She might easily become immortal. Then where would you be?'

'All I was going to say was, the more I talked about her, the more real she seemed to become.'

'Call her X,' he suggested, 'and faith, Y. Well, $X + Y = Z$, and Z's reality. It's all in that old book, worked out with graphs and things. Wish I could find it. Squeen, keep your eyes open for alchemy, will you?'

'Look here, father, I wish you'd be serious.'

'Serious! Never more serious in my life. Something very like this happened to me once. Better not tell your mother. I was in Basingstoke one winter morning; had an appointment to view some books at a sale. Well, something delayed me, don't know what it was, but anyhow I arrived an hour and a half late. By the way, very comfy little pub, the Blue Star; brewed their own mild in those days. The auctioneer was absurdly angry about me being late; said he'd held the books back specially, and so on. "Miss your train or something?" he said. "No," I said, "I don't suppose you'll ever believe me, but I got held up by an elephant." Of course I knew he would believe me. People always do if you tell them not to believe you and if you make it extravagant enough. It's when you try to make a lie sound like the truth that people get suspicious. Naturally.'

He leant down to a small cupboard near him and brought out a bottle of cherry brandy and two glasses.

'What's the time?' he asked.

'Eleven-thirty,' I said.

'H'm,' he said. He filled the glasses. 'Cheerio!'

'Thanks, Dad,' I said. 'Well, have you any advice?'

'Oh, I believe you,' he said. 'I sympathize. I understand in a way that most people wouldn't. Look at that! Red Queen's in check and I never noticed. It's that damned clothes-peg.'

'She doesn't play an oboe. You're wrong about that.'

'Pity. We might have managed one of the Brandenburgs.'

'What am I to do if she does turn up?'

'Yes, an elephant,' continued father, dreamily tipping up his glass. ' "Elephant?" said the auctioneer fellow. "Exactly," I said. "Broke loose from a circus. About a dozen of us were trying to catch the brute. Somebody brought a tennis net but the elephant ate it." "Well, did they get her?" asked the auctioneer. "Only after a struggle," I said. "A postman was killed." Well, do you know, Norman, my boy, I read in my paper that evening that *three* elephants had stampeded through Basingstoke that very day, upsetting a lot of carts stacked with celery, devouring the entire contents of two bakers' shops and killing a postman. *Three* elephants. So you see how careful you have to be. It shook me.'

'Yes, father. Yes, I can see.'

'Well, lunch-time, I suppose?'

We closed the shop and went round to the Swan.

*   *   *

The afternoon dragged on. Evensong passed in a sort of dream. I lost my place in a verse anthem (Battishill, I think it was) and plunged the boys into a wrong lead. I was nervous, terribly on edge. Back in the shop I had a cup of tea with father, then tried to work on a little counterpoint. But I couldn't get on with the stuff at all. I had another look at *Wayside Bundle*; I searched the shop in case there should be any more copies. I still half wondered whether Henry wasn't at the bottom of everything. Could he possibly have had the volume specially printed? But it was obviously perfectly genuine; the leaves spotted with age, and it had that dowsy smell about it which only years'll draw from a book. The title-page, the dedication and the binding might, of course, have been imposed upon a volume of poems by another writer. But was it likely? And could it all have been done in the time?

Many times I pondered over a sonnet which began:

> Belovéd bath wherein my tiréd feet
> Have oft-time plunged before the peaceful hour
> When sleep descends . . .

I didn't like it. I didn't like anything. And yet - and yet - (will you ever be able to understand this?) - I was already beginning to be curiously proud. Nobody but Miss Hargreaves could have written those poems, whatever Marjorie chose to say about them.

CHAPTER TWO

I went home about six, wondering what eight-fifteen would bring forth; hoping it would bring forth nothing, yet hoping too to see the realization of my invention. Even though it might mean hideous complications, I couldn't help hoping that.

Mother and Jim were out. I was rather glad about that. Because I should have found it hard to explain the enormous package in the hall. Janie told me it had just been delivered. It was addressed to Miss Hargreaves c/o Norman Huntley, Esquire, at 38 London Road, Cornford, Bucks.

It was a very large package indeed. It was done up in sewn sacking, wedges of newspaper and straw. It was, quite clearly, a harp. You could see the pedals.

H ENRY and I were waiting on the platform.
'Stupid waste of time!' he kept saying. 'Stupid waste
of time!' But I knew, by the way he was scratching the back
of his head with the stem of his pipe, that he was every bit
as nervy as I was. It was the harp that had upset him. 'People
don't go sending harps two hundred miles just for fun,'
he had said. I agreed. We stood and looked at it rather
solemnly for nearly five minutes, poking it gingerly now
and again, and half expecting that it would suddenly start
to play some ghostly tune from under its sacking. Finally,
we decided to taxi it to the Swan and leave it; I had already
reserved a room in case Miss Hargreaves should actually turn
up on the eight-fifteen.

The train was horribly punctual. I shall never forget that
train, the train that brought me my punishment. I remember
we were standing by the refreshment room and I sprang
nervously forward the moment I saw the engine. Henry drew
me back. 'Stay here,' he advised. 'You don't want to give yourself away, do you? After all, if this horrible woman *is* on the

train, how's she going to know you *are* Norman Huntley? She's never met you. If you rush about looking into carriages, she'll simply eat you up.'

It was good advice. Very slowly, oblivious to our suspense, the long line of carriages wriggled between the platforms, shivered a bit, clanked, and sleepily stopped. It looked as though it had crossed the frontiers of fourteen continents; very tired, very bored. A number of doors yawned open; about ten heads protruded from about ten windows. An old parson; a possible commercial traveller; the usual sailor; a fat woman with her baby. Obviously no Miss Hargreaves amongst that lot. By now passengers were walking towards the barrier; they were all unhargreavy-looking creatures, very simple and ordinary. Far away at the back a lot of luggage was dumped out from the guard's van. Apart from this rear activity, there was little movement.

I looked at Henry quickly.

'Not here,' I muttered. I felt half disappointed, half relieved.

'I told you it was all a waste of time,' said Henry. 'We'd better go. The girls'll be furious waiting for - '

I stopped him and clutched his arm.

'Hear it?' I muttered.

'Hear what?'

Henry's got no ear for music, that's the trouble. Suddenly I had heard something that I didn't care for at all. Far away, down at the back of the train, a raw, harsh voice, croaking, very slowly, very ill-temperedly - as though it hated the tune - Macheath's air from the *Beggar's Opera*, 'Were I laid on Greenland's coast.'

'My God!' said Henry. He had heard. We listened, our eyes turned to the back of the train. A dog had yapped; a dog was continually yapping. An irritable dog. Still the ghostly,

grudging tune went on, like a dirge. We saw a porter bringing something from the guard's van; it was a cage covered
by a black cloth. A large cage.

'Dr What's-his-name!' said Henry weakly.

'Exactly,' I said. 'Dr Pepusch.' I felt fatalistic; nothing
had much power to surprise me.

Henry stared at me. 'Are we going batty? Is this a dream?'

'Listen,' I said. 'Listen to that!'

A shrill, imperious voice had cried, 'Porter! Porter! Porter!'
Simultaneously the cockatoo, with a sepulchral growl on a
low D, stopped singing. By now everybody else had got out.
A porter sprang to a first-class carriage and opened the door.
With his assistance, slowly, fussily, there emerged an old lady.
She was carrying two sticks, an umbrella and a large leather
handbag. Following her was a fat waddling Bedlington ter-
rier, attached to a fanciful purple cord.

Old Henry went quite white. 'Here, let's go and have
a quick one,' he growled. 'This is killing me.'

We dashed into the refreshment room and hurled down
double brandies. We couldn't speak. Through the window
we watched, our empty glasses trembling in our hands.

'Henry,' I moaned, 'she is *exactly* as I imagined.'

Limping slowly along the platform and chatting amiably
to the porter, came - well, Miss Hargreaves. Quite obviously
it couldn't possibly be anyone else.

'At Oakham station,' we heard her saying, 'we have such
exquisitely pretty flowers. The station-master is quite an
expert horticulturist. Oh, yes, indeed!'

'Shall I have all your luggage put on a taxi, Mum?'

'Just wait! Kindly stay! A moment. Accept this shilling,
I beg of you. I am a trifle short-sighted, porter - oh, did I give
you a halfpenny? Here you are, then. Can you see a young

gentleman anywhere about? If so, no doubt but it would be my friend Mr Norman Huntley.'

I flopped weakly on to a chair.

'Can't see no one, Mum,' I could hear the porter saying.

'Then let us wait! Do not go. What a handsome train - what a most handsome train! I wrote a sonnet to a railway train once. In my lighter moments, porter; in my more exuberant moments. My Uncle Grosvenor was good enough to say it recalled Wordsworth to him. Do you read at *all*, porter? Tell me. Tell me frankly.'

'Well, Mum, I do read a bit. Detective stories, y'know.'

'Indeed! It has always interested me - what do these detectives *detect*? And *why*? Quiet, Sarah - quiet - ' The Bedlington was yapping spitefully. 'I am so interested, porter; I am interested in everything. Life, to me, cannot contain one dull moment. I do not believe in - but what *is* the matter, Sarah?'

Sarah was smelling me out; that was the matter with her. Tugging at her cord, she was doing her utmost to drag her mistress towards the refreshment room. They were only ten yards away from us now. Miss Hargreaves was scanning the platform through a pair of gold lorgnettes. I'd better try to describe her to you. She was very small, very slight, with a perky, innocent little face and alert, speedwell-blue eyes. Perched on top, *right* on top, of a hillock of snowy white hair: buttressed behind by a large fan-comb, studded by sequins and masted by long black pins, lay a speckled straw hat. Over a pale pink blouse with a high neck and lace cuffs, she was wearing a heathery tweed jacket; a skirt to match. Round her neck was a silver fur. Resting on one stick, she was holding the other, and the umbrella, on her arm; they were black ebony sticks with curved malacca handles.

I liked her expression. There was something mischievous and pensive, something very lonely, too, in the pursed-up lips and the fastidious little nose.

A feeling of pride stole over me. I couldn't help it. She was perfect; absolutely perfect.

'Henry,' I murmured dreamily. 'Pygmalion couldn't have done better.'

He looked at me sharply.

'Look here, Norman, *do* you know this old witch?'

I made the sort of mad reply you'd expect.

'Should have known her anywhere. And please *don't* call her a witch.'

Suddenly the Bedlington, frantic to make my acquaintance, broke from his cord and tore towards me. It was then I began to realize the awful danger of my position. If I acknowledged this old lady, even Henry would find it hard to believe I had actually never met her before.

'For God's sake, let's get away,' I muttered. 'Quick! There's still time.'

But there was not time. Miss Hargreaves had seen us. With a shrill, slightly coy cry, she tottered towards the refreshment room. From a luggage-truck, far down the platform, Dr Pepusch - inspired, no doubt, by the immensity of the occasion - shrieked in a shrill tenor, 'Were I laid on Greenland's coast, in my arms I'd hold my lass!'

I was face to face with my creation.

*   *   *

'My dear, dear boy! How well you look! How brown! Oh, dear, oh, dear - ! I am so excited. Hold me up, dear; hold me up! Porter, run and tell that silly old Dr Pepusch to be quiet - '

'Yap, yap, yap, yap, yap - grrrrrrr - '

'What shall I do with this 'ere bath, Mum?'

'And I would love you all the day - '

'Miss Hargreaves, I'm afraid you're making some mistake. I - '

'For God's sake, Norman, don't let her get away with it - '

'You naughty boy, hiding there in the doorway to surprise me! Sarah knew you! Just *listen* to Dr Pepusch! What gaiety! What spontaneity! He knows. You can never deceive the animal-world. *Can* you believe there is not an after-life for the dear creatures? Can you?'

'I tell you you're making a mistake - '

'Porter, *do* keep Dr Pepusch quiet. Look, here is a penny; run and buy him some chocolate, nut *and* fruit. Break it up for him. Norman, dear, give me your arm. I am quite exhausted. And who is this young man? Some friend?'

'Over the hills and - over the hills and - over the Greenland coast - '

'Dr Pepusch, stop that nonsense! Sarah, down doggie; down! Take her in your arms, Norman; she won't bite - anyway, her teeth are *old*. Oh, dear, I am quite unable to remain calm at these moments of reunion. Have you ever considered, Norman, that a railway station is the scene of some of the most poignant moments in life? Yes? I can see you, too, are affected. Introduce me to your friend. Let us all sit in this dreadful refreshment room while the porter collects my luggage. Have you a taxi waiting for me? Yes?'

*　　*　　*

Speechless, I sat down at a marble table and faced the Woman I had Made Up on The Spur of the Moment.

Henry was doggedly sucking his pipe, and looking at both of us under his black brows. I think the old devil was enjoying the situation; he's rather a hard-hearted brute at times.

Meanwhile, Miss Hargreaves talked. And when she talked there was no time for anyone else to get a word in.

'You cannot imagine how I have looked forward to this moment, dear. And I can see you, too, have looked forward to it. Pleasure is written boldly all over your face.'

Henry laughed sardonically. I scowled.

'It is such a very long time since we met; indeed, I cannot remember now when or where that was. My memory - alas! - works but spasmodically in this, the evening of my days. But *what* an evening! Oh, yes! It is no use disguising the fact; I am no longer young.' She leant forward across the table, tapped me on the chest with a silver pencil suspended from a chain round her neck. 'Eighty-three, Norman; eighty-three! Five reigns. And yet - I feel as though I had been born last week! Youth' - she declaimed, touching her heart - 'lives here. Not alone hope but also youth springs eternal. Shall we partake of a touch of refreshment? It will be dreadful food, of course, but still - Thank you, thank you! A little soda-water, perhaps one of those Chelsea buns. And who is this modest young gentleman who has never a word to say for himself?'

She whizzed round on Henry and examined him from tip to toe through her lorgnettes.

'He reminds me' - she spoke to me in a loud aside - 'of my dear Archer. He, too, had the Byronic black hair, the beetle brows. Ah, me! Time flies. What happened sixty years ago is as clear as crystal; yet, what happened yesterday - gone, gone!'

I handed her a glass of soda-water and a bun.

'Thank you, dear; thank you. But who *is* this young man?'

She did not seem to take to Henry somehow.

'My friend,' I said, 'Henry Beddow.'

'Beddow?' She wrinkled up her nose. 'Beddow? Grosvenor once had a parlourmaid by the same name. By any chance - ? No? So you are Norman's friend? H'm. It follows, Mr Beddow, that you are *my* friend.'

I smirked. 'Thanks very much,' said Henry.

'Ah, Mr Beddow! I wonder whether you can realize what Norman's friendship means to an old thing like me? Can I compare his appearance in my latter days to a shaft of pure sunlight warming the frail timbers of some old barn? Fanciful imagery, maybe! You need not blush, my dear Norman; you need not blush.'

'I should like to know,' Henry got in suddenly, 'just how long, Miss Hargreaves, you have known Norman?'

'I tell you, Henry - ' I began weakly. But she was off again.

'Oh - ' she waved her hand expressively. 'Years! I cannot remember. You must never talk of time, Mr Beddow. I am an old lady and an old lady does not care to be reminded of *time*.'

'H'm. I see.' Henry rose and knocked out his pipe. 'Well, I must be getting along. Very glad to have met you, Miss Hargreaves. I hope Norman'll show you the sights of Cornford.'

'Yes, yes, of course he will.'

It was unbearable, Henry's foul desertion of me. I ran out of the refreshment room after him.

'For God's sake, don't leave me alone with her,' I pleaded.

'Damn it, old boy,' he said, 'she's your friend; not mine.'

'You're as responsible for her as I am.'

He stared at me wonderingly.

'You surely don't expect me to believe in that rubbish any longer, do you? Why, anyone could tell at once that she's known you for years.'

'That may be. But I haven't known *her* for years.'

'You said yourself you'd have known her anywhere.'

'Yes - but that was - I meant - Oh, God!'

'I'm going along to the dance now. I'll tell Marjorie not to expect you.'

'No - no - ' I cried.

'Norman! Norman!'

Miss Hargreaves was standing in the doorway, calling me. Before I knew what I was doing, I had allowed myself to be led back into the refreshment room.

'A nice young man,' she remarked. 'But I confess I am glad that he has gone. Now we can have a cosy little chat together, before we return to your dear parents' house. Won't you have a glass of beer, dear? I like to see you enjoying yourself. I have never been against a simple glass of beer. My uncle's staff, the *male* members, that is, always had their own barrel of beer in the kitchen. I always think - '

*　　*　　*

As she continued to pour out her torrent of talk, the hideousness of the situation came home to me. I had accepted her. Over and over again I began to tell her that she was making some ghastly mistake; that I didn't know her, that my letter had been a foolish joke. But the devil of it was I couldn't convince *myself*. It seemed to me that I *did* know her. She never allowed me to say much, anyhow; always dismissed my remarks with a wave of the hands. Or else she completely ignored what I would begin to say. It was obvious that nobody in the world would believe I had never met her before; even father would find it hard to swallow. What was I to do? What would you have done? Run away, you say - run away and left her there in the refreshment room? What good would it have done? She would only have ordered a taxi and driven to my parents' house; and that, at all costs, I was determined to avoid.

'I am rested now,' she said, not long after Henry had gone. 'I am now fully prepared to meet your parents. Is it too much trouble to ask for a *fire* in my room? I am not fussy; I abominate fuss. Is there a south aspect to the room? I hope so. And tell me - has the harp arrived?'

'Yes,' I said. 'The harp's come. But I'm afraid, Miss Hargreaves - '

'Call me Constance, dear, when we are alone; perhaps not before others, perhaps not. But when we are alone, relax, I beg you; behave naturally. What were you about to say? You are afraid that Dr Pepusch will keep your parents awake? Not at all. I play him asleep every night.'

'Oh? You - play - him - asleep? Really?'

'Always. Eccentric, perhaps! But Orpheus achieved much with the lute and I - in my small way - do what I can with the harp.'

'Oh, really? I call that - topping! What I was going to say was - I'm afraid, well, I'm rather afraid we shan't be able to put you up.'

'Put me up? What does that mean, dear? A touch of slang?'

'Give you a room - well, I mean, you can't stay with us!'

'Oh.'

(Have you ever considered the word 'oh'? Have you? How it is full of an infinite variety of meaning? How it can be at moments the most sinister-sounding word in the whole language? '*Oh*.' In italics without an exclamation mark. '*Oh*.' Like that.)

Her sweet smile dried. It did not suddenly vanish. It dried up on her face like a crack in a sweet old apple. Into her eyes fell a steely glint. For the first time I began to be conscious of a feeling of fear.

'Mother is ill,' I said hastily. 'She's got' - (what was infectious?) - 'scarlet fever,' I added. 'We have to be very careful.'

'*Scarlet* fever?'

'Well, not exactly scarlet; but fever, anyway. You never know, you know. She's got an awful rash. I've made all arrangements for you to stay at the Swan. Best hotel in Cornford. Five stars. You'll like it.'

'But I feel sure I have *had* scarlet fever!'

'You can have it again. Besides, it may be smallpox.'

'Well - ' she shrugged her shoulders displeasedly. 'I suppose I must do as you suggest. But why should I not come and *nurse* your dear mother?'

'No,' I said quickly. 'She's funny.' I spoke in a lowered voice. 'She's difficult with strangers. In fact - ' I touched my forehead and sighed. 'There has always been,' I added quietly, 'a slight streak of - irregularity in our family.'

I hoped I might scare her away, you see.

'So there is in mine,' she said at once. A wild light came into her eyes. Like a flash the possible truth came home to me. She was an escaped lunatic. 'Calm,' I said; 'be calm, Norman. You'll have her in a strait-jacket in no time if you play your cards properly.'

'That is why,' she added, 'I play the harp. Music hath charms, as Dr Pepusch will tell you. Let us go now, dear; I am tired of this place. Take me to this hotel.'

I rose. 'Give me your arm, dear,' she said. 'Give me your arm.' I gave her my arm - ungraciously, I am afraid. Together we walked on to the platform. Before us, on a goods-truck, towered a pile of luggage. Miss Hargreaves had obviously come prepared for a long stay. There were hat boxes, two massive black trunks stamped 'H', several smaller cases, a gladstone bag, a leather portfolio labelled 'music', three butterfly nets, a large hip-bath peering rudely through half-torn brown paper, and, on top of the lot, Dr Pepusch in his cage, still covered by the black cloth.

CHAPTER THREE

Miss Hargreaves surveyed her belongings thoughtfully.
'Not quite so much this time.'
'What are the nets for?' I asked.
'Butterflies.'
'Oh. I see.'
'Not that I ever catch any,' she observed. 'But still - one
likes to be prepared for *everything*.'
(Had I made her a naturalist? I couldn't remember.)
Slowly we ambled out into the yard, the porter dragging
the luggage-truck behind us. I hailed a taxi.
'Can't take that there bath,' said the taxi-driver, a
lugubrious sort of fellow.
'Always *so* tiresome about the bath,' complained Miss
Hargreaves petulantly. 'After all, it is not a very *big* bath,
is it?'
'Can't manage it with all this 'ere stuff as well,' said the
driver.
She tapped the ground impatiently with one of her sticks.
'Well, well! Order another taxi. There is nothing to prevent our having two, is there?' She turned to me. 'These people are so lacking in imagination,' she remarked.
After a lot of arranging and assembling, the two taxis
drove off; Miss Hargreaves, myself, Sarah, Dr Pepusch and
various small bags in one: the bath and the two large trunks
in the other.
'And now we will have a nice little supper,' she said. She
rubbed her hands together and smiled at me. I thought of
the dance; Marjorie waiting for me, getting angrier and
angrier, old Henry telling her all about Miss Hargreaves.
'I'm afraid I can't have supper with you,' I said. 'I really
must get back to mother.'
'How disappointing! I have travelled so far. You cannot
leave me the moment we meet. It is cruel.'

'It can't be helped.'

'It *can* be helped.' Again that steely glint came into her eyes. 'I insist that you stay. Surely your sister can look after your mother for a little while? Ah, I can see what is really in your mind, dear. After so tiring a journey you think that I should retire early. Dear Norman! So kind - so thoughtful! How delightful Cornford is! Oh, that beautiful spire!'

We were coming through the North Gate into the Close.

'I am going to enjoy this,' she said. And again she rubbed her hands together and smiled at me.

'I'm sure you are,' I said wretchedly.

Just as we drew up to the Deanery, the Dean came out of his front door and stood under the arches saying good-bye to some friends. Miss Hargreaves fumbled quickly for her lorgnettes.

'The Dean?' she murmured. I nodded. She tapped on the window. 'Stop a moment,' she commanded. 'I must have a word with him.'

'Not now - please, not now,' I begged.

But already she was getting out of the car and walking quite briskly towards the group under the Deanery arches. Surprised, the Dean looked up. I heard her talking.

'My dear Mr Dean, pray excuse me. But on the privilege of my first visit to your Cathedral town, I feel that I must make myself known to you.' She handed him a card which the Dean could not very well avoid taking.

'My Uncle Grosvenor had a great attachment to Cornford,' she added.

'Oh? Indeed?' said the Dean. He turned pointedly to his friends. 'Well, good-bye, good-bye. Yes, we must certainly do something about those frescoes. Good-bye.'

'Sing unto the Lord! Sing unto the Lord!'

I jumped aside nervously, wondering for the moment who had shrieked out the harsh notes. It was, of course, that damn cockatoo. Miss Hargreaves laughed gaily.

'What is that?' asked the Dean.

'Oh, it is only Dr Pepusch,' she explained. The Dean glared over to the taxi and now noticed me. I slunk back trying to make myself invisible.

'Is that you, Huntley?' he snapped. 'Was that you crying out?'

'Oh, no, Mr Dean. Not me, not at all. I - '

'Well, good night to you,' said the Dean coldly. He turned, walked under the arches and shut his door loudly. Miss Hargreaves came back to the taxi and got in.

'Sing unto the Lord!' croaked Dr Pepusch, more in a minor key this time. It was funny, but that bird was never so certain of himself when Miss Hargreaves was near by.

'Yes, dear; *yes*,' she said indulgently. 'So you *shall* sing unto Him. He' - she addressed me - 'he is so proud of his *Venite*. He has not got it quite right yet. I taught it to him while we were at Hereford. The chant is by Samuel Wesley. I only hope that he understands what it *means*. I like you, Dean; a fine, scholarly, upstanding clergyman. He was Balliol, was he not? I hope he is not a modernist.'

*   *   *

We left the Close through Princes' Gate, drove up Canticle Alley and thus came into the High Street. In a few minutes we should be at the Swan. By now the other taxi had disappeared ahead of us.

Quite suddenly, out of the void of my half-fearful gloom a mad and wild idea lurched into my head; a burst of my old inventiveness, tempting me on to destruction. Another leap on to the ever-tempting Spur.

'And how is Agatha?' I asked.

(I suppose you understand that I hadn't the slightest idea who Agatha was? No good asking me why I do things like that. I'm made that way, as I told you earlier.)

'Sinking!' she replied promptly. 'Rapidly sinking!'

For the moment I was silenced; almost appalled by the immediate and totally unexpected response to my question.

'Tch! Tch!' I clicked sympathetically. 'But still,' I added gravely, 'it was bound to come, sooner or later.'

'Yes. We all sink, sooner or later. The bar must be crossed by all.'

'Does she suffer?' I asked. (I was now enjoying it.)

'Cruelly.'

'You will miss her.'

Miss Hargreaves touched her eyes with a fine lace handkerchief.

'Yes, indeed, I shall miss her - almost as much as I miss poor Seraphica Archer. I expect a telegram at any moment to say she has passed. I cannot pretend I shall be sorry. Protracted suffering is hard to understand. But it will be an old - a very old tie severed.'

'You will find it distressing,' I ventured, 'to return to Oakham without her.'

'I shall not return,' she said simply.

'Oh? You - will not return?'

'No. I am closing Sable Lodge. I shall live in Cornford.'

'Oh.' I relapsed into an awful gloom.

'*You*, dear' - she turned to me, touched my arm and smiled what the novelists call a 'brave' smile - 'you, dear, will have to take Agatha's place.'

*   *   *

The Swan is one of those old-fashioned, vast, rambling hotels where neither the food nor the service are particularly good. But it's so old-fashioned, and has been patronized by so many clergymen, that nobody has ever dared to criticize it. Miss Hargreaves, however, did not find it entirely to her liking.

We were standing in the hall, surrounded by her luggage. Mr Stiles, the manager, a rather pompous fellow (I remember he was dressed in staggering plus-fours that evening), was holding forth on the question of birds. Miss Hargreaves took very little notice of him; through her lorgnettes she was carefully examining some ancient oak panelling.

'We don't really reckon to take birds,' said Mr Stiles. 'And then there's the question of this bath - we're very well fitted up here, you know; hot and cold water in every - '

'What does he say?' Miss Hargreaves asked me.

'He says they've got hot and cold water in every - '

'I dare say - I *dare* say.' Miss Hargreaves acidly tapped the panelling with her stick. 'But the question of the bath is one upon which I am not prepared to enter into controversy.'

She bent down and rapped the panelling with her knuckles.

'Worm!' she exclaimed to me. 'I knew it! It really is shocking how people treat these priceless old things. Norman, perhaps we can find another hotel - '

'Of course,' began Mr Stiles, 'I'm ready to make a concession. Our terms are - '

Miss Hargreaves whipped round on him. 'My good man, will you stop talking and send the manager to me at once?'

'But - I am the manager.'

'You! The *manager*? Good heavens! How things are changing!'

'You've got Miss Hargreaves' room ready, haven't you?' I asked quickly.

'Yes, Mr Huntley. But the parrot - I'm rather afraid the other guests will - '

'You have a wooden swan over your front door,' snapped Miss Hargreaves, 'and you have the insolence to talk disparagingly of a live and well-educated cockatoo - even referring to it as a *parrot*. Scandalous! Monstrous!'

I caught Mr Stiles' eye. 'Come here,' I whispered. He followed me down into the passage that leads through into the kitchens.

'For God's sake, don't put her off,' I begged. 'I don't want to have to search the town for other rooms. She'll pay you well. Humour her a little and she'll pay whatever you ask.'

'I don't want to turn anyone away from the Swan,' he said. 'But really - if she's not satisfied with - '

'She's a niece of the Duke of Grosvenor, by the way.'

'Oh! Really?' Mr Stiles seemed more interested in her. 'Well, of course, I suppose - ' He went back to the hall. 'I dare say everything'll be all right, Madam,' he said to her.

'I trust it will be, manager. I trust so.'

'You won't object to a small charge for the animals?'

'I am accustomed to that. Poor Agatha,' she said to me, 'always cost me an extra half-crown a day, wherever I travelled.'

'Really?' I nibbled my fingers nervously. Was this damned Agatha a cat or a dog or a guinea-pig? Or an armadillo? 'I suppose she ate a good deal?' I ventured.

'Prodigiously!' She took my arm. 'And now, let us view my apartment.' Preceded by half the staff, we trooped slowly upstairs. Every now and again Miss Hargreaves stopped on the fine staircase to point out defects in the furnishing.

'Holes in the carpet, you observe, Norman. Oh' - she shuddered and pointed to a vile green glass vase standing in a large window-sill on the half-landing - 'what an appalling thing! Have people *no* taste?' She turned round and addressed Mr Stiles. 'I would like to buy that.' She pointed to it with her stick.

'Oh, indeed, Madam? It isn't usual, of course. But - '

'Will you accept ten shillings?'

'Yes, I suppose I - '

'Here you are. Have it sent up to my room at once.' She handed him a note, which he took with rather obvious eagerness. 'Wait,' she said. Fumbling in her bag she found another note, a pound this time, and gave that to him also. 'For the staff,' she snapped. 'I am not fussy. I abominate fuss. But I expect service.'

Eventually we came to room number 14, a large room looking out over the yard at the back of the house. Miss Hargreaves went straight to the window and peered out. A page-boy set down the bath and waited; a porter struggled through the door with one of the trunks; two chambermaids set down various smaller articles. Meanwhile, Sarah did the tour of the furniture legs.

We all waited. Finally, Miss Hargreaves left the window and came to the centre of the room. 'This will not *do*,' she said. 'I must overlook the main street - or a garden, if you have such a thing. I am not accustomed to overlooking stables. And a fire must be lit; several cans of hot - not boiling - water brought up.'

Mr Stiles sighed.

'I've got one room overlooking the street,' he said.

'Then let us examine it.'

We all trooped out again, except Sarah, who had found a comfortable home in the pink eiderdown on the bed. The other room, smaller but quite pleasantly furnished, seemed to satisfy Miss Hargreaves.

'But Sarah,' she remarked, 'clearly prefers the other bed. You will please have it moved in here while I am having supper. I abominate fuss.'

This was too much for Mr Stiles.

'Really, Madam, I can't go having beds moved for dogs to sleep on.'

'*Oh.*'

There was a dead silence. She stared at him slowly, up and down. A blush, the colour of the poor man's suit, flooded his usually colourless features.

'Did I understand you to say -' began Miss Hargreaves.

Mr Stiles held his ground. 'I don't move beds for dogs,' he said.

'Very well. Return me my pound, if you please. Norman, get a taxi. We will have to -'

'Look here,' I said desperately. 'Why not bring the eiderdown from the bed in number 14? That's what Sarah's taken a fancy to.'

Miss Hargreaves nodded. 'Possibly. Fetch it,' she said to one of the maids. 'And be careful you do not disturb Sarah. Carry her *in* it. Be most careful.'

The crisis had passed. Sarah was brought in, curled up in the eiderdown, one eye winking at her mistress as much as to say 'we've won again'.

'And now,' said Miss Hargreaves, 'when I have changed my clothes, we will have a little light supper.' With a wave of her hand she dismissed everybody from the room.

'Oh, this vase!' she cried. The page-boy had put it on the dressing-table. 'Take it, Norman. Take it!'

'What do you want me to do with it?'

'Oh, break it, break it, dear. Not here. Take it away somewhere; but do not let me see it again. What an abominably rude fellow that manager is! Why does he wear those clothes? What are they called? I believe they have a special name.'

'Plus-fours.'

'Indeed? Plus-fours! Well! Go along now, dear - go - oh, the harp! Where is it?'

'Downstairs, I think. I'll have it sent up.'

'Do. I cannot get along without my harp. Wait for me in the dining-room.'

I went downstairs, foolishly carrying the hideous vase. 'Here,' I said savagely to a waiter, 'hide this thing somewhere. And have Miss Hargreaves' harp sent up to her room.'

I waited in the dining-room.

*　　*　　*

Why did I wait? Curiosity? A sense of predestined doom? Mere laziness? I don't know. I could have skipped it. Yet there I sat, looking at the horrible marble clock on the mantelpiece (warriors with tridents sparring on the top of it) and thinking of the dance I ought to be at, imagining Marjorie's anger and all the explanations I should have to make up later on.

About nine-fifteen Miss Hargreaves came into the room and we sat down at a table near the window. Nobody else was there, for which I was grateful. She had changed her clothes and was now wearing a purple silk gown with a lot of lace about it.

'Now,' she said, 'to food!' She studied the menu for a few seconds, then threw it impatiently aside. 'Hopeless!' she said. A young waiter hung near us. 'Bring us,' she ordered, 'a little light supper. Nothing much. Clear soup, perhaps, with a few asparagus tops thrown in at the *last moment*. A little fish - I prefer mullet, red mullet, of course.' She changed her mind. 'No. It is not, I imagine, in season. Whitebait, then. They

must be cooked rapidly. No garnishing. I abominate fuss.
Have you any Dunstable larks? Yes? No? Tch! Tch! Then a
woodcock. And some fresh figs; I should very much like
some fresh figs. I do not care for cheese unless you have
Wensleydale. Then we will have coffee; I have brought my
own. Ask the maid who unpacks to bring it down. Have you
a mill here?'

'Mill?' stammered the waiter.

'Yes, yes! Mill. For the beans.'

'I'll ask in the kitchen, Ma'am.'

'Do. And Mr Huntley would like some beer; Norman,
order what you are accustomed to.'

I ordered a pint of old.

'Pint of old - ' The waiter sighed with relief and made a
note of it. 'We can't do you anything but cold beef and pickles now, Ma'am.'

'What?'

'Cold beef and pickles.'

'How exquisite those *putti* are!' she exclaimed, pointing
up to some plaster cherubs which adorned the centre of the
ceiling. 'Such innocence - yet such guile! What are you
waiting for?' she said to the waiter.

'I said we only had cold beef and pickles, Ma'am. Dinner's
off, see?'

'Pickles? *What* pickles?'

'Very good brand, Ma'am. Highly favoured by our
patrons.'

'Highly flavoured by your patrons - I do not understand.'

'Favoured,' I shouted, 'not flavoured.'

'Nothing but cold beef and highly flavoured pickles?
I have never heard of such a thing!'

I suggested an omelette. She sighed wearily. 'Always one
has to return to the inevitable omelette,' she complained.

'Still, what has to be, is to be. Yes. An *omelette aux fines herbes*. It must be done almost instantaneously, waiter. Have the pan boiling hot before you put the butter in; the egg should *almost* catch fire; not *quite*. No instrument must be used in order to disengage the mixture from the sides. What of the herbs? Not bottled, I trust! Have you a herb garden?'

'I'll ask in the kitchen, Ma'am.'

'Do. Thank you.'

Looking rather scared, the waiter hurried out.

'Let us move to this settee by the fire,' suggested Miss Hargreaves. 'The nights are drawing in; it is a little chilly.'

We moved and settled ourselves by a blazing fire. All thought of ever getting to the dance had now left my head.

'How kind people are!' she murmured. 'I expect little. All I demand is attention. Will you run upstairs, Norman dear, and fetch me my slippers? Thank you.'

I went up. A maid was unpacking and between us we found the slippers. Sarah was still fast asleep on the bed. Dr Pepusch's cage had been uncovered and stood on a chair. He was a green bird with a powerful bill and a temperamental-looking crest; he had a vilely malevolent eye. He growled something at me which I couldn't quite catch; sounded like 'avaunt'. I felt glad he was in a cage.

By the fireplace, in which a fire had just been lit, stood the harp, still wrapped up. The room was full of Miss Hargreaves' belongings; looking at it you would have said she had lived here all her life.

When I returned to the dining-room again, I found her holding out her stockinged feet to the fire. It wasn't a thing I should have expected her to do, yet somehow it didn't surprise me. She was perfectly at ease. She had the gift of being able to do unconventional things in the most casual manner, never losing her dignity thereby.

I gave her the slippers. 'Put them on for me, dear,' she murmured. She seemed a bit sleepy now. I bent down and eased the slippers on to her feet. 'And now,' she said, 'sit down and let me look at you properly.'

She looked at me properly. It took a long time.

'No,' she said. 'You haven't changed at all.'

I finished my pint. 'Since - when?' I asked.

'Since our last meeting.'

'Miss Hargreaves - ' I leant towards her and spoke solemnly, '*When* did we last meet?'

'I haven't the slightest idea,' she said simply.

I sighed and ordered another pint of beer; very good brew it is at the Swan. Miss Hargreaves murmured on, rather sleepily telling me tales about her old friend, Mr Archer. I drank more. A curious happiness, a contentment, a warm glow crept over me. It wasn't only the beer. I dare say, if you're a composer or a poet or a painter, you'll know that I-don't-care-a-damn feeling you get when you've finished what you reckon is a good piece of work. It's a grand sensation. That's how I felt.

*   *   *

I walked home about ten with very mixed feelings. Perhaps I ought to try to tell you about them, otherwise you'll be running away with the idea that this is meant to be a funny book. It is not; it is a very serious book; it is an account of the most amazing thing that ever happened to me, a thing that altered the whole course of my life. So please keep that clear. And remember it's true; I haven't made a thing up - except Miss Hargreaves in the first case.

I tried, on that queer walk home, to solve the mystery of Miss Hargreaves in various *natural* ways.

One. She was an escaped lunatic. Impossible. How could a lunatic know so much about me, having only that one letter to go on?

Two. Henry was playing some monstrous practical joke and this woman was his accomplice. Most unlikely. Henry's annoyance with me at the station hadn't been feigned; he, quite obviously, was firmly convinced that she was an old friend of mine whom I'd so far successfully concealed.

Three. As Henry himself had suggested, there had actually been a Miss Hargreaves staying at the Manor Court Hotel when my letter arrived. Now she, taking advantage of that, was playing a huge joke on me. Highly unlikely. Old ladies don't play such jokes.

Four. And this was the most convincing solution. I had actually met her somewhere in the past and, through some inexplicable lapse of memory, had forgotten her existence until, during that ghastly visit to Lusk church, she'd slipped out of my subconscious mind. It was a neat explanation; it fitted everything; it *was* possible for a person's mind to go quite blank. I decided that I'd go through all my old diaries to see if I could find any reference to a meeting with her or anyone like her.

Five. And this lingered; this really stayed in my mind. *What I had invented had actually come to pass.* Like that sermon years ago. Above all other possible solutions, this lingered. *I would like it to be so.* That was the danger. Always, simmering below every irritation, was a feeling of pride, a rich feeling. 'Mine,' I found myself murmuring; 'mine!' *My* work; my creation. Why not? Who knows anything? Thousands of mysteries all around us - stars, sky, chaps, girls, animals, flowers - and just why all of us are and do and die. Mysteries. Say what you like. Suppose this was simply another such mystery?

Proud of her. Yes. I couldn't help that. The way she had handled her affairs in the Swan had been magnificent. But she was a terrible strain on me; already a terrible strain. I felt worn out as though I'd been doing some really hard manual labour; and I had only had an hour or so of her company. What was I going to feel like after a few days - even weeks?

Thoughts like these soared in my mind, and I found I'd reached home without knowing how I'd got there. It was a lovely night; I yawned and went up the steps. I heard father's violin from his room, and guessed he'd taken the opportunity of mother and Jim being out to have a good go at the Kreutzer. I stood there for a few minutes, listening and looking at the great empty Queen Anne house caught in the moonlight over the road.

I yawned. 'Just the place for Miss Hargreaves,' I murmured.

I unlocked the front door and walked slowly upstairs.

*   *   *

I went to father's study. It's a wonderful room on the second floor, with a window looking along the back garden and up Candole Street where the Happy Union is. At the top of the hill you can see the Cathedral. Sometimes father lies on the sofa under the sill with the window open, and plays tunes on his violin to the spire. 'She's a lady, that spire,' he says, 'well bred; a proper lady.' And you feel he's right; particularly when you remember the Cathedral is under the patronage of the Blessed Virgin.

There are hundreds of books in the room; in bookshelves and stacked in piles on the floor. A large table in the middle is full of magazines, ink bottles, microscope slides, old cups of coffee, glasses, music, and tobacco tins.

A black Bord piano crosses the corner by the window. It's an ancient little piano, very far-away and pleasing in tone; the sort of piano you might hear playing from under the sea, if you know what I mean. A haunted piano, altogether. There's a picture above it of the Three Magi coming in procession to the Manger; by a chap called Dierich Bouts it is; very old, Flemish, full of colour, queerly like counterpoint. Bouts and Bord have always gone together for as long as I can remember; father says they're married. It's a funny thing, once, when the picture had to be taken away to have a new glass put in, the piano got terribly out of tune and some of the notes stuck. They're very fond of each other, clearly.

When I came in that evening he was sawing away at the rondo from the Kreutzer. A lamp was balanced perilously on some music on top of the piano. Father didn't stop. I sank into a chair, feeling very tired and muddle-headed.

Presently father laid down his bow and, finding an old hairpin of mother's, started to clean out his cigarette holder.

'Hullo, boy,' he said, 'come and play with me.'

'Too tired, Dad. I've been having supper with Miss Hargreaves.'

He nodded as though he'd known her all his life. Nothing ever surprises father; he can't even surprise himself.

'She bring her oboe?' he asked.

'I don't know what makes you think she plays the oboe,' I said.

'Well, come and try the slow movement of this Delius. It's a bit soggy, but it's got heart.'

'I'm very worried, Dad. I'm honestly wondering whether I oughtn't to see a doctor or something. I asked her how "Agatha" was - just making up the name on the Spur of the Moment, see?'

'I warned you years ago about that Spur, my boy.'

'And all she said was, "sinking". Like that. It was amazing. What do you think it means?'

'Delius is all right for a change; like going on to pudding after the joint. But you can't live on puddings. Take the Elgar *concerto - as a concerto* you can't beat it. Have an apple?'

'Do you think "Agatha's" a monkey? Oh, by the way, she stopped and actually spoke to the Dean. He was furious, glared at me. That horrible bird of hers screamed the *Venite* at him. He didn't like it, you could see that.'

'Monkeys like music,' he remarked, rolling himself a cigarette. 'If she plays the harp, as you suggest, probably she's got a monkey.'

'Do you suppose I've suffered some ghastly lapse of memory? I mean, I might have met her years ago, at Bournemouth.'

'Memory's a funny thing.' He twisted his moustache and a reminiscent light came into his grey eyes. 'I had a beard once. Before you were born, that was. Well, one night I shaved it off - or I suppose I did. Yet, to this day, I could swear I was trimming the veronica hedge in your grandfather's garden. He liked veronica very much, and I must say, one way and another, it does make good hedging.'

'I suppose Marjorie'll be furious with me for cutting the dance. Well, I can't help it.'

'Shall be glad to see her. Tell her to come round to the shop. By the way, who are you talking about? Agatha who?'

'Don't be silly. Miss Hargreaves.'

'Hargreaves? Oh. Ah. Yes. The woman you met at the Three Choirs Festival, you mean?'

'Oh, anything you like,' I sighed.

'It's astonishing what a number of interesting folk one does meet at that Festival,' he went on, tuning his G string as he spoke. 'I saw Tennyson there once, skulking behind a pillar and fumbling about in his beard. He dropped a bit of paper and I picked it up. There were only three words on it; I've got it somewhere in the shop. Remind me to look for it some time. Valuable, really.'

He started to play a tune he had composed for the G string.

'Come on,' he said, 'put in your accompaniment, then I'll give you some whisky.'

I went over to the piano and drifted in a few chords under his melody. It was a sort of saraband, very grave, soothing, yet - somehow - that particular evening, curiously disturbing. It was never quite the same each fresh time he played it. He'd never written it out. Towards the middle he invariably improvised something new. So my accompaniment had to be prepared for any modulation he might make, while the skeleton of the music remained always the same.

When we had finished, I sat for a long time looking up at the Three Magi and wondering, as I always did, whether any of them had moved while the music had been going on.

Father sighed, rather uneasily I thought, and looked out at the sign of the Happy Union - an old man and an old woman - swaying in the breeze from the red-bricked wall of the house.

'Can't help thinking,' he murmured, 'that the most lovely music is never written down. Like speech, like something said and soon forgotten, but still alive. You accompanied well, my boy; you've got real creative power, you know. Only, like me, you can't be bothered to control what you create. Well, perhaps we're not meant to; perhaps what we create ought to control us.'

'I don't like the idea of that,' I said. And I thought of Miss Hargreaves, perhaps at this moment playing her harp to Dr Pepusch. 'I don't like it at all. I - '

'Yes,' he said. 'Shaved it off. When I looked in the glass next morning, it had gone. Well, of course it had gone. You can't shave off a seven-inch beard and expect to see it on your chin next morning. But I never remember, and to this day I'll swear I was trimming your grandfather's veronica hedge.'

* * *

In my bedroom that night I sat up late, going through a lot of old diaries. There were a good many entries I couldn't make head or tail of, such as: 'Pall Mall ancients. Shove-'apenny sorrow.' But there wasn't anything that I could remotely connect with Miss Hargreaves. I gave it all up and went to bed.

TWICE a week, on Tuesdays and Fridays, I go to the Cathedral before breakfast to practise the organ. I always enjoy these early mornings alone up in the loft, particularly in winter when it's still dark and I and the bedesman who stokes up the stoves are the only people in the building.

Next day was one of my practice mornings. Before seven I was riding my bicycle up the High Street towards the Close. As I passed the Swan I glanced apprehensively up to the windows of a room on the first floor. Had all the events of yesterday, I asked myself, been a dream? I rode on quickly, trying to put the whole queer business at the back of my mind.

Going into the Cathedral by the little south door, I crossed the transept. It was a grey, gloomy morning; I felt rather depressed. Passing over the nave dais, I unlocked the gate to the north transept, left it open, and climbed the narrow, dark spiral stairway to the loft. The moment I saw the console, I felt better; I felt as though I had returned to an old friend, for ever faithful, of infinite variety of mood.

'Dear old Willis,' I murmured, gazing at his four silent manuals and smoothing my fingers tenderly over the yellowed keys. Switching on the current, I got out my music.

I had three-quarters of an hour before me, alone with the organ. Shortly before eight I would have to stop, as there was always a celebration of the Holy Communion in one of the chapels. Dr Carless did not allow me the use of any heavy work; I was expected to confine myself to the Great flue-work and, if I wanted a *crescendo*, the Full Swell. I never had found it easy to stick to this. A great organ is intoxicating; set yourself before one and see. Sometimes I had fallen to temptation, getting drunk on Great Reeds, disorderly on Solo Tubas, and ready to deal with all the miserably sober organists in the Royal College of them so long as I had the help of the Pedal Bombards.

I started on a Mendelssohn sonata, a soft movement, tricky stuff with a *pizzicato* pedal. Feeling complacent about my performance, I decided to go on to the third movement, a very flamboyant affair, brisk and battlish, in three-four. 'Damn Carless!' I muttered as the movement went on. I dragged out the four Opens on the Great and coupled the Full Swell; I opened the box and gave the Reeds their head. Sound soared above me, battering the immense Norman piers of the transepts. Within four bars of the end I read, printed in the copy, 'add Great Reeds'. Who could have disobeyed such an order? With a quick movement of my left hand over to the Great stop-board, I snatched out a handful of reeds - easy as plucking grass - Trumpet, Double Trumpet, Posaune and Clarion. Mixtures and mutations shot out almost without a hint. My right foot charged down on the Full Pedal composition. It was like accelerating to eighty on Salisbury Plain. Out shot the Bombards and the Ophicleide; a second later a sound like thunder filled the nave. My eyes strayed towards the Solo Tubas; somehow I resisted them and closed the movement on the Full Great and Swell, lifting my hands quickly from the final chord so that I might hear it rolling and rumbling about the nave and trembling in all the windows.

What a sound! Elated, I listened to it dying away like a tornado, chasing itself in and out of every arch and window in the building, up to the clerestories, until it was carried away to the very tip of the spire, out to the meadows, and so for ever lost to the ear.

Yes - but what was that I also heard? Faintly, far below, somebody clapping - somebody crying out: 'Bravo! Oh, bravo!'

Then footsteps on the spiral stairway, nearer and nearer, till they reached the top and the door opened.

*   *   *

'Oh, splendid, Norman! Splendid! What sound compares to that of a mighty organ? Perhaps you remember my sonnet; it appeared, I think, in *Wayside Bundle*:

'Roll out, ye thunderous diapasons, roll,
    And sound the battle-cry, ye roaring reeds -

and so on. But come, dear; play some more.'

Her face wreathed in a happy smile, she stood before me in the low little doorway.

'Oh, really Miss Hargreaves - ' I protested. 'You - you - '

'Well, dear? Well?'

I was speechless. She slid on to the seat beside me.

'You ought not to come up here,' I said. 'It's not allowed.'

'Tush! Fie! Play a hymn!'

'A hymn?'

'Yes. Let us have "Hark, hark my soul". And do the bells in the third verse. It is so hard nowadays to get anybody to make the bells in the third verse; they tell me it is old-fashioned to expect it. But no matter. I stick to the old things and I always will. Come, now!'

'Well, I'd much rather play you a Bach fugue. I can do the great G minor, if you like. You know. High diddle-diddle-dee; high diddle-diddle-dee - '

'No! No!' Her manner grew peremptory. 'I do not care for Bach at this time of day. No! No! "Hark, hark my soul." Come, here it is. Number 223.'

She placed the hymn before me. Fumbling about in her bag, she found her spectacles and adjusted them. Disagreeably, I started to play.

'Oh, slower, slower!' Her hand fell on my left elbow, checking the breakneck speed that I, in my displeasure, had commenced. '*Still* slower,' she commanded.

'You're digging into my arm,' I complained petulantly. 'I can't play if you dig into my arm like that.'

'Slower,' she said. 'How can my soul hark at that pace?'

I dropped into an absurdly funereal speed, thinking it would annoy her.

'Ah!' she said. 'That's better.'

At the end of the verse I stopped and turned over the pages of a Bach volume.

'Go *on*!' she said in surprise.

'What? Every verse?'

'Of *course*. A little louder now. Then go soft when you come to "Angels of Jesus".' She started to sing in a reedy, quavery voice. '"Angels of Jesus", softer, "Angels of Light"; now louder - more buzz, more buzz! "Singing to we-el-come the pilgrims of the night".'

CHAPTER FOUR

So we reached verse three with its celebrated 'Far, far away like bells at evening pealing'.

'Now make the bells,' she said.

I looked at the stops and considered how best to make them. Campanology has never been much in my line. 'Hurry up!' she said impatiently. I pondered. Nobody had ever asked me to make the bells before; it was a supreme test of my musicianship. Finally I decided to play the tune softly on the Choir, accompanying it with a quick downward E major scale on the Solo, using a very stringy Gamba, Harmonic Flute and a two-foot Piccolo, to get a tangy bell effect. It was fairly successful, though I got awfully tied up towards the end. Anyhow, it pleased Miss Hargreaves, who clapped vigorously when I had finished.

'Charming! Charming! Now the next verse. Louder now. Let me hear the Diapasons.'

After what seemed an eternity we came to the end. I closed the book firmly.

'Oh, more!' she cried. 'Unless you can remember Handel's *Ombra mai fu?*'

'You mean the Largo in G?'

'Precisely!'

'Oh, well, I suppose I can remember it.'

Disgruntled, I started to play. I don't think anybody else in the world would get me to do Handel's Largo at seven-thirty in the morning. As I played, Miss Hargreaves left the seat and wandered along the loft until she was over the chancel screen. Here she stood, looking down the nave. I watched her, and thinking of her my fingers strayed - all too idly - till I had lost the thread of the music.

'No - no,' she cried out impatiently. She hummed it as it should go.

'All right,' I growled angrily. When you're trying to remember a thing, nothing is more exasperating than people who hum you it as it should go. 'I can do it.' But the more I tried, the less I *could* do it. For some reason the wretched thing had gone completely out of my head.

Miss Hargreaves tottered quickly back to the seat.

'Move - move,' she commanded, pushing me aside imperiously. 'I can remember it. You do the stops; and the pedals. Oh, dear, how far away the seat is! Hold me! I shall slip off. Hold me!'

Very soon my petulance gave way to admiration. I don't know about you, but if a person's a good musician I can forgive them anything. And Miss Hargreaves *was* a good musician. I forgot all about last night. You may say that anyone could play Handel's Largo. You're quite wrong. Anyone can sentimentalize over it. But Miss Hargreaves made you feel you were hearing it for the first time; to her, obviously, the hackneyed Handelian cadences had never grown stale.

'I want more organ,' she murmured, gazing dreamily at the stops, her stiff little fingers working up and down as though in each one of them lay imprisoned a chord that had, with infinite care and love, to be given its freedom. 'Give me more buzz - more buzz!' she commanded. I coupled the Full Buzz of the Swell. 'Fine!' she said. 'Open the box, dear; open the box.' I fumbled about with my foot for the Swell pedal and pressed it down. About six inches away from the pedal-board her black shoes swayed helplessly.

'Hold me!' she cried suddenly. 'I'm slipping.'

She was approaching the climax. 'La-la-la la-la-l'la, la-la-LAH-l' Lah - ' she sang jubilantly. 'More buzz! The Tubas, dear! And why don't you put the pedal part in?'

The sound swelled out. I wouldn't give her the Tubas; I didn't see why she should have them, as I hadn't just now.

CHAPTER FOUR

I allowed her the Full Great; the performance was worthy
of that. Fascinated, I watched her, sitting almost on the
edge of the leather seat, her short arms stretched right out
to the Great keyboard, her little face beaming seraphically,
and the chains round her neck jangling to and fro as she
nodded her head to the beat of the music.

The last chord died away. 'There!' she said. 'I am quite
exhausted. Now you play, dear. Another hymn. Let us have
"For all the Saints".'

'We can't go all through that, Miss Hargreaves. We
simply can't.'

'The last two verses, then. "But lo! there breaks a yet
more glorious day." Oh, the *old* tune, I beg of you! None
of these dreadful modern tunes! Grosvenor *always* sang
Barnby. Barnby for me! Come on. Plenty of organ.'

I started on one of the Great Diapasons.

'Oh, more - more - ' she cried almost angrily. She
stretched rudely across me and grabbed a handful of stops;
amongst them were the Great Reeds. 'Still more,' she
demanded. 'The King of glory - how can He pass without
Tubas? More - more!'

The sound rocked about the roof. Infected by her extraordinary enthusiasm, I suddenly realized how magnificent
this old Victorian tune was. When we came to the last verse,
Miss Hargreaves was singing at the top of a voice which you
wouldn't believe *had* a top. Throwing all restraint aside now,
I unleashed the Solo Tubas and harnessed them to the
Great and Pedal.

'Bombards - Bombards,' she shouted above the glorious
din.

I released them. Loading the organ with its full charge,
I shot out the last line of the hymn; drunk with sound
I raised my head and sang.

'Everything - *everything*,' she was crying. Her hand snitched out a lonely Choir Lieblich that had been forgotten.

'That won't be heard,' I bawled.

'No matter. We might as well have it.'

The last cadence approached. There was a padding of rubber soles up the stairs. The door was hurled open. The Precentor stood there, his fat, red face sweating with anger.

*   *   *

'For heaven's sake stop this din, Huntley. Do you realize that Canon Auty is waiting to celebrate Holy Communion?'

'I'm - I'm awfully sorry, Mr Blow. I didn't know the time.'

'Why can't you look at your watch?'

'Yes - I see - it *is* a little after eight - '

'The Canon's been waiting up in the Innocents' Chapel for nearly ten minutes.'

'My dear Minor Canon,' purred Miss Hargreaves briskly, 'you are Minor, are you not? - is there any reason why the Holy Communion should not be celebrated with organ accompaniment?'

'Oh, do be quiet,' I muttered.

'Who is this - lady?' snapped Blow.

Miss Hargreaves pursed up her lips, took a small ivory-bound diary from her bag and made a rapid note in it. I could see danger in her eyes. 'I am not accustomed to being spoken to in this manner,' she said sharply. She went towards the door. 'Kindly move, sir! Kindly move! Make way. I wish to descend.'

'There's no need to talk to me like that, Madam,' began Blow. 'People below are trying to say their prayers and - '

Miss Hargreaves interrupted coldly.

'I think your name is Blow, is it not?'

'I don't see what that has got to do with it,' said Blow, feebly. But Miss Hargreaves had gone. Switching off the current, I hastily followed her down.

*   *   *

'Wheel your bicycle, dear. Then we can walk back together.'

'It's too bad of you, Miss Hargreaves. I warned you I'm not allowed to take anybody up the loft. There'll be an awful row.'

'Oh, tut! Life is made up of such little troubles. I abominate fuss. I shall see the Dean and make it perfectly clear that I am to blame.'

'No. I'd rather you didn't do that.'

'I most certainly shall, if only to report that wretched little clergyman. I am not accustomed to such insolence from a *Minor* Canon. Oh, dear, it is coming on to rain. Open my umbrella, will you?'

As we came out into Canticle Alley thin rain started to fall. Balancing my bicycle with one arm, I opened out the umbrella and handed it ungraciously to Miss Hargreaves.

'Oh, you hold it, dear! You hold it. I declare I am quite looking forward to breakfast, are not you? I ordered grilled sausages for two.'

'I can't have breakfast with you. I'm sorry.'

'You are very cross about something. Is it the weather?'

I was silent. I now loathed her.

'I hope,' she continued blithely, 'this is only the first of many such happy mornings. I must bring you some of my own compositions, a few meagre little hymn tunes, and you shall play them. Why do you not give a recital, dear?'

'Here's the Swan,' I said. I gave her the umbrella and leapt on my bicycle.

'The sausages - ' she cried, 'for *two* - '

'Give my share to Sarah,' I shouted. I rode on down the High Street savagely.

* * *

Breakfast was a very trying meal. Mother and Jim were in their most maddening moods. They never made any direct reference to my failure to turn up at the Clovertree Dance; in fact, they hardly spoke to me at all, simply went on talking to each other all the time about Miss Hargreaves. Henry had, quite obviously, most shamefully let me down.

'I'm sorry,' I began, 'I didn't turn up last night. 'I - '

Mother smiled sweetly. 'Oh, it doesn't matter, dear. We knew you were busy. Marjorie *quite* understood.'

My mother is a devil sometimes. I can't help saying it.

'I had an awful time,' I said. 'I think you - '

But mother was talking to Jim again. 'Of course,' she was saying, 'I know we are not out of the top drawer. And these chintzes are hardly as good as you'd find in the best houses.'

'You might hire a footman,' suggested Jim, 'and put a silver plate in the hall for cards.'

'I'm afraid it wouldn't ring true, my dear. People like us, very low, ill-bred people like us, we - '

'Oh, stop it, mother!' I said, miserably rearranging the bones in a kipper I had no interest in. I wasn't at all sure it wouldn't have been better to eat sausages with Miss Hargreaves. It was a rotten kipper, anyway.

'Oh, I'm sorry, dear,' said mother sweetly. 'I was merely wondering how we could make the house fit to receive Lady Hargreaves.'

'She's not Lady Hargreaves.'

'Countess Hargreaves, perhaps?' suggested Jim.

I lost my temper. 'Why do you both get at me like this? I've worked like the devil to keep her away from you; she'd drive you mad in a minute. You ought to be grateful.'

Father ambled in in his old green dressing-gown. He was eating a banana and reading *The Times*.

'Why aren't you using my new teapot?' he asked crossly. He rang the bell for Janie.

'I do wish,' said mother, 'you'd come down properly dressed in the mornings, Cornelius. It isn't nice for Janie to have to see you in your dressing-gown. The girl was strictly brought up in Suffolk and they're not used to such things.'

'Perfectly good dressing-gown,' mumbled father, dropping his banana peel in the coal-scuttle.

'I dare say. I gave it to you myself. But that isn't the point.'

Janie came in with father's breakfast. 'Make some more tea in the pot I bought yesterday,' ordered father. 'Oh, and Janie - there was a dead wasp in my shaving water this morning. Look out for things like that. I might have swallowed it.'

When Janie had gone out mother made a direct attack on me. Father was now muttering over the crossword.

'Anyhow,' said mother triumphantly, 'we've at last got the truth out of Henry.'

'What?'

'Oh, yes! He admitted that you'd both made up that tale about meeting her in the hotel and picking up her stick. He confessed you were both lying.'

I laughed bitterly. 'The whole thing's a lie from beginning to end. My God, if you only knew!'

'Are you after her money?' asked Jim. 'Because if you are, just say so. Nobody cares so long as you tell the truth.'

'Look here,' I said, 'you shall pay for this. I'll bring the old devil round here this evening. Then you'll see what I suffer.'

'There are people in Suffolk,' said father in sudden anger, 'who've never even heard of a railway train. They've got to grow up; they've got to gain experience. It's a perfectly good dressing-gown though I never did care for the colour. Give me a word in six letters meaning "this tree grows on paper".'

Mother, ignoring father as usual, came up to me, sat down by me and looked at me, quite kindly, yet searchingly, as though she were a sort of benevolent X-ray.

'Norman,' she said gently.

'Yes, mother?'

'It's quite obvious you're concealing something from us. We don't want to be unkind, my dear. If you've done anything unwise - you'd much better tell us all about it.'

I turned aside. It was so damned embarrassing.

'Thank you, mother. But I don't think you'd understand. I don't myself. I've told father the truth. Ask him if you like.'

'Well, Cornelius? What's all this about?'

'Eh? What do you want? Yes, I *did* put the orange peel there. What about it?'

'I wasn't talking about that. Norman says he's told you the truth about this mysterious friend of his.'

'Oh. Ah. Yes. H'm. Oh. Well - ' he scratched his head thoughtfully. 'Yes. H'm. Something like that happened to me once. I was in Basingstoke and - '

I groaned and went out of the room.

*   *   *

Half an hour later I was going down the Avenue on my way to the Cathedral for Matins. There was a wind blowing now; it was pouring with rain. The lime trees were shedding their leaves and everything seemed very grey and dreary.

I came down to the west porch and there, to my surprise, waiting under the porch, was old Henry, sucking away at his pipe, his hands shoved into his mackintosh pockets. He looked unusually thoughtful.

'What the hell are you doing here?' I asked. I felt about fed up with Henry.

'Thought I'd catch you,' he said. 'Let's go inside for a minute. I want to say I'm sorry, Norman, old boy. Felt I had to see you alone, at once.'

'Can't wait long. The last bell's going.'

We sat down on the bedesmen's bench under the statue of Charles the First.

'Well, I reckon you ought to be sorry,' I said.

'It just came over me, suddenly, in a flash. In bed last night. That damn bath. It stuck in my throat.'

'What do you mean?'

'I really did think, Norman, that you had been playing a game on me. I don't now. I felt furious with you on the station last night. It seemed to me that you *must* have known this old geyser. I was so angry with you that I didn't have time to realize what that bath meant. I saw it on the luggage-truck, you see. And it wasn't until I'd gone to bed and was thinking everything over, that it suddenly came home to me. See what I mean?'

'I certainly don't.'

'Well, you fool - *I* made up the bath. Not you.'

'Don't be an ass, Henry. Of course I made it up - '

'No, you idiot. I did. Last thing I shouted to you on Liverpool station. It stuck in my throat. To tell you the truth, Norman, Uncle Henry doesn't like it.'

'I'm glad somebody else doesn't like it. I simply loathe it. If you knew what I'd suffered this morning,' I told him.

'Of course,' mused Henry, 'you might have put the bath into my head. But I don't think you did.'

'Don't you feel rather - pleased?'

'Pleased?'

'Yes. I mean - about the bath. It coming true like that.'

'I don't know about being pleased.'

'The trouble with you,' I said, 'is that you're no artist.'

The last bell had stopped. Archie Tallents, one of the lay-clerks, came in from the west door, shaking his wet umbrella.

'Hullo, Norman!' he cried. 'When're you going to put up the banns, dear?'

*　　*　　*

If you know anything at all about cathedrals, you'll realize that if there's a story going round they'll have the cream of it in the lay-clerks' vestry. They talk about women gossiping. I don't mind telling you quite openly that a sewing-bee is a model of discretion compared to a lay-clerks' vestry. Take my advice: if you want to keep a secret, don't tell a lay-clerk - be he alto, tenor, or bass.

Not that I don't like the lay-clerks; I do. Particularly Archie Tallents, one of the altos, a very remarkable chap altogether with a gaiety that's almost goblin. Life's one long minuet to Archie. He has an enormous head, tonsured like a monk; great, furry eyebrows and a droll way of singing which has been the downfall of more than one chorister and has even been known to make an honorary canon giggle. If you were to wander about in the clerestory you'd find Archie immortalized in stone five hundred years ago as a gargoyle. (This isn't meant to be rude. Gargoyles may be ugly but they always have character.) When I say that Archie was also Jack Point and Lord Chancellor rolled into one,

CHAPTER FOUR

I give you him as nearly as I can. Everybody liked him. He ran a photographer's business up by the Milk Cross.

'Have you brought the harp, dear?' he said, as I came into the vestry. I saw at once they'd all been talking about me and Miss Hargreaves.

'What the devil are you talking about?' I growled.

Archie turned to Dyack, a jaundiced old bass who had been in the choir for centuries and still roared furiously through metallic moustaches. He was the world's worst singer, but he could sit on bottom D as easily as go to bed. A wicked old sinner, very rich in his language.

'Huntley's studying the harp,' said Archie, 'from the niece of the Duke of Grosvenor. Aren't you, dear?'

'Where's the Precentor put my bloody pitch-pipe?' muttered Dyack. The pitch-pipe is a long thing he blows when the service is unaccompanied - gives the note, you see. He always loses it and always swears at it.

Slesser, a smooth tenor - hair as smooth as voice - voice as smooth as silk - mewed from the cassock cupboard.

'Oh, naughty, naughty! Old ladies! Tchu!'

I drew Archie outside into the transept, and we sat on the monk's seat, an immense oak bench which is always reserved for the use of the lay-clerks.

'You've seen her, then, Archie? She's not in Cath, is she?

'Who? The celebrated niece?'

'Yes. Miss Hargreaves. I suppose that's who you mean.'

'I haven't seen her. Charlie Stiles told me all about her. I happened to run into the Swan on my way here. She's quite the rage of the town, dear. A crowd gathered on the landing last night, said Charlie, all listening to the Grosvenor harp. She played "The Bluebells of Scotland" three times. The cockatoo crooned a hymn. Very nice. I like a little bedtime music myself.'

'I wasn't there,' I said, 'I left before that.'

'Where did you pick her up, my child?'

'Oh, Archie!' I groaned. 'If you only knew!'

'Rescue her from drowning?'

'No.'

'Runaway horse?'

'No.'

'*Matrimonial Post?*'

'Don't be a fool.'

'All right, dear. Cheer up. The flowers that bloom in the spring have nothing to do with *this* case.'

'Absolutely not.'

Meakins, the Dean's verger, came up and tapped on the door with his wand. It was half a minute to ten. Under the tattered Crimean flags the boys were filing from their practice-room. The south door slammed and Dr Carless hurried in. Catching sight of me, he beckoned me over.

'I've had a complaint from Canon Auty,' he said. 'It really is too bad, Huntley. It reflects on me, you know.'

'I'm awfully sorry, Doctor.'

'The Precentor tells me you had some eccentric old woman up there. You know it's strictly against rules to take strangers up the loft.'

'I honestly couldn't help it. She came up of her own accord and - '

'No excuse. You should lock the transept gate. In future you're to confine yourself to the use of the Choir stops. I won't have you showing off the organ to strangers like this - '

'I wasn't showing off the organ - '

'You roar away on the full Great and imagine yourself to be an organist. Playing hymns - so the Precentor tells me! Haven't you got beyond the hymn-stage by now?'

Baker, that wretchedly supercilious solo-boy, was standing just inside the practice-room, adjusting his ruff in the
mirror and listening to every word the Doctor said. I don't
think I've ever felt so mortified.

The Doctor looked at his watch. 'Meakins early as usual,'
he muttered, hurrying away moodily towards the transept
gate.

Everybody was lined up and I went to my place. I saw
Baker whispering to young Hann. Devils, those boys are;
absolute devils.

The canons, like bees crawling out from a queenless
hive - the Dean was absent - emerged from the Chapter
Room. Old Canon Auty came last of all, fixing everybody -
including old Bishop Creighton in his alabaster tomb - with
a Mosaic stare and trundling his fist about in his enormous
white beard.

'The Lord is in His Holy Temple,' intoned the Precentor.

'Let all the earth keep silence before Him,' answered we.

'The Lord be with you.'

'And with thy spirit.'

'Let us pray. Wurra-wurra-wurra-wurra-wurra-wurra,
world without end.'

'A-men.'

Slesser's velvet tone rang the major third down the aisle.
We wandered in - boys with hands clasped in front of them;
men with hands clasped behind them; clergy with hands
unclasped. The Doctor trailed a sinuous tune from the Choir
Gamba. Meakins ostentatiously closed the gates. There was
a shuffling of knees upon kneelers. Matins began.

*   *   *

We had a busy morning at the shop. Father had bought
up a large country-house library, very cheap, and we spent

all day sorting the stuff out. The place was in the devil of a mess; no room to step anywhere.

'Put up the back-in-twenty,' ordered father. 'We can't have people coming in with wet boots and walking all over these books - not that most of them wouldn't best serve as doormats.'

Squeen demurred. He hates putting up that notice. I must say it's not particularly good for business.

'Do as I tell you, you withered jackanapes, you troll!' bawled father. 'And get some new strings for your violin, too. I'm arranging a concert. Back-in-twenty. Go on, you fool.'

Squeen sighed, hung up the notice and locked the door. Outside, the rain was pouring down, the wind howling. Winter seemed to have come in a night. For the first time in the season we had a fire in the shop. Cosy it was. I liked it. I was sitting on the floor under a table going through a pile of Caroline homilies in yellow binding. Squeen was very active, slithering up and down steps quicker than a piece of soap, and trying to find room for some of the new stuff.

'Alchemy,' said father, lifting up a massive octavo, leather-bound volume, very old. 'No,' he said, 'astrology. That's head bumps, isn't it? Catch, Squeen. Oh, you fool!'

He hurled the book at Squeen who tottered on the steps and came crashing down.

'My idea,' said father, 'is a quartet. Clarionet, two violins and piano. You'll have to practise, Squeen. I'll give you some time off.'

'Oh, Mr Squeen is no violinist.'

'I know that. But we can write an easy part for you. Don't know any music for the combination. We might arrange that tune of mine. I've always wanted somebody who could play the clarionet.'

'Who do you reckon *is* going to play it?' I asked.

'Now, here's Paley's *Natural Laws*; twelve volumes and leaves uncut. Might give it to Jim and Henry if they ever get married. They could use them as door-stops, I suppose. Clarionet? Miss Holway, of course.'

'If you mean Hargreaves, she doesn't play the clarionet.'

'This woman you met in Wales, Squeen, polish up this Surtees with some Ronuk and put it in the window with a notice, "Rare Copy". It's no value, but some fool of an American'll probably buy it.'

'Mr Squeen would like to remark that a lady is trying to get into the shop.'

'Pull the blind down then.'

I heard the yapping of a dog. Father went himself and pulled the blind down, blowing cigarette smoke over the glass. I stayed under the table. There could be no doubt as to the identity of that dog; I knew perfectly well whose stick it was that tapped so impatiently on the pavement.

'Must have that sign printed larger,' said father. 'Fools can't read it. Squeen, make a note. Why can't the damn woman see we're not back?'

Still the stick went on tapping; still the wretched little Bedlington continued to yap. She would get in; I knew she would get in somehow. Kneeling there under the table, a sudden insane feeling of rage came over me. Very strong it was; overpowering. I think I might have killed her had she come in at that moment. The whole thing was becoming too much for me. I can stand a good bit, but this was going too far. I've got a temper, as I dare say you've noticed, and when it's roused, well, it's roused, it's alive and awake, active and destructive. It wasn't that I actually *disliked* the old tea-cosy; no, not that. I liked her in a way. And that was just why I wanted to get rid of her; she was too power-ful an influence over me. I could see my whole life being upset by her. Already she'd caused a rift between me and Marjorie, got me talked about in the Swan and brought trouble upon me in the Cathedral. 'Damn her!' I muttered. 'Damn the old witch! Dog, cockatoo, harp, bath and all!'

But she was still standing outside.

'Yes,' father was saying, idly tearing a page out of Colley Cibber to make a spill for his cigarette. 'Time we had a bit of music. Wouldn't be a bad plan to give lunch-time concerts in the shop.'

'Go away. Go away,' I muttered. My face was turned to the floor. I saw a large, greasy, overfed spider crawling over one of the books. Black hate was in my heart. Flattening my hand upon the spider (a thing I couldn't ordinarily do), I savagely saw in it the face and form of Constance Hargreaves. 'Serpent!' I hissed. 'Depart from Cornford, serpent! Depart and trouble me no more.'

Squeen oiled his way round to a pile of books intended for display in the window.

'The lady's gone,' he remarked. 'Hobbling up the street. Mr Squeen thinks it a pity to have turned her away. Business, he thinks, should be as usual.'

'Stop talking,' said father, 'and take these Miltons up to the dump room. Nothing but Milton, always Milton in these country houses.'

I went cautiously to the window. Disappearing up Wells Street, almost lost under her umbrella, becoming fainter and fainter in the driving rain, went Miss Hargreaves. She looked so horribly lonely. I wanted to open the door, run out into the street and call her back into the shop. But she turned the corner just past Rawley's, the tobacconist, and I lost sight of her.

'Put some more coal on the fire,' said father. He thrust a red-calf Browning over to Squeen. 'Fuel,' he said.

'Browning, Mr Huntley,' said Squeen, fingering the book delicately.

'Fuel!' snapped father. He loathes Browning.

'That was Miss Hargreaves,' I said. 'You've missed her now.'

'Plenty of time,' he said vaguely. 'Yes,' he added reminiscently, 'only three words. There was old Tennyson, muttering bits from *In Memoriam*, skulking by a pillar in the retro-choir. He was tearing the band from his black felt hat, I remember. They were singing Parry's "Blest Pair of Sirens". It sounded more like a battalion of sirens to me. Never could bear Parry.'

'What were those words?'

'Damned if I can remember.'

*　　*　　*

Marjorie, as I told you, works in a cake shop. Not ordinary cakes. Special cakes, with walnuts, orange and coffee flavours, and a don't-you-dare-cut-me-with-anything-but-a-silver-knife sort of air. Jams, too; all arranged neatly on shelves with labels in their maker's handwriting. Autographed preserves.

I went round after lunch. I knew Marjorie would be pretty mad about last night. A spot of appeasement was indicated.

'Marjorie,' I said humbly, 'I'm damn sorry about the dance.'

'Oh, yes?' She was high-hat, you could see that; on a level with the cakes and fondants. I felt like slab-cake at sevenpence the pound.

'I honestly couldn't help it. You don't know what I went through. A wet bathing costume in a mangle goes through nothing to what I suffered last night.'

'They tell me you had a nice little dinner together. I suppose you bathed her and fed the dog and tucked her up in bed and gave her her bed-socks?'

'I shall kill myself if you go on like this, Marjorie.'

'Do. Here's a knife. It's quite sharp.'

'You don't seriously believe I'm in love with a woman that age who plays the harp, do you?'

'She plays the organ too, I hear. Did you spend the night with her in the loft?'

'You're a toad, Marjorie! That's what you are. A foul toad!'

'Don't call me names. I won't stand it.'

'I can't make out why you're like this. Miss Hargreaves is nothing to me.'

'She means enough to you to make you cut a dance I was specially looking forward to. Not that I missed you one little bit! Pat Howard thought my new dress was very nice.'

'I couldn't *help* it. Have you ever had a flea?'

'You needn't be rude.'

'Well, if you ever had a flea you'd know something of what I feel like. A sort of itching in the mind. I think I'm going balmy.'

'So does everybody else. I expect we shall get used to it.'

'I made her up. Can't you try to believe me? Henry was in it too.'

She sniffed and walking to the window started to fuss some honey pots. 'Perhaps it'd interest you to hear what Henry said last night?'

'Yes. It would.'

'He said you'd known this woman all along and wanted to hide her from us for some reason of your own.'

'Suppose it was true?' I cried. 'Would that be sufficient reason for behaving like a toad?'

She was silent.

'You're in love with Pat Howard,' I shouted, banging a toffee-hammer down on the counter. 'That's what it is. And you're seizing this as an excuse.'

'Pat Howard's got nothing to do with it. I'll tell you what we all think about you.'

'Do.'

'You've picked this poor old thing up somewhere without telling us, and you're hanging on to her in the hope she'll leave you her money. She's obviously well enough off by the way she flings tips about.'

I was amazed.

'Did Henry say that?'

'Yes. He did.'

'Well, of all the - I!' For a moment I was absolutely speechless. 'Why,' I cried suddenly, 'for that matter it *is* my money, anyway.'

'*Your* money?' Marjorie looked quite scared.

'Yes!' I was thoroughly worked up by now. 'I endowed her with a fortune. She could have been a pauper if I'd said the word.'

'Norman, you're *mad*!' exclaimed Marjorie.

'It's you who are all mad!' I cried. 'Not me. And if I did make the money, you needn't think you'll get a penny of it. Not even to buy you another new frock for Pat Howard to admire.'

I slammed the door and charged out of the shop. I rushed round to Beddow's garage. Will-hounding! Me - sniffing round a last testament! It was vile. It was conspicuously unpleasant. Anyway, Agatha would probably inherit every penny. It was just the sort of thing that would happen.

*　　*　　*

I was really angry with Henry.

'You,' I bellowed, 'you - who ought to be the first to realize your responsibility in this matter. You - who lured me on. You - who started the bath and the harp, who - '

'Damn it, Norman! I had nothing to do with the harp.'

'You - who insisted on going into that pestilential church, who dragged me into - '

'Don't dance about like that, old boy. You'll burst something, you really will.'

'I don't care if I burst everything.'

'All right, Norman. All right. Only do stop stamping in that oil. You'll ruin your trousers.'

'What are trousers compared to truth? My honour's at stake. They're saying now that I'm after the trout's money. And you started it - '

The puddle of oil splashed up into my face. I calmed down. 'Sorry, Henry,' I said, 'but I'm going to pieces.'

'Smoke a cigarette. And don't be so unkind to your Uncle Henry. I've told you I'm sorry for last night.'

'God! I've been a fool!' I moaned. 'I ought to have said straight out - "Madam, I don't know you".'

'Well, it would have been better, of course.'

'I'm going round to the Swan now, and I'm going to tell Miss Constance Hargreaves precisely where she gets off. And she can get off. She can fall off. You're coming with me.'

'I think it'd be better if you went alone, old fellow.'

'No. You're coming. You half made this creature. You're going to help me unmake her. If you don't, I shall black your blithering eye.'

'Norman, you really are quite excited, aren't you?'

'Get your jacket on, you ape.'

We went to the Swan. I was spurred, booted, ready for action, ready for any foe, ready to face Dr Pepusch even if he should sing the whole of the *Beggar's Opera* at me. Oh, I tell you - I was angry! I was the angry one!

'Miss Hargreaves,' I said to the girl in the office. 'I wish to see her at once. Send for her.'

'Miss Hargreaves has left,' said the girl acidly.

* * *

It bowled me over. It caught me fair and square in the middle of the eyebrows and sent me rolling. It weakened me.

'When did she go?' I asked faintly. I suddenly remembered that spider under the table; remembered seeing her disappear up the rainy street.

'Only a few minutes ago. She had an urgent message calling her away.'

'What about her luggage?' asked Henry.

'She only took a small bag. She said she'd instruct us about the rest. I suppose she's an old friend of yours, Mr Huntley?'

'She damn well is not!'

'Hush, Norman!' murmured Henry. 'These little paddies get you nowhere.'

'I don't mind telling you,' said the girl, 'that Mr Stiles wasn't sorry when she went.'

'Bit eccentric, isn't she?' said Henry sympathetically.

'Eccentric! I think she's mad. Do you know what she was doing all the morning? Running round from room to room collecting vases.'

'What on earth for?'

'For the dustman. What do you think of that? I won't deny she paid well enough for them. Mr Stiles is out now, as a matter of fact, buying some more; fortunately they've still got some of the same sort in stock. There'd hardly have been an ornament left in the place if she'd stayed any longer.'

'Henry,' I said, 'can you *beat* it?'

'What about the dog - and the parrot?' he asked.

'Oh, she took them. We saw to that.'

'Has she left any address?'

'No. But I should think Colney Hatch would find her, wouldn't you?'

With incredible rudeness the girl slammed down the glass door before the counter and went on with the novel she had been reading. Girls aren't courteous nowadays; you can't get away from the fact.

It was only two o'clock. 'Come and drink,' said Henry. I tottered weakly into the bar after him. 'What?'

'Scotch,' I said. I passed my hand across my brow. Sweating. Leaking. Shaking. All that anger and nobody to vent it on. Bad as having a broom and no dust.

'Well, anyhow, she has gone,' remarked Henry.

I groaned. 'Yes, and you don't realize the awful part of it. I made her go.'

'You - made her go?'

'Yes. Simply sat under the table and willed the old serpent away. Oh, it's awful - awful - '

'Why is it awful?'

'Because I want her back.'

'What the hell for?'

'I don't know. I'm getting fond of her. And I want to have it out with her once and for all.'

'I don't think that'd be easy, somehow.'

'Why?'

'I don't know. She struck me as being - ' He paused. 'Do you know,' he added presently, 'frankly, I was the smallest bit scared of her.'

'Scared of her? You! Scared of an old thing of eighty-three?'

'The way she looked me up and down through those what-d'you-call-'ems. Made me curl up inside and go to sleep.'

I nodded. 'Yes,' I said. 'I know. And yet I *like* her; I can't help it. I've got a wonderful sort of feeling of pride about her. I feel I've got to look after her. When she wandered up Wells Street this morning she looked so terribly lonely.'

'For God's sake, don't get sentimental about her.'

'I hate her and I love her and - I'm half afraid of her.'

'I think we ought to try to get her right out of our heads,' said Henry over his third whisky. 'You'll probably go mad if you talk about her too much. I've got a feeling it only aggravates things.'

'Yes, you're right, Henry. I see what we must do. We mustn't talk about her again, not to anybody. You must help me. Don't let her name once cross your lips; not to a soul.'

'It's not going to be easy.'

'We've *got* to do it,' I said. 'And if she does turn up again - I'll - I'll - I'll damn well ignore her.'

I knew it would be about as easy to ignore a boil on my nose.

'I've got an idea,' suggested Henry. 'Suppose we run the car up to Oakham on Saturday and see if they know anything about her there? I'd give anything to see if there was such a place as Sable Lodge.'

I thought about this for a long time. It did, of course, seem the obvious thing to do. But I could see dangers bristling ahead.

'No,' I said finally. 'It's tempting; but it's dangerous. Something would happen up there we didn't expect. We should only find ourselves making up fresh stories about her. We've simply got to behave as though there isn't such a person.' I slapped my knee. 'What we've got to try to do is to convince *ourselves* there isn't such a person.'

We were silent for a few minutes. I drained my glass. 'Miss Hargreaves?' I murmured. 'Never heard of her.'

'Who were you talking about?' asked Henry.

I rose. 'That's right. Keep it up.'

* * *

I went back to the shop.

'Telegram for Mr Norman,' said Squeen.

I ripped it open. 'Agatha sinking Hargreaves.' That was all it said. Handed in at Reading station.

I was beyond being surprised by now. I showed it to father without a word.

THREE weeks passed without a sign of Miss Hargreaves. Not even a letter came from her. Henry held his tongue; so did I. But I don't mind telling you I never found a tongue so hard to hold.

Mother was really very nice about it all. I overheard her talking to Jim one day.

'Jim, I think we'd better not say anything more about Miss Hargreaves to Norman. The poor boy goes quite pale when I mention her.'

'It's a funny business, mother.'

'It is. Very funny. But I'm sure Norman wouldn't do anything dishonourable. From all I can hear of Miss Hargreaves, she was a pretty terrible old woman.'

'You don't think she's blackmailing him?'

'My dear Jim, what a horrible suggestion! No! Norman's like his father. He gets himself muddled up with all sorts of ridiculous people and tells stories he hardly knows are true or not. Cornelius is just the same. He used to tell me he spent his boyhood in Canada; then, one day, it was

New Zealand. I shall never know the truth. But there - he's made like that. We mustn't judge people.'

'Yes, but all this talk of "making up" Miss Hargreaves. It's quite mad, mother.'

'Of course it is. But we must try to forget it. I suppose the boy isn't bound to take us into his confidence if he doesn't want to. I do wish he'd settle down, though.'

Mother sighed and I felt quite sorry for her. After all, father and I *are* a rum pair.

In a sort of way I did settle down; told myself that I would never be able to solve the Hargreaves mystery and that somehow I had stumbled upon something out of time. I'd read Dunne's books on the past, present and future; and though I couldn't follow half of what he said, it did seem to me there was a quality about time which had nothing whatever to do with clocks and calendars. But thinking only muddled me. So I stopped thinking. If I decide to dismiss a matter from my mind, I can do it. So can father. We're not the brooding sort.

I suppose now is the place to tell you something of the daily routine of my life. It centres round the Cathedral, of course. Matins every morning, except Mondays and Wednesdays; Evensong every afternoon, except Wednesdays, at four. 'Plain day', we call Wednesdays, which means that the services are said, not sung. On Sundays - Matins at eleven, when all the County big-wigs swarm up in their cars; Evensong, without sermon, at three-thirty, attended solely by people who come to hear the anthem; then an extra Evensong at six-thirty, which is what you might call a town service, when we have a lot of hymns, tubas from the organ and a straight-from-the-shoulder sermon.

I only had to go to the Sunday evening service every other week. It always bored me. What were called supernumeraries flowed into the choir stalls; dreadful people who hadn't a note of music in them. As the Dean was hardly ever there, nobody cared how they behaved. The boys used to read bloods or play tip-up during the lessons and sermon. Once there was a craze for cards. A pack of cards came sliding down one evening from Rapley's stall and lay scattered about on the ground in front of King John's dark old tomb in the centre of the choir. Meakins was leading Canon Padge up to read the lesson. It was a dreadful moment. Old Padge looked stonily before him as though nothing had happened. I remember he trod on the ace of spades. Nobody had the courage to remove them or could even look at them directly while the lesson was being read. Meakins wisely waited till the *Magnificat* had started.

If I hated that Sunday evening service, I hated the stuffy Sunday morning service almost as much. The truth is, cathedrals aren't meant for crowds. The less people you have in them, and the less chairs, the better. Even if you don't find people and chairs, you find tombstones and monuments to old generals or bishops nobody has ever heard of. It's all a great mistake. If I were a dean I'd do something about it. But deans aren't what they were.

The times when I really loved the Cathedral were weekdays when you could look right down the great nave, seeing perhaps only one tripper creeping from pillar to pillar with a guidebook, a vigilant verger stalking him and ready to net him if he so much as sneezed. In winter you'd see nothing at all except the light from one gas-globe plunged smokily into the remote and vast darkness of the nave roof. Then you really felt that Evensong and the Cathedral *meant* something. Heralded by old Dyack and his pitchpipe, Tallis in the Dorian Mode would float down the aisles; a motet by William Byrd weave its intricate pattern upon the dark silence. At such times I believe we all felt, even the boys, a relationship to the great roof that soared away above us and to the wonderful old monks and people who'd built it all, and wrote that glorious music, centuries ago.

*   *   *

The usual handful of queer people regularly haunted the Cathedral. Amongst them was Colonel Temperley, who had a very roving face and a very purple nose. The boys called him the Purple Emperor. He loved music, this old buffer; particularly jammy things like the oboe solo in Stanford's *Nunc Dimittis* in A major. At such moments he would weep; you expected him to roll right down the nave in his ecstasy. Afterwards, he'd tip any of the boys who cared to dog his footsteps, a half-crown or two.

Then there was Miss Linkinghorne. I am told by a friend that you can find a Miss Linkinghorne in every cathedral in the United Kingdom. But I like her so much I am going to put her in. She was an elderly lady whose outstanding eccentricity was to dress always in the colours of the Church's seasons. During Advent and Lent she would wear purple, which was very suitable; but then would occur Whitsun or a Martyr's day, and lo - she would appear in scarlet. In the long Trinity period, from about June to November, she was decently garbed in shades of green; at Easter, Christmas, All Saints and such major festivals, she blossomed out in white or cream. At Easter, adorned also with primroses, actual and artificial (I believe she somehow connected Lord Beaconsfield with the Resurrection), this purity of costume did not appear incongruous. But I never thought the effect was so happy on Christmas Day when she contrived somehow to make herself look like a snowman. She was very thorough in all her colour schemes, carrying it down to such details as gloves, handbag, even handkerchief. In the hall-stand in her house were five parasols: white, purple, green, red and black (for Good Friday, not rain). She talked excessively of Jerusalem, and once a year had the choristers to a party which had become the season's best joke.

Dear Miss Linkinghorne! My heart goes out to you - and to other persons, less noteworthy - canons, minor canons, choristers, vergers, bedesmen and lay-clerks - who almost daily were to be found in Beauvais' ancient building. I could tell stories of all of them; stories that would not be believed. How old Canon Hepple, for example, wandered up to read the Litany with a mouse-trap trailing from his cassock. But this is the history of Miss Hargreaves, not of Cornford Cathedral.

*   *   *

One Saturday afternoon towards the end of September, I came out of a cinema with Henry, Marjorie and Jim. Marjorie and I had patched up our quarrel and I was in a very light-hearted mood. The film had been a comic, and we were all talking about an absurd hat which one of the female characters had worn.

'Nowadays,' I said jokingly, as we turned into Dumper's for tea, 'girls haven't the courage to wear something out of the way like that. You're all fettered by fashion.'

'If we did wear such hats,' said Marjorie, taking me seriously as usual, 'you men wouldn't be seen dead with us.'

'On the contrary,' I said, 'I'd be proud to be seen out with you in something really original for a change. Girls are all too much alike.'

I winked at Henry, who was ordering crumpets and tea.

'That's right,' he agreed cheerily. 'You want to learn to brighten things up a bit, you girls. That's what you're here for, anyway. Pity you didn't study Miss Hargreaves more.'

There was an uncomfortable silence. I glared at Henry and studied the menu card. Connie's name hadn't once passed our lips in the last week or so. It was mad of him to revive her again just when people were beginning to forget her.

'How about having some meringues,' I began.

But Jim, who really never could get her knife out of Miss Hargreaves, said bitterly, 'To hell with Miss Hargreaves!'

Of course that set me off. Certainly, to hell with her; but not at Jim's behest.

'There's not the slightest need to be unkind about the poor old thing,' I said.

The tea and crumpets came. In a few minutes the conversation had swept me along against my will and we were all arguing hotly. It was utterly maddening. I didn't want to talk about Miss Hargreaves. But I never could bear to hear her attacked.

It broiled up to a proper row.

'You're absolutely potty about her,' said Marjorie. 'I call it rather indecent the way you went on. I was sorry for her.'

'I don't need you to be sorry for her!' I snapped. 'Anyway, I'm not a little bit potty about her.'

'Oh, yes, you are! Just because you won't talk about her that doesn't mean to say you're not always thinking of her. I know perfectly well when you're thinking of her. A sort of soppy air comes over you.'

'You screamed her name in your sleep last night,' said Jim.

'It'd be a good thing if you kept your ear away from my bedroom door.'

'Of course,' remarked Marjorie airily, 'you're really peeved to death because she's gone away and not written to you.'

I laughed scornfully.

'What piffle! Why, if I wanted her back, she'd come back. I don't want her back. I'm glad she's gone. I made her go, anyway. And as I did it solely for your benefit, I'd be grateful if you'd stop nagging.'

'Oh, so I nag, do I?'

'Nag! You'd nag the wool out of the woolsack.'

'I wish you two would shut up,' complained Jim. 'Everybody's looking at you.'

So they were. And listening. When we stopped talking the room was as quiet as the North Pole. Henry rose and went to the pay-desk to settle the bill. I followed him moodily.

'You do get sizzled up about Connie,' he said irritably.

'It was mad of you to bring her name up like that,' I told him.

'It slipped out. Anyway, that was no reason for you to get so worked up. You just don't seem able to keep calm where Connie is concerned. It's ridiculous.'

'I can't help it, Henry. Somehow, I simply can't bear her to be attacked. I believe I'd give anything to see her again. Just once so as I could know she was really real.'

'Whistle and she'll come to you, my lad,' remarked Henry lightly.

We all went out into the street and stood watching a flame of sunset over the market buildings. It made me feel rather ashamed of myself. Sunsets always do.

'I'm sorry, Marjorie,' I said.

But she was chillily silent as we walked home. I tried to talk lightly; to pretend we hadn't really quarrelled. I stuck my hands in my pockets and whistled casually in the way one does when trouble is near at hand. I sometimes think that that fellow who faced the fat bulls of Bashan closing in on him must have known a thing or two about whistling.

*   *   *

I shan't forget Michaelmas Day that year. It was a beautiful afternoon, very warm. The great west doors were wide open at the bottom of the nave, and through them, firing the thousands of chipped colours in the mighty window that Cromwell had smashed, streamed the sun, dark gold and growing deeper as Evensong went on. I was feeling happy, loving the Cathedral, loving everything. From one of the little windows high up in the choir clerestory a ray of sun struck upon King John's tomb. The Doctor started quietly to play the introduction to the *Magnificat* (it was Stanford in A), increasing his registration bar by bar until that thrilling moment came when we all crashed in at the words 'My soul doth magnify the Lord'. Colonel Temperley clung to the wooden pillars of his Miserere seat, dabbing his eyes with a check handkerchief. Miss Linkinghorne, veiled in warm tones of red, gently waved her fingers to the beat of the music. A stray honorary canon tried to look over Archdeacon Cutler's copy, but receiving no encouragement, turned aside petulantly. The Precentor, as usual, was writing something in his diary. Archie Tallents turned to Slesser, bowed and cooed sweetly. Meakins, always on time and never caring how long the *Gloria* was, approached the Dean's door and, undoing it, waited with his wand over his shoulder. The Dean rather wearily snapped his horn glasses into their case, blew his nose with an enormous silk handkerchief, and followed Meakins up, past the pool of sunlight, to the lectern.

We sat down for the second lesson, and I studied my copy of the anthem. *And I saw another Angel ascending in the East, having the sign of the living God.*

Wonderful words. Almost automatically I looked east, up the choir to the great reredos.

The sign of the living God?

Well, I don't know whether you could call a hat a sign, but I certainly never had seen a hat like that before.

*   *   *

Archie Tallents, who missed nothing that went on in the Cathedral, wrinkled his brow and gazed up to the Bishop's Throne, near the south door to the choir.

'The Angel *has* ascended in the east,' he murmured.

It was true. Reposing calmly in the rich cushions under the carved canopy of the throne, sat Constance Hargreaves. On her head was a truly remarkable hat; a strange and very wonderful hat. It was cylindrical in shape, taller than a topper, with barely any brim, made of some smooth cream-coloured fur and softened by many veils. On anyone else it would have looked quite ridiculous. But somehow, as usual, Connie got away with it. You couldn't laugh; you could only hold your breath and wonder. Sublimely unconscious of the attention she was attracting (the Bishop's Throne is the most conspicuous seat in the Cathedral; more than a seat, it is really a house, with its own door, roof, and stalls for chaplains, amply furnished with octavo leather-bound prayer-books and tasselled cushions) - sublimely unconscious of the attention she was attracting, Miss Hargreaves sat in this sacrosanct place, idly gazing through her lorgnettes at the emblems of Our Lord's Passion in the roof.

'Ye gods!' exclaimed Slesser.

'And fishes great and small!' added Archie.

'That 'at,' said Dyack, 'would 'old about ten bloody pints.'

And I heard Baker, the solo-boy, say, 'Mr Huntley's friend's come back again. Won't he be pleased?'

A chorister giggled; the four probationers tittered. The clatter of a lozenge tin was heard; a service-book came tumbling out of Baker's scob. The Dean hesitated, looked round sharply, then hastily went on with the lesson. Meakins stared up to the throne, half rose, sat down again, frowned and importantly adjusted his gown.

The lesson ended. We rose for the *Nunc Dimittis.* So did Miss Hargreaves. It was now clear that Meakins was prepared for action. Rushing the Dean home again, he gave a twist to his white moustache and set off at almost a sprint for the episcopal quarters. The boys, all eyes turned upon him, struggled weakly to reach the top F sharp in the *Nunc Dimittis.* Meakins had got to the throne; we could see they were arguing, though we couldn't, of course, hear what they said. After a few seconds Miss Hargreaves, looking very angry, limped ostentatiously down the choir, making far more noise than was necessary with her sticks, and finally seated herself in the Canonry stalls, bang in front of Miss Linkinghorne. In order to advertise her disapproval for all of us, she sat down during the rest of the *Nunc Dimittis;* she did not even rise for the *Gloria,* only slightly bowed her head. And I can tell you, it's not easy to remain seated for the *Gloria* in Cornford Cathedral. People don't like it at all.

Archie turned his large head to me and cooed, 'Lord now lettest Thou Miss Hargreaves?'

'Depart in peace,' I sang. But I couldn't see her doing that.

* * *

I suffered afterwards in the lay-clerks' vestry. Archie had no mercy. Everything was brought up. Dr Pepusch, Sarah, the Duke of Grosvenor, the harp, the bath, the visit to the organ-loft. I was spared nothing.

'Always knew you were one for the girls,' said Slesser, 'but old ladies - that's vice, Huntley! Pure vice!'

'Don't you take any notice of these nasty remarks, dear,' said Archie; 'remember you have to live up to a nine-foot hat and be brave.'

'Might 'a' been a mitre from the size of it,' buzzed Peaty. He is a little alto with a voice like a starving fly in a bottle. Sir Hugh Allan, who once attended Evensong, mistook him for a bassoon.

Archie put his head round the door and looked out into the transept.

'The Queen of the May is waiting for my Norman,' he said.

At this point Pussy Coltsfoot, one of our ancients, who always made the same sort of noise, whether he sang or spoke, asked whether we had observed the woman with the queer hat sitting in the Bishop's Throne. Being deaf, he had heard nothing of the talk.

'Huntley's girl-friend,' shouted Slesser above the organ. (The Doctor was wallowing in an endless Rheinberger sonata.)

'I didn't notice a bend,' murmured Pussy. 'It seemed quite straight to me. Like a drainpipe in the snow.'

'Concubine,' hummed Peaty right in his ear. 'Huntley's concubine.'

'You needn't be disgusting,' I said. I don't know about you, but I loathe that word 'concubine'.

Wadge, the other tenor, a pleasant fellow who has a habit of putting in aspirates in unlikely places (he has a favourite solo in which he sings 'Thou crownest the h-year') turned and patted me on the back. 'A faithful female friend is very nice for a h-young man,' he said.

'Wonder if that bloody 'at folds up?' growled Dyack.

The voluntary had finished; it was time to go into choir for the full practice. Already the boys were trooping in with piles of music. I peered round the door. There she was, prowling up and down, tapping the pavement tiles critically with her stick. You immediately felt they were second-rate tiles; you would have said that she had always been used to walking on the best Roman tiles.

The Precentor came in. 'Hurry up, gentlemen,' he said. He looked at me with a slight smile. 'Friend of yours waiting for you, I imagine.' He went out, giving the others a vile leer. I don't like that man.

Archie was just going out. I called him back. 'Look here,' I said, 'there's been some ghastly mistake. I want you to understand, Archie, that I do not know this damned woman. Somehow she's managed to hook herself on to me.'

'Hook, dear? You supplied the eye?'

'Don't joke. It's terribly serious. If she comes up and tries to talk to me, I've simply got to ignore her. I want you to help me, Archie. Walk out with me and talk loudly all the time. I shan't look her way.'

'Come on,' he said. 'Blow out your chest. Scowl and be a man. Take a deep breath and look at her boots. Glare critically at her boots and you're safe. Come on, dearie.'

Together we left the vestry and started to cross the transept. She was standing by Bishop Creighton's tomb, examining some alabaster cherubs, and for a moment didn't notice us.

'Quick!' I hissed. 'Quick!'

But she was too sharp for me. Whipping round, she cried out and tottered towards us.

'*Dear* Norman!' she cried jubilantly. 'It is so nice to see you again. What a truly beautiful anthem! Though I cannot imagine why you were not given the solo. Surely - '

'No talking allowed in the transepts,' said Archie severely. 'Haven't you seen the notices?'

'Notices? What notices?'

Archie looked round him. 'Ah!' he said. 'Meakins has taken them away to be cleaned. But the order still stands. Nothing but singing allowed in the transepts. Come along, Huntley.'

'Ridiculous! Ridiculous!' exclaimed Miss Hargreaves, flushing angrily. She followed us, talking all the time. 'I have been in a score of cathedrals and never yet have I been told not to talk in the transepts. I shall report the matter to the Dean.'

'The Dean himself made the transept by-law,' said Archie, 'and he will not tolerate it being broken.'

'I shall write to Grosvenor about it,' she snapped.

I bit my lip and said nothing.

'My dear lady,' said Archie, allowing her to catch up with him for a moment, 'transept talk is strictly forbidden, even to royalty. Read the notices when they have been cleaned.'

'We are now in the aisle,' she said triumphantly.

'Aisles, too,' said Archie. 'Except on Sundays.'

Slesser joined us, blithely humming 'h-where did h-you get that hat?'

'Norman,' panted Miss Hargreaves, in a voice that broke my heart, 'Norman - how can you - '

God! How unbearable it was! I hurried on, loathing myself.

'We are all very busy now,' said Archie. 'The music of the Cathedral must come first.'

Baker was standing by the choir gates, his hands in his cassock pockets, an insolent smile on his face. Still she followed us. At the gates she was stopped by Meakins. Hurriedly we went inside.

'Now, now,' we heard Meakins saying, 'we've had enough of you.' (Oh, it was *intolerable* to hear her spoken to like that.) 'No, you *can't* come into choir. Sitting in the Bishop's Throne - never heard of such a thing!'

'I had no intention of trespassing upon the dear Bishop's Throne,' we heard. 'I have never willingly sat on a throne, and I never will. Here is my card. I am a friend of Mr Huntley's; a close friend. Kindly move. I abominate fuss.'

'There's a practice on, Ma'am. You can't come into choir.'

'Tut! All these absurd restrictions - ! Why do you not have a notice forbidding one to use this ridiculous throne? Unless you are cleaning those notices too - come, come, my good fellow - perhaps - ah, I see we understand one another!'

We heard the jingling of money. Baker came sauntering in and pushed his way up decani side to his place.

'Tipped old Meakins half a dollar,' he said.

'We shall have to get the Doctor's permission,' I heard Meakins say. I saw him take her arm and lead her gently round to the north transept.

Baker turned and spoke to me gravely.

'Did you make that hat, sir?'

'You turn round!' I snapped. 'And give out the music, you brat!'

'Really, sir!' said Baker.

A moment later the Doctor came into choir; he looked very irritable. 'Huntley,' he called. I left my seat and went down to him with a sinking heart.

'This - er, lady friend of yours - she wishes to come into choir for the practice. Of course, you understand - '

'But, Doctor,' I began, 'she is *not* - '

' - you understand we can't start a precedent like that. For years I've been fighting to keep people out of choir while the practice is on. Go and tell her, if you please. Of course she's at liberty to wait in the nave.'

Anger mounted in me. I suppose because I loathe being made to look ridiculous. As I marched out on to the dais, I heard Collins say, 'Mr Huntley didn't half look furious, didn't he?'

I stamped across to her.

'Miss Hargreaves,' I said, 'nobody is allowed into choir during the practice. Dr Carless says you may wait in the nave.'

For a moment she said nothing; only looked at me reproachfully. I turned my head away.

'What have I *done*,' she said, 'to deserve such treatment from you?' Her voice rose; I felt that every ear in the choir was straining to hear her. 'What have I *done*? If you knew what trouble I had been through lately' - her voice broke - 'Agatha - gone!' She buried her face in her hands for a moment; her shoulders shook. 'Dr Pepusch suffering from psittacosis,' she continued. 'And now - I return to my beloved Cornford, expecting to be greeted by my old friend, and - '

The choir had started on 'O, where shall wisdom be found,' by Boyce; I was supposed to be singing in the verse.

'I'll see you presently,' I muttered, avoiding looking at her directly. It was no good. The moment she turned that heart-rending expression on me, I knew I was beaten.

*   *   *

The practice was misery. I generally never make mistakes (I'm an utter fool, but I'm not an utter fool at music), but that evening there were two tricky bars in Boyce's anthem which for the life of me I could not get right. Carless kept running along the loft like a trapped and angry beast, shouting down at me: 'Whatever is wrong with you, Huntley?

Take it again.' I would take it again, and again take it the wrong way. 'Stop! Stop!' The Doctor clapped. And when the Doctor clapped it didn't mean applause either. For the sixth time he jammed his white face through the brick-coloured curtains.

'Wadge, you take it!' he snapped.

It was dreadful. I had never been disgraced like this before. The boys, heartless creatures, turned and looked at me with a new sort of interest. Baker wrote something on a bit of paper and passed it down to that lout Tonkin at the bottom of decani; Tonkin burst into laughter. 'Silence, boys!' cried Carless. I looked down the darkening nave as Wadge went on with the solo I ought to have been singing. One lonely, forlorn-looking figure was sitting in the front seats, apparently writing something in a note-book. The practice dragged endlessly on; still that lonely figure sat in the empty nave.

*　　*　　*

The Precentor said the Grace; the boys rushed from their stalls as though unchained from a prison. The men went out. Slowly I wandered towards the gates with Archie.

'Now, Norman,' said Archie, 'take a pinch of snuff and go to it.' He offered me his little black box, but I pushed it aside. What's the use of snuff when you're in trouble?

'I can't face her,' I groaned. For she had risen now and was slowly coming up the dais steps. 'Archie,' I begged, 'tell her I've got an appointment. Say I'm ill. Anything. I shall slip out by the north door.'

Quickly I went up towards the reredos and thus out into the retrochoir. But luck was against me that evening. I saw Meakins disappearing along the south aisle, jingling his keys; he had locked the north door, the little door near the

Lady Chapel. To run after him now would probably mean meeting Miss Hargreaves and Archie in the transept. Yet if I stayed up here, I might be locked in for the night.

Unable to make up my mind about anything, I sat down on a seat near Cardinal Beauvais' Chantry. My eyes wandered to his opulent figure, lying stretched out in his magnificent red hat, a green ring, like an eye that sees all things, watching me from his finger. He'd have sent her to hell-fire, that's what he'd have done; sent her to hell-fire as a witch and thought nothing more about it. Nowadays one couldn't even arrest her. She could wear a hat like a wedding-cake, lounge about in the Bishop's Throne, and there was nothing you could do about it. If that throne had been the Cardinal's, she wouldn't get away with it so easily.

It was getting dark. One by one I heard the boys and the lay-clerks slam the south door. In a few minutes Meakins would be locking up. I couldn't stay here all night. Already that damned Cardinal was beginning to make me twitch. They said he came out from his chantry at night. I could believe it. I could fancy he was studying me, knowing that I was caught up in some vast spiritual problem utterly beyond me, and amusedly wondering what I would make of it.

I went to the aisle gate, peering down the steps to see if anyone were there. Not a soul. Except for the footsteps of Meakins far away at the end of the nave, all was quiet. Perhaps Archie had been able to get rid of her. Slowly I walked down the steps, pausing and listening and looking. I passed the Saxon kings; the tomb of Thomas Weelkes. I was in the south transept. I had only to skim round Bishop Creighton's tomb and I should be out by the little south door.

Suddenly I remembered my hat in the vestry. It was rather a special hat: green, with a nice tilt to it, a Bing Boys

air and a feather in the band. I was going round to see
Marjorie that evening. I knew I wasn't in her good books
and that hat would help me. The sort of hat Churchill
wouldn't mind having.

Well - all I can say, vanity gets its right reward.

Miss Hargreaves was kneeling on the floor in the vestry,
studying the lettering on the tomb of Jacob Burton, the
fisherman and naturalist.

*　　*　　*

She rose slowly to her feet.

'Fishing,' she observed, 'must, in those days, have been
such a noble pastime.'

There was a long and awful silence. I breathed heavily.
I knew we were heading for a crisis.

'Grosvenor,' she added, 'was fond of trout. Cooked with
a little orange-juice, it was his opinion that no fish could
be more succulent.'

'This is no time for talking of fishes,' I said.

She sighed. 'They are very soothing creatures,' she
remarked. 'Very bloodless.' She sat down by the table and
toyed with a pencil hanging on the chain round her neck.
'I once wrote a few lines that would seem to be appropri-
ate to this moment.'

'I haven't time for poetry,' I warned her. Neither I had.

She shrugged her shoulders. 'I would not pretend that
my poor lines were poetry. Mere verse. Nothing more.
They ran like this:

> 'I talk to them of candlesticks and pears,
> 　Of clothes lines, postal orders, wheelback chairs,
> 　Of plants (in pots), of pans, e'en polar bears -
> 　　To hide my woe.'

'Yes, very nice,' I began. 'But - '
She held up her hand. 'Wait. There is more.

'They talk to me of coal and china tea,
Of politicians, fonts and kedgeree,
Of saucers, sheets, hemp and the honey-bee -
'Tis better so.'

'That's all very well,' I said.
Suddenly this pensive manner changed. She rose and wrung her hands. She started to talk passionately.
'I come back after having buried poor Agatha. I look forward to meeting my dearest, my oldest friend again. What does he *do*? *What* does he do? He ignores me. Nay - more! He is actually rude to me! Norman - I can bear much. But not this - not this!'
'The time has come,' I said sternly, 'to get things straight.'
'Explain, I beg you!'
'Why' - I burst out the words - 'do you follow me about like this? I don't know you. I never did know you. I never met you before in my life.'
'Stop! Stop!' She tottered forward and clutched on to a chair for support. 'Not know me - never met me - how can you, how *can* you say these wicked, wicked things? Much have I travelled in the realms of gold but never suffered such a bruise as this!'
Her voice rose and echoed in the silent building. Far away I heard Meakins locking the west doors; then his footsteps along the nave.
'Do you' - she tapped her stick menacingly on Burton's grave - 'do you deny that you wrote to me while I was at Hereford? Dare you deny that?'

I gulped. 'No. I can't deny that. But all I can tell you is that I never knew of your existence before I wrote. I wish you'd put that whistle down.' She was shaking a little silver whistle at me; it lived on her chain with the pencil and the lorgnettes.

She stared at me. 'Tell me frankly. Is your mind wandering, my dear boy? Or perhaps I have offended you in some way. Tell me quite frankly. Is it my - hat?'

'Well, it is pretty awful!' I mumbled.

'I wore it for you, too!' Tears came into her eyes. 'I thought that you, with your love of the bizarre, would appreciate it.'

'Don't cry. For heaven's sake, don't cry!'

'I did not *know* it was a bishop's throne! There is no notice. I went to the first seat I saw. Heaven forbid, *Heaven* forbid, Norman, that I should in any way make myself conspicuous.'

This wouldn't do. We were getting away from the point. I was determined, once and for all, to make her see the truth.

'I don't care about your hat,' I cried untruthfully, 'or your sitting in the Bishop's Throne. I don't care *what* you do - so long as you don't drag me into it. That letter I wrote to you from Lusk - it was a joke, Miss Hargreaves; nothing more than a joke. It may have been a mean joke, and I'm sorry for it. We've never met before. You know perfectly well that - '

Her sticks clattered to the floor. I stopped, suddenly appalled at the effect my words had had on her. She had almost collapsed. Clutching the table for support, her head was lolling from side to side, her mouth open as though she wanted to speak and had no power to do so. It was terrible to see her like that. I rushed towards her and helped her gently into a chair. Weakly, she sat down, her fingers fumbling at a service list on the table and twisting it up into a ball.

'A joke,' she muttered, 'a *joke* - '

Shrilly, almost hysterically, she laughed. It was a laugh that made me go dead inside - so contemptuous, so ironical, yet so pitifully forced.

'Don't - don't, Miss Hargreaves!' I begged. 'I'm sorry for what I said. Awfully sorry.'

A deathly silence fell over us. She sat there with a fixed stare, looking at the crumpled-up service paper in her hand.

*　　*　　*

Meakins would, of course, choose that particular moment to come into the vestry. 'Well, I never!' he said. 'Her again!'

'You shut up!' I hissed. 'Can't you see she's ill?'

Still she said nothing at all; did not move an inch.

'Well, I'm just locking up,' said Meakins, taking off his gown.

'Miss Hargreaves,' I said gently, 'we must go.'

'Water - water - ' she whispered in a funny, sad, faraway little voice.

I filled a glass from the carafe on the table and handed it to her. For the first time she saw Meakins. A slow, bewildered smile broke over her face.

'Is that you, Archer?' she murmured.

'Wandering,' said Meakins, tapping his head unkindly.

'You hold your tongue!' I hissed again.

She was looking at me as though she had never seen me before. *As though she had never seen me before.*

'Where am I?' she murmured. And, looking at me as though struggling to remember, 'Who - are you?'

'Why,' I said, 'I'm Norman Huntley. You know me, Miss Hargreaves?'

The words were out of my mouth before I realized what I had said. Escape had been offered to me; I had rejected it. To this day I always believe that if I had not told her my name then; if I had been hard and denied all knowledge of her - she would never have troubled me again. Without my realizing it, the opportunity had been put into my hands; and I had thrown it away.

It was no good now. The moment she heard my name the bright expression came into her eyes; the old unquenchable spirit was returning.

'Norman!' she cried. 'Norman' - then, suddenly with a burst of recognition - 'oh, my dear, dear boy! My head is throbbing so! Oh, for a cup of tea!'

'Poor lady!' said Meakins, no doubt remembering her half-crown. 'Poor lady! You'd better help her home, Mr Huntley. You can see how she depends on you.'

Yes, one could see that; one did not need to be reminded of that.

'Come along,' I said to her. 'You - you'd better take my arm.'

She rose slowly and came towards me. 'Thank you, dear. I feel better now. Forgive me. I am an old woman. I get confused. It is the music in my brain; there is always music in my brain. How strong your arm is, dear! Where should I be - where *should* I be - without the life you put into me?'

'I'd very much like to know,' I said grimly.

We went out by the south door and walked slowly along the Cloisters towards the Close.

'The beautiful autumn air,' she explained. 'What power it has to revive one!' We came out into the Close. 'This exquisite September sun,' she murmured. 'Ah, Michael, Michael! What fire you pour upon the old!' She was as light as a leaf on my arm. 'You know poor Agatha has gone?' she said.

'I'm so sorry,' I said lamely.

'Ah, me! A lovely soul! So simple! So faithful to me! I have no friends left, Norman - except you. Remember that, dear: always remember that.'

'All right,' I muttered. Did she realize that it wouldn't be long before I had no friends left except her?

Suddenly she came out of this contemplative mood.

'And now,' she said briskly, 'let us meet your dear parents. I called upon your father at the shop on my way to Evensong. What a truly *charming* man! One can easily see, dear, where you get your brains from. Such taste - such a flow of eloquence! He asked me to come and have tea with you and your mother. Shall we walk or take a cab? Is it far? Yes? Yes? Don't walk *quite* so fast, dear; and speak up, I beg you; I am a *little* hard of hearing in one ear, I cannot remember which. Look at the rooks! Oh, that I might flee away and be at rest!'

'It would be nice,' I said.

'How often have I longed for it! But, alas, we are called into the world by the power of the Creator and must needs play our appointed part before the time comes for departure.'

We passed the Dean and Archdeacon Cutler. They stared at us for a moment, then hurriedly resumed their conversation.

'A beautiful evening!' observed Miss Hargreaves, as we passed.

The Archdeacon frowned at her.

'No, of course' - he went on talking to the Dean - 'we can't use the funds for - '

'The fire of Michael is upon us all,' remarked Miss Hargreaves to everybody in general.

'What - what? Michael? Oh, yes - yes. I suppose so.'

We passed on. 'Who on earth *is* that woman?' I heard the Archdeacon mutter. 'Relation of Huntley's?'

The Dean laughed. 'I really don't know. But I thought she made quite a passable bishop, didn't you?'

I heard them both laugh. Then we came to the north gate and Miss Hargreaves stopped by the trunk of a large elm that had just been felled.

'Let us sit down for a moment,' she suggested.

'You'll catch cold,' I said.

'Fiddlesticks! Colds are not caught; they are begged.' She sat down and beckoned me to sit beside her. In the distance I could see the Dean and the Archdeacon looking at us. 'Ah - the autumn leaves,' she exclaimed, 'spinning earthwards, to their common home! Ah me, life is strange! Would you care to hear my triolet on the leaves?'

'Later,' I said.

'No, here. I would like the leaves to hear it too. A simple little thought, but expressed, I tell myself, not unworthily. Thought cannot be new, Norman; it is the expression that matters.'

She rested her chin in one of her hands, gazed dreamily at the leaves, and declaimed:

> 'Sweet little leaves so brown and thin,
> Sycamore, beech, oak, elm and lime;
> Soon will your year again begin,
> Sweet little leaves so brown and thin.
> Sycamore, beech, oak, elm and lime,
> Victims of winter, weather and time -
> Sweet little leaves so brown and thin,
> Sycamore, beech, oak, elm and lime.'

*　　*　　*

We took a taxi home. Apart from the fact that she was very tired, I really couldn't bear walking down the High

Street with that hat. As we came to number 38 I saw mother and father sitting at the tea-table. Jim wasn't there, for which I was glad.

I unlocked the door and ushered Miss Hargreaves in. Owing, perhaps, to her interminable stream of talk, a curious stupefied feeling had overcome me. I didn't much care about anything. Let it happen, I thought; whatever it is, let it happen. I don't care.

I opened the dining-room door. Mother rose hastily, gulping down her tea when she saw Miss Hargreaves and the hat. Father looked up for a moment, said nothing at all, dropped three lumps of sugar into his tea, then looked down to the evening paper again.

'I've brought Miss Hargreaves,' I said. 'I understand father asked her to tea.'

Mother forced a smile as Miss Hargreaves sailed valiantly forward.

'So glad,' she cried, extending her hand cordially, 'to meet you! I have already had the pleasure of a chat with Mr Huntley amongst all the books. Books - books! My dear Mrs Huntley, where should we be without them? *You*, I can see at once, reverence literature as I do.'

'Oh, yes. I like a good book,' said mother shortly, fussing cushions into shape in her usual tea-party way and looking into the teapot. 'I wish you'd told me you were bringing Miss Hargreaves,' she said to me, 'then we would have waited tea.'

'Didn't father tell you?'

'Of course not.'

Father spoke for the first time. 'Miss Holway, isn't it?'

He offered her his hand which she took warmly. 'How do you find the weather in your part?'

'Oh, very fair - very fair!'

'Let me see, you play the clarionet, don't you? Now I've always thought that the clarionet wants very special handling. I'm thinking of giving a concert, and - '

'Oh, but the harp is my instrument, Mr Puntley.' (I couldn't make out whether she got his name wrong on purpose.) 'I toy also with the piano and the organ. But I fear a clarionet is rather beyond me. I am always ready to learn, of course.'

'H'm.' Father munched a cream bun. 'Can sell you a book on the clarionet, very cheap. Don't think much of these buns, mother. Not enough cream in them. Are they Dumper's?'

Miss Hargreaves sat down in father's special old leather chair with the ash-trays on the arms. Her eyes caught an old photograph of me, taken when I was two. Full of curls and petulance. I hate it.

'Norman?' she murmured.

My mother nodded and rang the bell for Janie. Miss Hargreaves had taken the photograph from the mantelpiece and was studying it closely.

'What *extravagant* curls! How proud you must have been!'

'Yes,' said mother shortly. 'Not a bad baby.'

'Children are *quite* certainly the arrows in the hand of the giant. Eh, Mrs Huntley?'

'Could tell you a thing or two about giants,' put in father, looking rather anxiously over to mother, who always scotches his yarns if she can. 'Knew a giant once. Strange case. Grew every time he stretched. Melancholy chap, too. Said he'd eaten something from the garden, some weed, and that did it. It started with his legs one night when he stretched, feeling very tired. Then he yawned and he could never quite close his mouth after that. Positive chasm, that chap. He was a gamekeeper. Some weed, he said. Wife ate it, too. She died when she'd reached fourteen feet. Went on tour in a circus. Funny things happen. You never know, Miss Holway.'

'Oh, *do* tell me what the weed was, Mr Puntley!'

'Nothing in particular. Just a weed. Have some salad?'

He pushed a bowl of lettuce and cucumber towards her.

'We're waiting for some fresh tea,' explained mother. 'And don't take any notice of Cornelius' stories, Miss Hargreaves. Are you staying long in Cornford, by the way?'

'I think of coming to live here. It would be an excellent place in which to spend the twilight of my days, near your dear boy, yourself, and that splendid cathedral. I shall give a few little musical parties. But one or two matters have to be arranged with Grosvenor first.'

'We close at one on Thursdays,' remarked father. 'Norman, pass Miss Harton the anchovy paste.'

Janie came in and mother ordered some more tea rather curtly.

'Talking about twilight,' said father, who seemed to be in a very communicative mood that evening, 'did you ever go to Norway?'

Miss Hargreaves, instead of answering, looked over to me. 'I cannot remember,' she said. There was an expression of uncertainty in her face. '*Did* I ever go, Norman?' she asked.

I paused. How the hell should I know? But supposing - 'I think you did,' I said, plunging wildly and hopefully.

'Of *course*,' she said instantly. 'It all comes back to me now! Those beautiful fjords - the midnight sun - the folk-tunes on the long pipes and all the icy glamour of the Scandinavian *geist*! Shall I ever forget how - '

'I was just going to say,' continued father, 'that before I was married - did you hear me, Dorothy?'

'Yes, I heard you, Cornelius. Before you were married.' She smiled indulgently as she took up some needlework. All the things that happened to father were before he met mother.

'Before I was married I spent some time in Oslo. Now, there isn't any twilight to speak of in those parts; you go from one thing to another. I found that this curiously affected one's behaviour. Did you, Miss Harton?'

'Oh - decidedly!' She nodded her head rapidly.

'How did it affect you especially?' asked father.

'Ah!' she said. No more. But father seemed to understand.

'H'm,' he said. 'Funny things go on. Have some salad?'

* * *

One of the most surprising things about Miss Hargreaves was the way she immediately took to my father and he to her. For what seemed hours they talked, neither paying much attention to the other, of course. Mother and I spoke hardly a word.

'Yes, I should like to start an archery club,' father lit his fifth cigarette. 'Ever tell you, Miss Holton, how the poet Swinburne took to archery?'

'I think not, Mr Hunkin. My name is Hargreaves, by the way.'

Mother sighed.

'Amazing!' said father. 'He made his own arrows, you know, and used them to write with as well. *Atalanta in Calydon* was written entirely with arrows, Miss Hargreaves. He'd take the manuscript, pin it to the board, and fire at it. Any words that the arrows pierced, he'd take out. Like that. You know the verse:

> O, thy luminous face
>   Thine imperious eyes,
> O the grief, O the grace,
>   As of day when it dies!'

'Ah, yes,' she said. 'I remember. Beautiful!'

'Well, before Algernon Charles aimed at that verse, it ran:

> O thy lustrous and luminous face,
>   Thine inclement, imperious eyes.
> O the grief, O the gall, O the grace
>   As of darkening day when it dies!

Algy killed about three million adjectives with those arrows. He used to say, "the pen that writes them in can shoot them out".'

'How very remarkable! Then, we might say, had not the poet indulged in this archaic sport, many gems might not have been lost to English poesy?'

'H'm. It depends, Miss Holgrave. Depends what your idea of a gem is.'

'Ah. Yes. True. I myself, Mr Puntley, have - '

Father rose quickly. 'Must go now. Got some microscope slides to go through. You must come up to my den one day, Miss Halton. Bring your harp.'

Almost immediately father had left the room, mother put down her needlework and asked the question I knew would come sooner or later.

'And how long have you known Norman, Miss Hargreaves?'

She smiled. 'Ask him,' was all she said. Stretching out her hand to a cigarette box, she took one and asked me for a light.

'An occasional vice!' she murmured.

'Oh - we've known each other for a - long time,' I said vaguely to mother.

'Really? And where did you first meet, then? It's funny, Miss Hargreaves, but Norman has kept us quite in the dark concerning his friendship with you.'

'In the dark? Tut! I do not care for that!'

'There's an ash-tray on the arm, there.'

'Thank you; thank you.' She smiled and blew a puff of smoke towards me. 'I really cannot remember a time,' she said, 'when I did not know Norman. We are such very old friends.'

'Well, fancy! I thought I knew *all* Norman's friends.' Mother laughed a bit petulantly. 'I do think you might let me into the secret now that Miss Hargreaves is here,' she said to me.

It was a critical moment. What should I say? Could I say I didn't remember? Should I again try to tell the extraordinary truth? No. It was too dangerous. She would probably collapse in her chair, even die, and we should have the frightful task of burying her, advertising in all the papers for a possible Duke of Grosvenor who would, if he ever came to light at all, be as difficult to get rid of as his niece. The hat would be kept as a relic to be stowed away in the theatrical chest on the landing; every time I saw it I would choke a sob and remember my villainy.

Hastily I searched my mind for an answer vague and yet satisfactory. Where *does* one meet people? From what sort of a place might one begin a friendship with an old lady? Church? Theatre? Cinema? (She might have been grovelling for her gloves in the darkness.) Concert hall? Pleasure gardens? Bookshop –

'In Blackwell's, at Oxford,' I said, hardly realizing the words were out of my mouth. Mother looked at me quickly. It was a plausible lie, of course, because I often had to go to Blackwell's to buy or sell books for father.

'Ah, me!' murmured Miss Hargreaves, heaving a reminiscent sigh and spilling ash down her blouse. 'Ah, *me*! *What* a memorable day that was! You know Blackwell's, Mrs Huntley?

Yes? Yes? You remember the little iron spiral stairway which leads up to foreign books? I had been up there referring to some Norwegian literature - it must have been shortly after I returned from the Land of the Midnight Sun. Shall I ever forget the dreadful moment when I lost my footing and fell crashing to the bottom? Ah, well, Mrs Huntley - we are sent many a blessing in disguise. For, without that catastrophe, I should never have met your good son.'

'Really? What did he do?'

'Everything, my dear Mrs Huntley. Everything! A compound femoral fracture could not, I am sure, have met with wiser treatment. Oh, those splints, Norman! Oh, dear, dear, dear!'

She burst into little peals of delighted laughter. Did I remember 'those splints'? I shifted about uncomfortably in my chair.

'The ones I made from the newspapers?' I suggested, knowing that, once again, I was on the Spur; once again, could not turn back.

'Precisely!' she said. 'Nobody, my dear Mrs Huntley - except perhaps my dear Uncle Grosvenor - could have handled a critical situation with keener presence of mind. If it were not for your brave son, I doubt whether I should be here - I very much doubt it.'

'Well, fancy! Who'd have thought it! Fancy Norman never telling me!'

Mother stared at me, half admiringly, half suspiciously. I smiled sheepishly. 'Oh, well,' I said, 'one doesn't talk about such things, you know.'

'Not alone flowers,' declared Miss Hargreaves, 'but many good deeds were born to blush unseen. Not that this is desert air, Mrs Huntley - not that this is desert air, indeed!'

'After that,' said mother, 'I suppose you saw quite a lot of each other?'

There was a tense silence. I was aware that Miss Hargreaves was leaning forward towards me, almost impatiently waiting for me to open the game.

'I met her again' - I gulped - 'in the - in the - Albert Hall.'

I sank back in my chair, pleased. I didn't care a damn now. Nothing mattered. You had to go on at this game.

'You mean when you went up for that big Choir Festival?'

'Oh - the heat that day!' cried Miss Hargreaves.

'Shall I ever forget,' I murmured, 'those' - (raspberries?) - 'strawberries?'

Miss Hargreaves clapped her hands.

'Oh, how happy we were! Happy - and foolish! There was an interval, you see, Mrs Huntley, between the rehearsal and the actual festival. Norman and I suddenly felt we must have strawberries; nothing but strawberries it must be! So we bought a little punnet and set out for the park. Norman suggested it would be pleasant to eat our fruits on a boat in the Serpentine. So off we set, Norman handling the oars most *awfully* well. And then' - she raised her hands - 'the catastrophe!'

She paused and looked at me. It was my move.

'The strawberries fell overboard,' I ventured.

'And *you* stretched out your hand over the side - ' she continued.

'And *you* did the same - ' I said.

'And - '

'The boat turned turtle - '

'And there we were,' she said, crying mate as it were, 'floundering about in the Serpentine!'

'Good heavens!' exclaimed mother. 'You might have caught your death, to say nothing of drowning!'

'It is such incidents,' remarked Miss Hargreaves, 'that link Norman and me very closely together. *Very* closely.'

The door opened and Marjorie came in. I wasn't prepared to face her, leave alone Jim. Suddenly my courage deserted me; I felt the ground slipping away from under my feet. Excusing myself vaguely, I rushed out and went up to father's room.

* * *

He was seated before his roll-top desk, examining a water-beetle under his 'scope.

'My God!' I groaned. 'I'm going mad!'

I fell down on the sofa by the window. Horace, the penny-coloured Tom, spat at me and leapt on to a pile of George Eliot stacked on the floor.

'You wouldn't believe these things had so many legs,' said father. 'I've counted eighteen already. Or are those whiskers? Come here and have a look. What's the matter with you this evening?'

'That woman. She mesmerizes me. What am I to do? I went crazy. Made up tales about us both, and she confirmed them all - even added to them.'

'Women are like that. Dare say the female of this species here are constantly saying they've got more legs than they really have. Wish I knew which were whiskers.'

'Damn your water-beetles! There she is downstairs, probably spinning the most ghastly yarns. I wanted to make it up with Marjorie this evening, too. What am I to *do*?'

'Have a drop of whisky. There it is, on *The Times Gazetteer*.'

'I honestly believe,' I said bitterly, 'that if I was to say I'd been up in a balloon with her, she'd agree with me.'

'I was impressed with that story of hers about Norway,' said father. 'Wonder if she ever met - who's that fellow? Wrote plays - ah, Gynt, that's the chap. Lord Gynt.'

'I never heard a story about Norway.'

'You never do listen. I say - look at this - this beetle's not dead. It moved.'

'Why shouldn't it move if it wants to?'

'But it's dead. Remarkable. Pity we can't get your Miss Molway under this thing. No knowing what we might not see.'

Jim suddenly came in. I could see she was cross.

'Oh, there you are, Norman!' she said. 'What the devil do you mean, leaving us stranded with this wretched woman?'

'I'm sorry, Jim. She got too much for me.'

'Well, she's certainly too much for us. Looks as though she'll stay all night. Come down and get rid of her.'

'She hasn't said anything about a balloon, has she?'

Jim looked puzzled. 'Balloon?'

'Oh, all right,' I said hurriedly. 'I'll come.'

When we got downstairs Miss Hargreaves was still holding forth. Marjorie looked at me coldly as I came in; poor mother was stifling her yawns.

'*Oh*, yes!' Miss Hargreaves was saying. 'Norman and I have had many adventures together. And I have no doubt but that we shall have many more. Old I may be, but I am still ready for - '

I interrupted. I didn't want to hear what she was ready for.

'Isn't it time Dr Pepusch was covered up?' I suggested.

She looked up. 'Ah, there you are, dear! Yes. Perhaps I had better go. Will you see me to my lodgings? Yes? I am temporarily staying in Canticle Alley, Mrs Huntley. My furniture is in store, of course. But as soon as I find a suitable property, I hope to get settled. Then you must all come and dine with me. I look forward to many musical evenings, many feasts of reason. By the way, my dear Mrs Huntley, I completely forgot. Are you quite recovered from this unfortunate fever?'

'Fever?'

'Scarlet, I believe.'

This wouldn't do at all.

'Come along, Miss Hargreaves,' I said very loudly.

'Who on earth told you I had scarlet - ' began mother. But I interrupted with a shout.

'Look!' I cried. 'A stag-beetle! Mind out, Marjorie - '

Marjorie, who is really soft about the mothiest moth, screamed and waved her hands round her head. I flew to the curtains and poked about noisily.

'Must catch it!' I said. 'Always wanted to breed them. Mother, call father. He'd be furious to miss this.'

'Oh, what nonsense - '

'Go on! Get father, I tell you.'

'Wait!' cried Miss Hargreaves. 'Let us be calm. Close all the windows and place this screen before the chimney. I will get my butterfly net - '

'Too late!' I screamed. 'He's escaped. All your fault, Marjorie. Miss Hargreaves, run out and see if you can shoo him back.'

'Father!' mother was crying from the hall. 'There's a stag-beetle here.'

For a few moments the wildest confusion prevailed. Fever, scarlet or otherwise, was forgotten.

'No good getting father now,' I said.

Miss Hargreaves returned from the front door. 'It has often occurred to me,' she said a little breathlessly, 'that since there exists a beetle who resembles a stag, there may possibly exist a stag who resembles a beetle. The frolics of nature tend often to mimicry.'

While she spoke she went to the mirror and adjusted her hat which, in all the sudden rushing about, had sustained a slight list. We all looked at her wonderingly as she patted it more to one side and carefully arranged the veils.

'That's a - ' Mother paused, then smiled and spoke. 'That's a very original hat, Miss Hargreaves.'

'You like it?'

'Well - ' Mother pursed up her lips thoughtfully. 'Yes, I think it suits you, really. Not everyone could wear it, of course.'

'I made it myself, Mrs Huntley. It is Lapland beaver.'

Marjorie giggled.

'Really?' said mother. 'Lapland beaver! Well, fancy!'

'Hats,' remarked Miss Hargreaves, 'were getting so abysmally *dull*. I felt a gesture had to be made to the world. Of course, you will understand' - her voice sank reverently - 'while dear Agatha was alive, it was not possible for me to appear in anything but the most sober apparel. But now that she rests - we *hope* - in peace, I do feel I am more free to express my true nature.'

There was a moment's silence. Everybody was wondering, of course, who Agatha was; nobody liked to ask.

'So,' continued Miss Hargreaves, 'I feel the time has come for me to strike a new note in the harmony of the trivial round. You girls are not going to have *all* the fun! Oh, no! The hat - of course - is a mere symbol - worthy enough, I trust, to be flung over the windmill, if there are any windmills left in the modern world.'

'You can always tell a person by their hat,' said Marjorie rather spitefully.

Miss Hargreaves looked her up and down in one second, from tip to toe. It was like the look she had given Henry on the night of her arrival, as though she were weighing the value of an object offered for sale at an auction. A devastating look. Marjorie coloured.

'Precisely!' remarked Miss Hargreaves. 'I abominate the commonplace!'

She walked rather stiffly to the hall. I followed her uneasily. 'Good-bye, my dear Mrs Huntley,' she said, 'and you, dear Miss Huntley. So you are called Jim? How quaint! A family version of Jemima, I presume. Yes? No? Good-bye. *Good*-bye!'

She ignored Marjorie. As I opened the door for her she said to me, loudly enough for the others to hear, 'Is there something wrong with that poor girl's finger-nails, dear? I noticed they were a most extraordinary colour.'

*　　*　　*

It was a rapturously beautiful night. By the gate she stopped and pointed with her stick up to the sky.

'The Seven Stars and Orion!' she declaimed. 'I feel I could seek Him who made them. But not in one of these dreadful aeroplanes. No! Balloons for me!'

'What - did - you say?'

'Balloons, dear! Balloons!'

'What made you think of balloons, especially?'

'How can I tell, dear? A floating thought. No more.'

Uneasily I suggested calling a taxi, thanking God there wasn't such a thing as a balloon-rank. 'It's too far for you to walk,' I said.

'No, dear! I prefer to walk on such a night. Give me your arm.'

Slowly we crossed the road. Here, again, she stopped, right under the board which announced that Lessways, 'this highly desirable property', was for sale. Little did I realize how dangerous a place it was to stop at.

Pensively she looked up to the starry sky.

'We are breath from the mouth of God,' she stated. 'For a time we remain anchored in the harbour of this little planet, but somewhere, beyond the starry oceans, lies our true home. Do you not sometimes feel you could sail there, dear?'

'You can go if you like,' I said brusquely.

'Shall we,' she continued, 'like the beautiful picture of Lord Leighton - a distant connection of mine, by the way - together twine heavenwards? Ah, me! What would I not give to shatter this sorry scheme of things and - '

Instead of shattering the sorry scheme, she shattered, with her stick, in a histrionic gesture, the agent's board above her.

'What is that?' she snapped. 'What hit my stick?'

'You hit the board.'

'What board?' She turned, looked up at it and read, in the light of the street lamp, 'This highly desirable property for sale'.

'Oh, I must take a note of the agent's name!' she cried. Out came the little ivory diary. 'Dictate to me, dear!'

I did so, never guessing what would be the consequences. I was glad to find anything to distract her mind from heavenly excursions. 'H. Carver & Co., Larkin Street, Cornford,' I read.

'And now' - she snapped her diary sharply into her bag, and grabbed my arm tightly - 'let us proceed. Do not hurry, dear; do not hurry.'

Ashamed to be seen with her - frankly I admit it - I avoided the High Street and led her by many side streets towards Canticle Alley. Over and over again she would stop, treating me to a long semi-metaphysical discourse. Once she stopped in Dome Place where some urchins were playing marbles.

'Ah!' She pointed over to them. 'The working classes at play. How very charming!'

'Hi, Alf!' I heard a shout. 'Got your catapult?'

'Come *on*,' I muttered, almost dragging her along, 'otherwise these brats will get difficult.'

'Let them, dear. Let them! Why not?'

A marble whizzed past her hat, missing it by one inch. Four ragged pairs of legs went scuttling round a corner; four heads popped out by the shelter of a faggots-and-peas shop.

'Dear me!' she murmured, mildly surprised. 'Did somebody throw something?'

'Yes, a marble. Come *on*. I shan't be responsible for your safety if you insist on standing here.'

After the longest and most tiring walk in my life we reached her lodgings, one of the stucco houses in Canticle Alley where every other window displays a notice 'room to let'. She made me go in with her. She had taken two rooms, a sitting-room and a bedroom. It was very dowdy and close and smelt rather of stale food.

'A dreadful place!' she said. 'But there are times, Norman, when I like to taste the dregs of life. I was perhaps too strictly brought up. I remember, even as a small child, I was constantly finding my way into Grosvenor's stables. All my life I have been too restricted, Norman. Now that Agatha is dead, I mean to sow what has long been unsown. It is a little withered, perhaps; but it is still an oat.'

'I shouldn't if I were you,' I said. I jumped back. Sarah had flopped down from a chair and was scratching ambiguously at my legs. 'Down, doggie, down!' I kicked the brute furtively; I always have loathed dogs who sniff and scratch at your legs.

'Where's Dr Pepusch?' I asked.

'Oh, in my bedroom. He always stays by my bed. You must come in and say good night to him.'

'No, thanks. I must be going now.'

'I would ask you to play to me, dear. But the piano - I see it is a Wade and Meggitt - is really only fit for firewood.'

She took off her hat and rang the bell for her landlady, Mrs Beedle. Then she sat down by the fire and warmed her hands while Sarah cowered defensively at her feet, showing her teeth at me. 'I wonder,' murmured Miss Hargreaves pensively, 'why my mind turns upon balloons?'

'I shouldn't think of things like that,' I said uneasily, edging back to the door.

'Those dreadful finger-nails!' she murmured. And louder, 'Who *was* that young woman, dear? No friend of yours, I hope?'

This was too much for me. I left the house without saying good-bye to her. The rest of the evening I spent alone in the Happy Union, drinking tastelessly. I was filled with foreboding.

I HAD splinted a broken leg in Blackwell's bookshop;
I had sported about in the Serpentine with an elderly
lady. The stories - with variations (some of them indelicate) - were soon buzzing round Cornford. I did not attempt
to deny them. What was the good? Mother, after her first
suspicions, fully believed both tales and was embarrassingly
sympathetic towards me. She also liked Miss Hargreaves far
more than I had supposed she would.

'Whatever you may say about her,' she was arguing
with Jim, 'she *does* wear that hat well. I call that an accom-
plishment.'

'But, mother, it's a *fantastic* hat!'

'Of course it is. But Miss Hargreaves is a fantastic person.
You know, I can't help liking her. Of course, I can easily
understand how difficult it must be for you, Norman dear.
I think one would get quite fond of her, and yet never want
to set eyes on her again.'

'That's exactly how I feel,' I said.

'Well,' said Jim, 'I think she was an impossibly rude old
woman. Look at the way she talked about poor Marjorie!'

'As for that,' said mother, 'I absolutely agree with her. I can't bear these painted finger-nails and I've always told Marjorie so.'

I went to the Cathedral with a low heart the following morning. I fully expected her to be there. But for some reason she didn't turn up; neither did I see her all that day. I kept well clear of Canticle Alley, of course. Every minute I expected I should bump into her somewhere; but I didn't. Had she chartered a balloon and floated away to her home beyond the stars? Who knew?

It was early-closing day and happened also to be a plain day at the Cathedral. Marjorie and I had arranged to spend the afternoon on the river - perhaps the last trip we should get that season. I rather doubted whether she'd come with me after what had happened last night. (Marjorie hates being criticized.) So I went round to Beddow's in the morning to see if I could borrow Henry's two-seater, instead of having to take the bus to Cookham as we generally do. I knew Marjorie wouldn't find it easy to resist a drive in the car; she's mad about driving.

'Well,' I said, 'Connie's back!'

'Good God! No?'

Apparently Henry had heard nothing about yesterday. I told him everything. To my annoyance he was very critical about the new stories Miss Hargreaves and I had made up. (I don't mind telling you I was awfully pleased with those stories. Who wouldn't be?)

'You've only got yourself to blame,' said Henry, 'if you *will* go on making up these mad yarns.'

'But, Henry - what the devil was I to *do*?'

'You should have sat quiet and said nothing at all.'

'With mother pumping me all the time and Connie glowering at me from her chair. Yes, I should like to have seen you sit quiet.'

CHAPTER SIX

'The truth is,' said Henry, 'you just can't resist taking people in.'

I was furious with him for that; furious because it was true.

'It's all very well for you,' I said, 'but you're not plagued by her as I am. I don't see why you should be.'

This was a deliberate threat. Henry knew it. I saw him go quite white at the thought of it.

'Well, old boy, I'm sorry, I really am. But to tell you the honest truth, I'm downright sick of the whole queer business. Don't get mad with me, now! Whatever happens, I'm going to hold my tongue from now on.'

'If you'd held your tongue from the beginning, we might not be in this fix.'

'*I'm* not in a fix,' he said truthfully. Which made me damned angry. It seemed so unfair. Why shouldn't he be in a fix too?

'I shall turn her on to you,' I said. I left the garage so fed up with him that I forgot to ask him to lend me the car. However, I phoned him later and he was quite nice about it; said I could have it as long as I liked.

* * *

Friday, September the thirtieth. Another dreadfully memorable day. Turning back to my diary I find this cryptic entry: 'Swans in tall hats.' Means nothing whatever to you, does it? Wish it meant nothing to me. Or rather, I wish I knew what it *did* mean.

It was another beautiful day and ordinarily I should have been looking forward to our trip on the river. But I couldn't. I felt something unpleasant was going to happen.

Parking the car at the Ferry-Boat Inn I chose a punt from Cooper's boat-house and we set off down the river.

'We're very quiet, aren't we?' I said.

'Yes, we are, aren't we?' she agreed, looking up from her novel. I extricated my pole from some weeds and for about ten minutes we sailed smoothly down towards the lock. I didn't know what to say. So I waited to see if *she'd* say anything. It was a lovely day, the sun mellowed in the faintly misty sky, the great banks of trees round Cliveden House turning to a rich gold. A lovely day, but rather a sad one. A long way away somebody was ringing the six little tubular bells of little Hedsor church; I don't know why they were ringing, but to me it sounded like a farewell to summer. Bells are like that; they cry a *vale*, never an *ave*. We passed hardly any other boats. Floating on the water were hundreds and hundreds of dead willow leaves; they, and the six little bells, made me think of all the hundreds of days and millions of minutes of my life that I couldn't account for. I got so melancholy that I knew there was only one thing to do.

'I think I shall swim,' I said.

'Do,' said Marjorie. If I'd have said 'drown' I think she'd have still said 'do'.

We entered the lock, the only boat to go in, and while we waited I lit a cigarette.

'Good book?' I asked.

'Very.'

'Who's it by?'

'Oh, I don't know! What's it matter?'

'Of course it matters. I can't understand you saying a thing like that, Marjorie.'

'I can only remember the titles of books.'

'Titles! As though they were anything!'

'Oh, do be quiet!'

'You're very good company to-day,' I said bitterly. It's always the way. Whenever I get depressed I quarrel with somebody; then I feel better.

'I just happen to be interested in my book,' she said.

'Well, I think you might be interested in me. A fellow expects a girl to say something when he sweats away with a pole all the afternoon.'

She laid down her book rather deliberately. 'You know perfectly well what's on my mind,' she said. 'If anyone talks about it - you only fly into a rage.'

'Well, go on. Risk that. Better than sulking.'

'Wait till we're through the lock.'

If you've got anything to say, it might as well be said in a lock as out of it, I thought. However, I waited, prepared for the worst. As soon as we were through the gates I coaxed the punt into the bank, laid down the pole and turned firmly to Marjorie.

'*Now*,' I said. It's a word I know how to use.

Again she put down her book and looked at me straightly. 'I don't believe that story about you meeting Miss Hargreaves in Blackwell's shop,' she said. 'I should like you to tell me the truth, Norman.'

I was silent for a long time. 'If I were to tell you the truth,' I said, 'you'd simply say I was mad.'

'Then it *was* a lie?'

'Yes.'

'Well, tell me the real truth then, Norman. It's rotten, the way you're going on; absolutely rotten.'

'Look here, Marjorie,' I said earnestly, 'I know my behaviour must have seemed funny, but if you'd gone through what I had, you wouldn't criticize. You'd be glad of a friend. I tell you I'm doomed - I'm cursed.'

'That hat!' she sniffed. 'I wouldn't mind so much if she didn't make you look so ridiculous. Everybody in Cornford's talking about you. And who is she to talk about me in the way she did?'

'If I do tell you the truth and nothing but the truth, will you *try* to believe me?'

'I shall do what I like with my own finger-nails,' muttered Marjorie.

'Oh, damn your finger-nails!' I cried. 'Sorry, darling - didn't mean that. They're lovely finger-nails - glorious!'

'You *do* still love me, don't you, Norman?'

'Darling, I - ' I kissed her. They always believe you when you kiss them. 'I wish all this had never happened,' I said.

'Darling, you talk as though it was something awful.'

'It *is* awful.' I told her everything then, from Lush church onwards.

'Henry'll tell you the same,' I said. 'He's as mystified as I am.'

For a long time she was silent, and I couldn't tell whether she believed me or not. It was very calm and cool there and I felt happier now I'd got it all off my chest. After all, she is a topping girl, really; it would be awful to lose her, I told myself. She's got such grace, such poise. I looked at her in her white dress and compared her to a swan who sailed up near us. Of course, she hadn't got such a long neck, or anything like that, but she had the same sort of dignity.

'The awful thing is,' I added presently, 'everything I now make up about the wretched woman comes true.'

'You mean - like Blackwell's shop and the Serpentine - and - '

'Yes.'

'Did you *really* make those tales up, Norman?'

'Of course I did.'

'But she talked about it too. When you were out of the room she said how noble you'd been to her - how she would never have lived if it hadn't been for your quickness. Although I couldn't bear the old thing, I couldn't help being proud of you.'

'But you said, just now, you didn't believe those stories.'

'It wasn't true. Of course I believed them. I said I didn't believe them because I felt certain something must have happened between you and Miss Hargreaves which you were hiding from us. I thought if I said I didn't believe all that, you might get angry and blurt out the truth.'

'I've told you the truth, Marjorie.'

'But - Norman darling - if you really can invent things which come true, why don't you simply get rid of her?'

'Do you hate her as much as that?'

'Don't you?'

I evaded this. 'I did try to get rid of her,' I said. 'I told you. I sat under the table and willed her away. She went.'

'And came back.'

'I *wanted* her back. It was my fault. I didn't really believe she'd gone for good. I tell you what, Marjorie; I reckon that if I could really bring myself to believe she didn't exist - well, she wouldn't exist. But that's damned hard when you see her sitting in the Bishop's Throne with a fifteen-inch hat. Isn't it?'

'What about the Duke of Grosvenor?' she asked. 'There *is* such a title, isn't there? I thought they used to live at Cliveden.'

'Yes, they used to - about a century ago. That's probably what brought the name into my head. But I think the title's extinct now. I believe there's a branch of the family in Ireland somewhere.'

'Couldn't you find out from them whether Miss Hargreaves is - '

I grew impatient. 'What's the good?' I snapped irritably. 'The more I try to find out about her, the more tied up I'm bound to get. Henry wanted to go to Oakham. I said no. Can't you see how dangerous it would be? Why, for all I know, I might actually have created a Duke of Grosvenor. And Agatha - look at that! She's dead. But there's a corpse somewhere which I'm responsible for. And I don't even know what *sort* of corpse.'

Marjorie shuddered. 'It's horrible,' she said. She withdrew from me a little, I noticed. 'If you can really do these extraordinary tricks,' she said, 'why don't you try something big?'

'Big?'

'Yes.' Marjorie smiled. 'You might turn her into that swan, for example.'

'I see,' I said bitterly. 'You don't believe a word.'

'I haven't said so.'

'Turn her into a swan! It's an absolutely mad idea! Besides, think how damned uncomfortable it'd be for her.'

Marjorie shrugged her shoulders. 'Well, you say you invented her. If you turned her into a swan, I might begin to believe you.'

She smiled at me mockingly. It was obvious that she didn't believe a single word I'd told her. If I *could* do it, I thought; if I could really turn Miss Hargreaves into that swan, Marjorie would simply have to believe me then; nobody would ever doubt my word again. The immensity of the job frightened me. Suppose I tried? Or - would it be better to try to turn the swan into Miss Hargreaves - so that Marjorie would really have her evidence at once? No.

Because if I succeeded in doing that, we should have her here floating about in the river, making an awful nuisance of herself. Besides, she might not be able to swim. Hargreaves into swan was the trick.

... It was done. In my mind, I mean. Almost before I could argue the wisdom of it, I heard myself muttering with terrific intensity, 'Miss Hargreaves - turn into that swan; Miss Hargreaves, turn into that swan. Don't dare to disobey me. Turn into that swan and no more nonsense. Don't come here, either. Change somewhere else.'

'What's that you're saying?' asked Marjorie.

'Nothing,' I said quietly. I held on to the side of the boat, feeling a bit queer.

'Why, what's the matter with you?' she cried. 'You've gone white, Norman darling. What's wrong? Do you feel ill?'

'I feel sick,' I said, in that lumpy sort of way in which you speak when you feel you're going to be sick.

She drew away hurriedly. 'Lean over the side,' she advised. 'Shall I thump you on the back - ?'

'Leave me alone,' I gasped. 'Don't talk. I shall be all right in a minute - '

It passed. I was staring at the swan. Nothing whatever had happened. The swan floated gracefully away from us, disappearing regally round a bend in the river. I had been mad to imagine I could ever do it. But the effort had given me a turn. Funny how the brain works on the body like that.

'Better now,' I said.

'What on earth came over you? Something you ate?'

'I tried to turn Miss Hargreaves into a swan. It tired me.'

'You needn't be funny, Norman.'

'I'm not being funny. I tried to do what you suggested. And it tired me. Damn it all!' I cried, getting suddenly angry with her. 'Damn it all! Turning old ladies into swans isn't easy work. You try it yourself.'

She looked at me very queerly and didn't say any more.

*　　*　　*

I swam presently. Slithering about under water I got back some of my composure. I don't know about you, but I can always believe in myself more under the water. The fact that I haven't got fins yet can still go on living with several gallons of that watery stuff above me, always gives me confidence in myself. Lately, I'd begun to doubt a good many things. Whether life wasn't one long dream: whether dreams weren't really life: whether I actually existed. Under water, I knew, at any rate, that I existed; I knew that because I knew that if I stayed there much longer I should cease to exist. Funny way of proving it, but it *is* proof.

I came up, spluttered, and looked about me. Immediately I doubted everything again. Miss Hargreaves - *was* she real? I'd seen her eat. But was the *food* real? Damn it all - this was a pure nightmare! I swam quickly down to the bed of the river again. Suppose she died? Then I should know she had existed. Well, suppose I killed her? I might be hanged. Didn't want that to happen. The parents wouldn't like it. Marjorie would get into the papers. No. Suppose, with all the power I was capable of, I willed her for ever away? It could never be done unless I could convince myself that she wasn't real. Had I believed in her when I had first brought her to life? Yes, firmly; she had grown more and more with every fresh thing I made up about her. Could I compel myself to behave as though she wasn't alive? Henry and I had tried that; and it had broken down.

A sentence of father's came back to me. 'Like me, you can't be bothered to control what you create.' Suppose - the dreadful possibility lurched into my mind - she were to control me?

My lungs were bursting for air. I shot to the surface just in time.

*　　*　　*

On our way back to Cookham I finally challenged Marjorie.

'You might as well admit it, you don't believe me.'

'No, darling, I don't. I'm sorry. How can I?'

'Well, whether you believe me or not,' I said, 'I don't see why you should allow her to come between us. She's done you no harm.'

'She's made you the laughing-stock of Cornford.'

'I don't care. Let them laugh. Miss Hargreaves is original, anyway.' I laughed ironically; but Marjorie didn't see my point. 'You're simply jealous,' I told her, 'that's all it is. Jealous of an old lady of eighty-three!'

'I don't know the meaning of the word "jealous".'

'Oh, yes, you do!' I dug about with my pole. I was angry with her now. It did seem to me that people ought to *try* to see, at least, how remarkable Miss Hargreaves was. 'Jealous,' I went on, 'because she's got style, and you haven't.'

'Oh. I haven't got style? I see.'

'There are hundreds like you. But there's only one Miss Hargreaves. You ought to be proud to know her. She's out of the rut. You ought to be proud to know *me*. It isn't everybody could do what I've done.'

'Look out for that pole, you idiot!'

'Oh - sorry!' I said to a beetroot-faced old gentleman in a motor-boat, who'd somehow got in the way of my pole.

'Another thing,' I continued, 'Miss Hargreaves *has* got a mind. Thinking that the authors of books don't matter! Huh!'

'You needn't say any more. This is the end.'

'Amen,' I said.

'You're not a man.'

'No,' I said. 'I'm a magician.'

Marjorie suddenly burst into tears. 'Oh, you beast!' she sobbed. 'You horrid beast! Saying I've got no style when everybody knows I'm the best-dressed girl in Cornford. Even Jim admits that. You beast - you horrid beast!'

'Oh, God!' I groaned. 'Don't cry! I'm awfully sorry. You've got tons of style. You're marvellous. You're grand. Miss Hargreaves doesn't come in it.'

'Give her up - never see her again. Then I'll know you love me.'

'I wish I could, darling.'

'Well, why can't you?'

'She won't let me,' I said. We didn't speak another word.

* * *

I dropped in to see Archie Tallents early that evening. He was in the dark-room when I arrived at his studio and he asked me to wait. When he came out a few minutes later he was holding a plate up to the light and looking at it. 'Just a minute, dear,' he said. Resting the plate on a dish, he went over to the telephone.

'Is that the *Cornford Mercury*?' he asked presently. He continued: 'I've got a nice picture of old Jezebel. Yes, got it this afternoon. Any use to you? All right. Send your boy round for it in half an hour. Good-bye.'

He rang off. 'Always carry a camera with you,' he said to me. 'Never know what you might see. Look at that.'

He showed me the negative. It was a group of people in Disraeli Square, some on the pavement, some in the middle

of the road. A long line of traffic was held up and a policeman was poking at something with a stick.

'Can't quite make it out,' I said. 'Somebody run over or something? Oh, yes - I can recognize the Dean. He seems to be back-
ing away from - my God!' I held the plate against my sleeve in
order to see it more clearly. 'This - isn't a - swan, is it?'

Archie nodded. 'That's Jezebel,' he said. 'The oldest royal
swan on the river, so they say. She always was a spiteful one.'

I began to feel a little faint.

'Will you open a window, Archie?' I asked. 'Bit close
in here.'

He opened the window for me. 'What's the matter, dear?'

'Nothing, Archie. I'm all right. Tell me about - this Jezebel.
What time did she turn up in the Square?'

'About four. Dear old canary came waddling out of
Canticle Alley - '

'Did you say Canticle Alley?' I asked faintly.

'Canticle Alley, I said. She stopped in the middle of the
road, by the traffic lights, as you can see. The policeman
got a little huffy. So did Jezebel. She seemed to want to lay
an egg or something. The Dean went for her with his
umbrella. Most undeanly.'

'Did they - catch her?'

'Catch Jezebel? Not likely! They had to turn the fire-
hose on her.'

'Fire-hose? Good God! She'll catch cold.'

'Is this fowl a friend of yours, Norman?'

'She - Never mind. Go on.'

'Well, she toddled away after that. Back to the river.'

'I suppose, Archie, you're quite sure it *was* Jezebel?
I mean - there wasn't anything unusual about the bird, was
there?'

'Unusual? Jezebel's a very unusual sort of bird. Very old bird.'

'Yes. A very old bird.' I agreed. I turned to the door. 'Well, so long, Archie,' I said. I felt I couldn't talk to him now. Something had to be done at once.

I rushed straight round to Canticle Alley and knocked at Mrs Beedle's door. Mrs Beedle came herself.

'Is Miss Hargreaves in?' I asked. I was shaking so much I could hardly talk.

'No, sir. She went out this afternoon and she ain't come back yet.'

'Oh. Do you know where she went?'

'Over the hills and far away - ' croaked Dr Pepusch bitterly from a room upstairs.

'Drat that there bird!' exclaimed Mrs Beedle. ' 'Uman, I calls that bird, simply 'uman. Miss 'Argreaves, she goes to the river. "Mrs Beedle," she says to me, "I feels like a blow on the river." Those was her words, her very words, Mr 'Untley. "What!" I says. "You go on the river, Mum! Well, just you mind you don't catch a chill, then." Because she's the sort that *do* catch a chill, Mr 'Untley, and go off sudden.'

'I know,' I said. 'I *know*, Mrs Beedle.'

' "There are times," she says to me, grave-like, "times there be, Mrs Beedle, when I am driv willy-nilly to do things as don't proper become a lady of my years." Willy-nilly - they was her very words. And she puts on her 'at, the one like a chimney-pot, and off she goes.'

'Oh,' I said. 'Yes, I see.' I felt numbed.

'She's a very funny lady, ain't she now?' said Mrs Beedle. 'Last night, look, you wouldn't believe her, her 'eart were set on a balloon, nothing but a balloon it must be. Well, look, my little girl got a balloon or two, see, so I blows one up - took a lot of breath it did and I'm ashmatical too - and

I gives it to her. "There," I says, "there's a balloon, Ma'am." But she says, "That ain't no good to me, Mrs Beedle. It's a real balloon I want." And she looks kind of wistful-like. She affect me, sir.'

'Affects you? Oh. Does she?'

'Affect me, she do. I don't believe she's got a friend in the world except you. She think the world of you. She tell me how you saved her life. Lonely-like, she is. Of course, she do wear odd 'ats, but look - '

I suddenly came to my senses. 'What time did she go out?' I snapped.

'Well, it would have been about four, Mr 'Untley, yes, about four, because look, the wireless was playing that minuet what they call it and - '

'Thank you,' I said. 'Good evening.'

'They go off sudden,' shouted Mrs Beedle after me. 'The nights is damp and she'll catch 'er death. They go off sudden.'

I reeled out into Disraeli Square, Mrs Beedle's gloomy words ringing in my ears. It was time for me to go home to supper, but I knew I shouldn't be able to eat anything. A drink was what I wanted. I turned towards the Swan. The very sight of the great golden bird with his wings outspread above the doorway made me feel sick. A coincidence. I muttered to myself over and over again; a coincidence. It must be, it must be, it must be. A picture soared into my mind: the picture of a swan in a balloon sailing away into the clouds, over the hills and far away as Dr Pepusch had prophesied. 'God!' I said aloud. 'No balloons - *please*. Whatever else has to happen, let there be no balloon. Change back, *dear* Miss Hargreaves; change back at once. Wherever you are now, change back to your proper self.'

I was staggering up St James' Street, making for Henry's house and hardly knowing what direction I was taking. I felt giddy and sick; I felt as useless as a pin without a head; I felt drunk with the knowledge of power that terrified me; I felt afraid.

I knocked at Henry's door. 'Damn fool,' I muttered to myself. 'There's nothing in it. It *can't* be true. Coincidence - coincidence - coincidence - '

*   *   *

He was having a late tea; deeply immersed in a book propped up on the teapot. I flopped down by the fire.

'Half a mo,' said Henry. 'Just finish this chapter. Most extraordinary story about a stockbroker who fell in love with his wife's boots.'

'Thanks for offering me tea,' I said.

'Sorry, old boy.' He poured some out and gave it to me. 'Been wenching on the Thames?' he asked presently. I nodded blankly. I felt unable to talk.

'Bit late in the year,' he observed, lighting his pipe and sitting in an armchair opposite me. 'Had a good time?'

'Interesting.'

'Made it up with Marjorie, I hope?'

'No. Made it worse.'

'Oh? I hope you're not throwing her over in favour of Connie.'

'Shouldn't be surprised at anything. Or rather, no - ' I added hastily. 'I am *not* throwing her over in favour of Connie.'

'How is the old fowl?'

I groaned. '*Need* you call her a fowl, Henry?'

'Well - hen, then.'

'I haven't seen her since yesterday. I believe she's changed a bit.'

'Oh? Dyed her hair, or something?'

'No. She's gone - rather white.'

'White?'

'Yes. White. And her neck's a bit stiff.'

'Oh.'

Henry glanced at me rather strangely. Then he walked up and down the room in an uneasy sort of way, jabbing the stem of his pipe in the nape of his neck. You could tell he was thinking hard.

'Look here, old boy,' he said, 'I've got an idea about you.'

'Have you? That's nice. Want me to see a doctor, I suppose.'

'No. Not a doctor. This psycho-analyst fellow. I think you might see him.'

'Who do you mean?'

Henry took up the book he had been reading. 'Fellow who wrote this,' he said. 'Marvellous book! I've found out a whole lot about myself I never knew before.'

'Why - do you think there's something wrong with me?'

'You never know. You're looking rather peeky. And you're growing extraordinarily absent-minded.'

'I never had much of a mind to be absent, Henry.'

'Well, it might as well be present, whatever it is.'

'Wonder if I could work her into a flea?' I mused, half to myself.

'What?' said Henry.

'Flea. I should have her under control more. I don't suppose a flea could hold up a line of traffic.'

'What the hell are you talking about, Norman?'

'Oh nothing. Let's have a look at that book.'

It was a green book, with a long list of contents under several sub-headings. It was called *The New and the Old Self*, and it was by a Doctor Birinus Hals-Gruber. I opened it at random and read a bit. There was a lot about the *Sesame*

Impulse and the *Agamemnon-Reflex* which made, as they say, fascinating reading. But I couldn't relate Miss Hargreaves to any of it.

'It mightn't be a bad plan,' suggested Henry, 'if you took Connie and had her psychoed too. You'd probably find she ogled you in your pram centuries ago.'

'You can take her, if you like.'

'Not me. No, thank you, old boy. Anyway, I've got a feeling that Connie doesn't much care for me.'

'You're damn lucky.'

'Well, what about it? He might help you. There's no getting away from the fact, Norman, you're up against something that we can't understand at all. And, after all, these fellows know more about minds and subconsciousnesses and what-not than I know about cars or you know about organs.'

'I don't know, Henry. I don't much believe in them. I tell you - ' A sudden idea came to me. 'I tell you who *might* help.'

'Who?'

'Father Toule.'

'What? That comic little R.C. with a face like an egg?'

'I reckon he'd understand this sort of thing somehow. It's - well, it's a miracle, and Roman Catholics know more about miracles than most people.'

'Why don't you go to the Dean? He's a kind old bird. He'd listen.'

'Yes. And think I was mad. Father Toule wouldn't think that.'

'I don't see why.'

'He came into the shop one day, Henry; and bought an old book about some queer saint-chappie. Joseph, he's called; Joseph of Cupertino. He used to fly.'

'First time I've heard of an aviator-saint.'

'Idiot. This was in the seventeenth century. Nothing to do with aeroplanes. He used to fly all over the church. The monks had a job to keep him down. It's a fact, you needn't laugh. At least - it is to the R.C.s. He hadn't much brain, either. Like me in that way.'

'Well, I don't see what flying's got to do with Connie.'

I shuddered. 'It might,' I said cautiously, 'have more to do with her than you imagine.'

'You've got something fresh up your sleeve about Connie,' said Henry suspiciously. I was silent. I felt I didn't dare tell him about the swan. It might not be true, after all. And, if I blabbed about it, it might yet come true. Which was the last thing I wanted, attracted as I was by the miraculous.

'Well,' said Henry, 'I think you'd far better go to this doctor fellow. There's nothing supernatural about it. Something's just gone askew in your mind - that's what it is.'

'Thank you, Henry,' I said bitterly. 'And in your mind, too, I suppose.'

Henry ignored this. I could see that bath sticking in his throat again. He swallowed rapidly. 'Suppose,' he said, 'he could prove you *had* known Miss Hargreaves years ago? That'd get you somewhere, wouldn't it?'

'It's too damn prosaic an explanation,' I objected. 'I don't want it.'

'You don't *want* it?'

'No. I - ' I hesitated. I was burning to take him into my confidence about the swan. I couldn't resist throwing out a hint.

'I might have done something pretty big to-day,' I said. 'I don't know yet. I'll tell you when I'm sure.'

'You haven't murdered her, have you?'

'Not quite. Just a little metempsychosis.'

'A little what-osis?'

'Metempsyche.'

Henry stared at me.

'I wonder if - ' I mused to myself, looking at a vase of montbretias on the table. I was suddenly tempted to try to turn them into a cotton-reel. Don't know why. Just came into my head. Another peak.

'Be a reel of cotton!' I hissed, throwing a lot of invisible dust at them.

Nothing happened. The clock ticked on. I laughed weakly.

'Only my little joke,' I said feebly. 'Only my little joke. So long, Henry.'

I left him. Through the window I could see him holding up the montbretias and looking at them. There was a rather scared expression on his face, I thought.

*   *   *

Things fly round a bit too quickly in Cornford. I believe if you sent a telegram to yourself you'd get it before you sent it.

'Marjorie's broken-hearted,' said mother, the moment I got in.

'Don't you believe it,' I said. 'Hearts don't break as easily as that.'

'How *can* you be so unkind? Marjorie actually told Jim she was certain you were going to marry this wretched woman. Of course, I don't believe anything so fantastic as that, but I do wish you would tell us the *truth*, Norman.'

'Truth!' I laughed cynically.

'First you say one thing, then you say another. What *are* we to believe?'

'I'll tell you something about truth,' I said bitterly.

'What do you mean?'

'They say Truth lies at the bottom of a well. I've got drowned in it. That's what I mean.'

'Norman, I really believe you are ill.'

The way my mother said that word 'ill'. I wish you could have heard it. 'You can't go on like this,' she continued. 'You've dropped your work completely; you won't settle down to a thing. And it's all because of this Miss Hargreaves. I - '

I suddenly lost my temper.

'Damn Miss Hargreaves!' I cried. 'Blast Miss Hargreaves! To hell with - ' I caught back my words, appalled at what I had said. Who knew what might not happen to her now?

'I'm sorry I swore,' I said. 'Is father upstairs?'

'Father is in his room, messing about as usual.' Mother turned rather coldly away from me, obviously offended. I went upstairs. Father calmed me. He always does. He's never yet told me I'm a liar. He doesn't necessarily believe what you tell him, but at any rate he never voices his disbelief.

I had to tell him all about the swan; it was intolerable to keep it to myself any longer.

'I know it's impossible,' I said. 'But still - '

'H'm.' He was very slowly tapping out letters on an old Oliver typewriter. 'Swans are funny creatures. I wouldn't trust a swan with a five-pound note. No, I wouldn't.'

'Yes, but the point about this swan - ' I began. Then I stopped. What was the use of talking about it? Somehow I had simply got to convince myself that the whole thing was pure coincidence. A good many things that seem surprising *are* coincidental. I dare say my being alive and writing this book is a coincidence, really, if one could only get to the bottom of it all. What a damn mystery life is!

'Give me a drop of whisky, will you, father?' I asked.

'Go ahead, my boy. You'll find the siphon on the top of the butterfly cabinet. You might put back those oak-eggars, will you?'

I drank and fell back into a chair; I felt like drinking myself silly. Father lit a cigarette and poured himself a drink.

'Do you think I'm batty, father?' I said.

'Battiness,' he remarked, 'is far more common than one supposes.'

'Nothing seems real to me to-day.'

'Reality isn't what it's thought to be,' he said, blowing out great clouds of smoke, then blowing them away from himself to me. 'No. Reality is - well - there's that fellow who talks on the wireless - who is it? Lord Elton, or is it Eddystone? No! Edison, that's the fellow. We're here to-day gone to-morrow and some say to-morrow never comes, so perhaps we don't go. Who knows?'

'Do you believe in psychology, father?'

'How do you *know* you're real? You might not be here at all. There's only one thing I'm certain of, my boy; and that is - I'm not certain of anything. You can't prove a damn thing. Two and two make four; so they *say*. But who the hell knows what two is?'

I helped myself to some more whisky. For several min-utes we were silent. It was queer how I felt that my father had the key to the whole mystery of Miss Hargreaves, if only he could find the right lock to put it into. But you never could pin father down to anything definite; if you could, he wouldn't be father.

'Music now,' he said presently. He rose, stubbed out his cigarette in an old bowler hat he uses as an ash-tray, and found his violin.

'I can't play,' I said. 'I've got an addled mind.'

'Well, you can listen to me, then. Music's the only thing in this world that isn't addled.'

He stood by the open window and started to play one of his own tunes. I wish I could write it down for you, but it would lose something if I tried to tape it out to minims and quavers and so on. It was, as usual, the long *cantabile* type of melody that always seemed to grow as naturally as speech from him. More naturally. I knew that when he started he hadn't the slightest idea what he was going to play. He gave the violin a life of its own; never interfered with it. The violin had a song to sing; father was merely there to help it.

'There,' he said, laying down his fiddle. I was moved and I said nothing. 'I,' continued father, 'and this gut and carved wood - animal and vegetable - together we combine to produce something that's never been in the world before. Listen.'

I listened. 'Can't hear anything,' I said.

'That's the point,' he said. 'Neither can I. But if you had sharp enough ears, you'd be able to hear that tune going on somewhere. You don't suppose it's dead, do you?'

'What're you getting at, father?' I sat up, keenly interested.

'An idea of mine,' he said. 'Just an idea of mine. About sound. Go and strike a great fat *arpeggio* chord of D flat on the piano, boy.'

I went to the piano.

'Hold the loud pedal down,' he said. 'Strike bass D flat - then A flat a fifth higher - then tenor F - and so on right up the piano to the highest F. Then sit still with your foot down on the loud pedal. Listen. You'll understand something.'

I did as he commanded, very slowly and powerfully striking the notes, then sitting silently, the loud pedal down, and listening. Slowly, slowly, the great chord trembled away into space. For nearly a minute we could hear it. It was hard to break the silence afterwards - a silence that was no longer a silence and never, never could be again.

'My God!' I said.

'Hush!' whispered father. He stood at the window, looking out. 'Still there,' he murmured. 'Never dies, you know. Never dies. Going on, all round the world, my boy. You can't cancel it. That's my idea. You and your Miss Holgrave - that chord, my tune. Mysteries, boy; all mysteries. Don't be surprised at anything. When you understand what that chord does, you'll be near to understanding everything.'

Mother came in. It's always the same. Whenever father and I get talking, mother comes in. And, of course, she doesn't *know*; she doesn't understand the sort of things father and I talk about. Not that we understand them ourselves, as a matter of fact.

'Have you heard the news?' mother asked. You could tell she was bursting with something important; I knew it was Hargreaves news.

'Jim's just met Mr Carver, the house-agent who was handling Lessways. Miss Hargreaves has bought the property.'

Somehow, it didn't surprise me. Vaguely I knew that I must be responsible, though I didn't know exactly why.

*   *   *

About half-past ten, feeling terribly uneasy, I went round to Canticle Alley again.

Mrs Beedle shook her head mournfully.

'No. She ain't come back. I were thinking about these 'ere S O S's, sir. They'll be dragging the river, mark my words. Willy-nilly, she say to me, and those was her very words ...'

*   *   *

CHAPTER SIX

I tried to sleep. The moon straggled through on to my pillow. The infinite chord of D flat reverberated in my brain. I tossed about. I dreamt of swans wearing tall hats sailing over the hills in balloons to the perpetual accompaniment of father's violin. Awful. About three I rose, put on my dressing-gown and went to the window. Below me, on the other side of the road, Lessways rose emptily to the moony sky. The board had gone. I thought of Miss Hargreaves in residence there. It was incredible. Baffled, bewildered, I gazed out at the night. Everything looked very cool and silvery. Far away, beyond the Cathedral, I could see the winding arc of the Thames.

I went back to bed, but sleep wouldn't come. Again I rose. This time I dressed quickly, putting on an old sweater and a pair of flannel trousers. Creeping downstairs, I got my bicycle out of the shed, wheeled it down the garden and leapt on the saddle. In twenty minutes I had reached Cookham Bridge.

*   *   *

I was glad I had come out. If you've got any serious thinking to do, you must do it at night. The longer I stayed on that bridge, listening to the lapping of the water against the boats, the greater was the sense of mystery which filled me. Father was right; we didn't understand a damn thing. Old professors might tell me that the moon was carbon monoxide, or whatever they like to call it, but that didn't make the moon any simpler. They might tell me that I, Norman Huntley, was only a mass of electrons formed in certain shapes to produce heart and lungs, brain and limbs. I was still a mystery.

Take Miss Hargreaves, I said to myself. Another mystery - the only difference being that she was an *unfamiliar* mystery.

There was simply, so far as I knew, no precedent for the way Miss Hargreaves had appeared in my life. And yet, actually, she wasn't any more of a mystery than my little finger.

Anything was possible. That's what I felt that moonlit night as I leaned over the bridge. On the far bank of the river, beyond Hedsor wharf, was an apple orchard; sheltering behind it, graced by beautifully mown lawns, an old house that I had often admired. Why shouldn't it be mine? Far away at the top of the hill, Lord Astor might be asleep in his bed. Why shouldn't I be there? (Not as *well*. Instead of.) Move him out, I said, and put yourself there, the master of Cliveden. Or - instead of there being the apples of autumn in that orchard, let there be the blossom of spring. Let there be light now; no darkness.

My gosh! I thought - how grand God must have felt when He'd said 'let there be light' - *and* it worked. After all that darkness, how He must have revelled in His new creation, making things because He'd made light and now had got nothing to look at in the new light.

Everything, it seemed to me, was just within my grasp. (Yes, I know it was all a horrible blasphemy, but there it is.) For that moment I accepted Miss Hargreaves without question or complaint. I felt proud of her; I realized these things didn't happen to everybody. Naturally there were going to be complications. One couldn't learn in a minute how to manage her. If she was still a little out of control - well, don't *all* created things get out of control before long? Well, I mean, look at us ... God thought we were a very good job. And *look* at us ... Well, I mean ...

'Oh, Miss Hargreaves!' I breathed her name upon the cool night air. I longed to see her again. Couldn't bear the thought of her going just when I was beginning fully to understand my responsibilities towards her. Whatever embarrassments she plunged me into - she was my own handiwork. Never again must I be tempted to play about with her. A strict sense of form must inspire all my dealings with her. No good getting drunk on swans and such like. Slowly I must adapt her to the conditions of Cornford society and guard her from all dangers of my impetuous will.

Thus I thought, that autumn night over the Thames. And, even as I thought, my eyes were fixed on the bit of river running past the orchard.

What was that strange melancholy singing? What was that boat doing out in mid-stream? Whose form huddled in the bows? Whose hat?

Whose hat?

'My God!' I muttered. I rushed across the field to the bank.

* * *

'Miss Hargreaves!' I cried from the bank. 'Miss Hargreaves!'

Whether she heard me or not, I don't know. At any rate, she paid not the slightest attention. I called again, louder, a little exasperated. What in God's name did she imagine she was doing?

'Can't you hear me?' I shouted.

She looked up. I could just see that she was writing something in her note-book.

'Who is that?' she called irritably.

'Me. Norman. What on earth are you doing?'

'Oh. *You!* Do you want anything?'

'I want to get you home. You'll die of cold.'

'I'm busy now,' she said. 'Come and join me if you wish. But do please be quiet.'

'How on earth did you get there?' I asked.

But she was writing in her note-book and did not answer me.

'Where are your oars?' I bawled.

'I can't hear you!' she snapped. 'If you *must* talk, come closer. I am not accustomed to shouting across a river.'

There was only one way to reach her, short of swimming. I walked along the bank till I came to Cooper's boat-house, nearer the bridge. Luckily there was nobody about, not even a prowling policeman. Taking one of the rowing-boats, I unmoored it, and rowed up to the little tributary. In a few minutes I was alongside her.

'You'd better get into this boat,' I said, 'and I'll row you back. What have you done with your oars?'

'A minute! Wait - wait - ' She wrote rapidly. 'I was hoping to set it to music,' she murmured, pausing with her silver pencil tapping on the side of the boat, 'but I cannot quite get the tune. No matter. I will read you my verses.'

'They can wait,' I said. 'We've got to get you home some-how. Don't you realize Mrs Beedle is worried to death about you?'

'I do *wish*,' she said petulantly, 'you would not keep interrupting. What is this Beedle woman to me? Listen.'

Before I could say any more, in a low vibrant voice she started to recite.

'River at Night. A Lament. I hope you follow me. A *Lament*.'

'Yes, yes,' I muttered. 'I get you. Go on. Hurry up.'

She cleared her throat. 'Strike a match, dear,' she said, 'and hold it over the manuscript. I cannot see too well. Keep striking matches as quietly as you can.'

I struck a match and held it near her note-book. Very tempted I was to set the thing on fire.

She read:

> 'Oh, water and breezelight and magical moon,
> And me all alone on the river!
> They tell me that dawn will be here very soon -
> They talk of a chill on the liver.'

She paused. 'You like it?' she asked anxiously.

'What was the first line again?' I asked.

'"Oh, water and breezelight and magical moon".'

I frowned. 'Breezelight?'

'Precisely. Breezelight.'

'Don't you mean moonlight?'

'What does it *matter*?' she cried. 'If I write "magical breeze" the rhyme is annihilated. In any case, the breeze is not magical; the moon is. How stupid you are! This is verse two:

> Oh, for the wings, for the *neck* of a swan!
> To swim all the night and not shiver.
> Oh, say not the hour is eternally gone
> When I floated like floss on the river!'

'Yes. I - I like that,' I said uneasily. 'But really now - I think we'd better - '

'Verse three,' she said, 'goes like this. Why don't you strike another match? I cannot be expected to read in the dark, can I?'

I struck another match and she read verse three.

> 'God made reservations to human desires,
> And though He's a bountiful giver,
> He turned a deaf ear to the mind that aspires
> To sport *all* the night on the river.'

'Is it blasphemous, do you think?' she asked anxiously. 'I trust not. I have always had a very high regard for my Maker.'

'Who *is* your Maker, that's what I want to know!' I said.

'What did you say, dear? Speak up! Speak up!'

'No. This isn't time for talking. You must come home at once.'

'How extraordinarily prosaic you are! Alone on the river "night with her train of stars" - Henley, dear; the poet; not the place - alone, you and me - and you must talk of going *home*. Fie! Come and sit in my boat. If you must pursue me, at least you need not be unsociable.'

'Good God!' I exclaimed. 'You're moored to the bank!'

'Am I? Possibly. I attempted to engage the oars, but they are such clumsy things. I let them go.'

'Oh, Miss Hargreaves!' I cried, 'you're really too bad! There'll be an awful row about this if anyone finds us. Do come into this boat at once and let's get home somehow.'

Her boat was moored, I had now seen for the first time, to a tree stump at the bottom of the orchard.

'I can't understand how on earth you got here,' I said.

'Got here? Really - it is so many hours ago. How can I be expected to remember everything? In any case, I see no reason why I should account to *you* for all my movements.'

'All right,' I said hastily. 'You needn't get huffy. Read your poem again.'

I knew that would pacify her. Miss Hargreaves never could resist reading her poems. When she had finished her second reading she tore the pages out of the book, wrote her name at the bottom and gave them to me.

'Keep it, dear,' she said. 'Perhaps it is not my best effort. Not, I fear, on the high level of the verses in *Wayside Bundle*. But no matter. A poet cannot *always* roam on Parnassus.'

'Jolly true,' I agreed. 'Personally, I like this poem. It seems so - well, so much from your heart.'

'*All* my poems,' she said, 'emerge to the world *directly* from my heart. They always have and they always will.'

'Quite. But this - well, you know, it's packed with experience. Why, one would almost think from reading it that you had actually been a swan.'

'That is precisely what it is meant to convey. Pavlova was a close personal friend of mine.'

I was silent for some moments. Then I made another attempt to get her into my boat. 'Come on,' I said. 'Take my hand. Be careful. We must get home.'

But she would not stir. 'Do you remember the Serpentine, dear?' she said. 'How luscious those strawberries were! How I wish we could partake of some such refreshment now. But, alas - ' Then she suddenly pointed to the apple trees. 'But look! The forbidden fruit! It is Providence, dear. Providence!'

'When you get home,' I said uneasily, 'Mrs Beedle'll make you a nice cup of tea and boil you an egg.'

'We could light a fire,' she mused. 'There are plenty of sticks. Possibly we could *roast* the fruit. Raw apples lie none too easily within me. Get into my boat, dear. Pull on the rope. You will soon draw us into the bank.'

'If you talk like this,' I cried, 'I shall go away and leave you here.'

'Do!' she said coldly. 'What do I care? I have the stars. I can *look* at the fruit. No doubt I shall die of cold. But no matter - no matter. Connie Hargreaves has ceased to interest you, that is quite clear. Leave me. Go!'

She shivered petulantly and drew her fur more closely round her neck. Of course, I couldn't leave her. I decided it was best to humour her; to land on the bank, perhaps eat an apple or two, then find our way through the garden somehow to the road. I only hoped we shouldn't wake anybody in the house.

I clambered into her boat with some difficulty and pulled it into the bank, mooring the other boat to the same tree stump.

'Ah!' she said warmly. She took my hand and stepped nimbly on to the bank. 'Ah! Apples now!' She rubbed her hands together almost avariciously. 'Get my sticks, dear. And now you must light a fire. It is quite simple. I abominate fuss. Let an adventure have more spice in it than dough. An old Norwegian proverb, dear. Light me a fire and I will do anything you wish. Yes, anything!'

'You mean that?' I said sharply.

'Most certainly. Anything within my power.'

'Then,' I said, 'oblige me by getting rid of that hat.'

There was an awkward pause. Suddenly she wrenched it from her head and flung it into the river.

'You are right,' she said. 'It was a mistake. It was a little too low in the crown.'

*   *   *

'Oh, my bag!' she exclaimed. 'Please get it out of the boat, dear. There is nothing of any value in it - except to me. My diary - a little miniature of Mr Archer - Agatha's licence - trivial things, but precious to me. Thank you, dear, thank you.'

She was shivering a little; her hair was blowing about in the wind.

'Perhaps you would lend me the coloured handkerchief from your breast pocket,' she said. I gave it to her and she wound it round her head, tying it at the back. It was queer how completely it changed her appearance.

'You look like a gipsy,' I said.

'Ah!' She wagged a diverting finger at me. 'What blood, I wonder, flows in my veins? One never knows, dear; one never *quite* knows. But these are indelicate topics. Come - come - what about this fire. Look sharp. This wretched dawn will be here before very long. How feelingly one echoes Swinburne's complaint - "Ah, God! Ah, God! that dawn should come so soon!" I have never approved of the particular circumstances which drove the poet to resent the dawn, but I entirely endorse the sentiment. Give me a cigarette.'

I gave her one and, seeing there was no way out of it, began gathering sticks to light a fire.

'These are moments to be remembered, Norman,' she said. 'Let us not waste them in soft thoughts of bed and blankets. Be sturdy. Be different. Pick me an apple.'

'Damn you!' I muttered, crouching over my sticks and striking a match. 'Damn you!'

But I picked her the apple. In spite of my annoyance, I realized I was half enjoying this adventure.

'Did you - have any trouble with the traffic to-day?' I asked. (Supposing, I was arguing, I *had* managed to turn her into a swan? It was quite possible that she herself had never realized the change.)

'Trouble?' she echoed. 'Oh, I might have done.' She shrugged her shoulders. It was easy to see how easily she would have shrugged wings. 'I might have done. It is really so long ago, I cannot remember. Oh, yes! I stopped to do up my shoe-lace and I seem to recollect a lot of motor-horns sounding. A rude sound. Most offensive!'

'H'm,' I said thoughtfully. I snapped some sticks with my foot. They were damp and wouldn't catch. 'I supposed you don't remember seeing the Dean, do you?' I asked.

'The Dean? Possibly. But why are you asking me all these questions? I cannot understand you.'

I said nothing. The clock up at Cliveden struck four; far away I heard the chimes of the Cathedral. Something else I could hear too; footsteps crackling the twigs in the orchard.

'Listen!' I whispered. 'Somebody's coming!'

'Well? What of it? As I was saying, many a time Marie Corelli said to me how - '

A light was suddenly flashed in our eyes. A deep voice said, 'May I ask what you imagine you're doing here?'

*   *   *

It wasn't at all an easy question to answer. If I had it in an examination, I don't suppose I should be able to fill up both sides of the paper. Miss Hargreaves, however, seemed to find it simple.

'By all means,' she said crisply. 'You are certainly at liberty to ask.'

A man came through the trees, flashing his torch down on my twigs. 'Damned impertinence!' he muttered. 'Well,' he said aloud, 'I *am* asking what you imagine you're doing here. And I should like an answer.'

'We're trying to - that is, we're lighting a fire,' I said feebly. 'But the twigs are rather damp.'

'And eating,' added Miss Hargreaves, 'your excellent apples. A superb flavour, if I may say so. Do you use any special manure in the soil?'

'I can see perfectly well what you're both doing.'

'Then,' remarked Miss Hargreaves rationally, 'why *ask*? I imagine, my good sir, that what you really desire to know is *why* we are doing what we are doing? Is not that so?'

The fellow grunted. I could see now that he was a very tall, square-shouldered chap, with a rather sallow face, a flattened boxer's nose. He was wearing a dark, close-fitting overcoat; it seemed to me to fit a little *too* closely.

'I don't know who the hell you both are - ' he began.

But Miss Hargreaves cut in on him. If there was one thing she could never tolerate, it was loose language. Dropping the apple as though it had been a live coal, she rose from the felled tree she had been sitting on, and addressed me. 'Norman, we will go now. Get the boat ready.' She opened her bag and fumbled about for some money. 'Perhaps,' she said to the chap, 'you will be good enough to tell me the *price* of your fruit. I have consumed half an apple. Incidentally, I have also used your boat and lost your absurd oars. Kindly name a price.'

'Well, that's cool!' said the fellow. I thought he seemed quite disposed to be friendly, so I spoke quickly before Miss Hargreaves should say any more.

'We're awfully sorry,' I said. 'The truth is, Lady Hargreaves and I were - '

Immediately he looked at Miss Hargreaves with considerably more interest. Wonderful what tricks you can work with a title.

'*Lady* Hargreaves?' he said.

I nudged her.

'Precisely,' she said, playing up magnificently. 'I have, unfortunately, no card upon me. Why are you nudging me, Mr Huntley? Is anything amiss?'

(Oh, bravo, bravo! I said to myself.)

'Well, come inside,' said the chap. 'Perhaps you'd like some refreshment. I don't know what on earth you're both doing here, but anyhow, it's warmer in the house.'

I didn't, of course, want to go. But it was kind of him to ask us and hard to know how to refuse. So we followed him up through the orchard and across the lawn.

'I'm Major Wynne,' he said carelessly, over his shoulder. 'What do you think of my house? Rather good, eh?'

Miss Hargreaves swept a glance at it through her lorgnettes. 'H'm,' she said. 'I think you should cut back that Virginia creeper. And these yews want clipping. This tulip tree is sprawling, positively sprawling, Major. But perhaps you prefer them to sprawl. How many gardeners do you keep?'

'Oh, I do most of it myself.'

'Indeed! I suppose that is rather the modern habit, is it not?'

We followed the Major through some french windows that opened into a drawing-room. Switching on the light, he quickly whipped some dust-sheets from the chairs and invited us to sit.

'Sorry the place is covered up,' he said. 'Fact is, servants all away - house is really closed up. I came down unexpectedly from London on business and thought I might as well picnic here for the night. I only use the place in the summer, of course. Wife in Italy.'

'Bordighera, I presume?'

'Yes. That's right. Now, what'll you drink, Lady Hargreaves?'

'I suppose you have gin?'

I stared at her. Drinking gin? It was the last thing I would have expected.

'Oh, yes,' said the Major. Miss Hargreaves sat down on a sofa. 'Dear me!' she exclaimed. 'How pleasant it is to rest. I see you have one of these electric heaters. Detestable things, but they have their uses. Can you switch it on? These autumn nights are a little chilly.'

'Oh, certainly.' The Major turned the switch with his foot. 'Excuse me a moment,' he said. 'I'll get the drinks.'

He went out. Miss Hargreaves, after having surveyed the room rather disdainfully, held her hands out to the heater.

'You did that jolly well!' I said to her.

She stared at me displeasedly. 'Did *what* jolly well?'

'That Lady Hargreaves business. Rather a good idea of mine, wasn't it? I thought it would impress him.'

To this remark she vouchsafed no reply except a cold stare which rather puzzled me. While we waited I examined the room. It was very comfortably furnished. Chairs of a deep strawberry shade; carpet a pale rose; walls, white. The furniture was 'modern antique', heavy stuff with synthetic worm-holes. There were a lot of unread-looking books in fine bindings and one or two dim oil paintings - the sort that are 'reputed to be by Canaletto'. It wasn't an original room. But it was warm and inviting.

I yawned. I was dead tired now. 'What are we going to say to the Major?' I asked her.

'I don't see that there is any need to *say* anything.'

Major Wynne came in, carrying a tray with bottles and glasses on it. Miss Hargreaves accepted gin and soda; the Major and I drank whisky. Presently, when we were all settled, the Major turned rather apologetically to Miss Hargreaves.

'I'm afraid I was a little short with you just now,' he said.

'No matter. No doubt it was a little surprising for you.'

'Lost your way, or something?'

'More or less,' she said airily. She pointed over to the books in the bookcase. 'You admire Meredith?'

'Eh? Who's Meredith?'

The Major followed the direction of her finger. 'Oh - books! No. Afraid I don't read much.'

Miss Hargreaves smiled, sipped her gin, and waved her silver pencil at the Major. 'A man of action, eh, Major?'

'That's right,' he agreed. 'Do you live in this neighbour-hood, by the way?'

She crumbled a water biscuit thoughtfully. 'My uncle,' she said to him, 'once had property here. Cliveden, you know. A pleasant little place. But that was years ago. The river became too popular, Major Bin, far too popular. I am at present residing at Cornford.'

'Oh? Well, hope we may see more of each other.'

'My circle' - she snapped a piece of biscuit sharply in two - 'is small. Most of my old friends have crossed the bar. I detest people of low family, Major Bin; I positively detest people of low family.'

Uttering this remark with the most marked venom, she popped the piece of biscuit into her mouth and carefully wiped her fingers on her handkerchief.

'Oh, quite!' said the Major quickly. For a man who'd had a blow below the belt he behaved rather well, I thought. 'So do I. So many bally rotters about nowadays, what? Never know where you are with people.'

There was a long and rather awkward silence. I felt my eyes nodding. I could see that Miss Hargreaves, too, was very tired. Presently the Major rose, collected the glasses, and went towards the door.

'Would you care to stay the night?' he suggested. 'It's rather late to get anywhere else now. You're welcome, if you wish.'

Miss Hargreaves nodded sleepily.

'A capital suggestion,' she murmured. 'Five blankets. And put a glass between the sheets to see they are properly aired. I like water - Vichy, if you have it - and a Bible by the bed. Authorized Version. Mr Huntley, please see to every-thing.' Her eyes were drooping; already she was nearly asleep. 'Three pillows,' we heard her say, 'and buttered eggs at ten. I hope the water is soft.'

'Don't you bother,' I said to the Major. 'Anything will do.'

'Anything will certainly *not* do,' snapped Miss Hargreaves, suddenly wide awake.

'Well, I'll go and see to the beds,' said the Major. 'I suppose,' he said to me, 'you're her chauffeur, or something, aren't you?'

Before I could deny it he had left the room.

* * *

I woke with a start. Over the misty river the autumn sun was streaming into the room. Blackbirds and thrushes were singing. A cherubic gilt clock on the mantelpiece struck a quarter to seven.

At first I couldn't place my surroundings. Then I saw Miss Hargreaves curled up peacefully asleep in her chair and all the wild events of yesterday rushed back to me with what they call sickening reality.

I rose, stretched, and wandered to the window. I remembered suddenly that it was one of the mornings when I was supposed to be at the Cathedral to play the organ. I remembered also that there was an early bus from Cookham to Cornford at seven-ten. If we hurried there would be just time to catch it.

It was queer that the Major had never come back. Or perhaps he had, and finding us both asleep, had decided to leave us. My whole instinct was to leave the house without seeing him again; but it didn't seem right. After all, he'd been very decent to us. It was up to me to thank him, at any rate, and try to offer some sort of explanation.

Without waking Miss Hargreaves (let sleeping dogs lie, I thought), I went upstairs, thinking I'd try to find the Major's room. There were three doors on the landing. I opened each one gently, but the rooms were empty, all the furniture covered up as it had been downstairs last night. I tried another wing; the attics; then downstairs - smoking room, dining-room, boudoir. But it was no good. There wasn't a soul but us two in the house.

'Extraordinary thing!' I said. But I couldn't pretend. I was sorry. It simplified matters, the Major not being there. It meant I should be spared trying to explain our trespassing in his orchard.

I returned to the drawing-room and found Miss Hargreaves standing by the open bookcase, turning over a volume of Jorrocks.

'Major Wynne isn't here,' I said. 'We'd better scoot pretty quick. We can catch a bus if we hurry.'

'Why this ridiculous hurry? Is there no morning tea?'

'Oh, don't be absurd!'

Without making any reply she walked over to a chair, sat down, and started to read.

'Come *along*,' I cried impatiently. 'We've only just time to catch the 'bus.'

'*Bus?* I am not accustomed to travelling in buses. Ring a garage and order a car - a large one. I cannot bear being cramped. Do it at once. I abominate - '

Before she could say 'fuss' I rounded on her.

'Are you *crazy?*' I shouted. I was mad to get out of the house in case the Major should return. He might have gone for an early dip in the river, for all I knew.

She ignored me completely. 'Where is the toilet?' she asked. 'And *why* is there no tea? *What* a place!'

'Look here,' I said, 'you've got us into this fix - '

'Fix?' she said. 'I do not understand. Who is in a *fix?*'

'You've got us into it,' I went on, 'and you're going to let me get us out of it in my way, not yours.'

Very slowly she walked to the shelves, returned the book to its place, took off her spectacles, put them away in her bag, and finally addressed me.

'Mr Huntley,' she said gravely, 'it seems that I had the misfortune to spend an entire night in this room with you. Do not assume - do *not* assume that such close proximity to my person for so long a period entitles you to any *sort* of familiarity. Kindly ring the garage and instruct me as to the geography of the house - if such a poor place *has* any geography. There need be no argument.'

'Upstairs. First floor,' I said savagely. I was so angry I could hardly trust myself to speak.

Slowly she walked up. I went to the phone in the hall, took up the receiver, hesitated, hooked it back again. No, I was damned if I'd be browbeaten like this! Fuming impatiently I strode up and down the hall. After an intolerable time she came down.

'Is the car ready?' she asked.

I lied quickly. 'It'll be waiting for us on the road,' I said. I led her out through the drawing-room.

'Appalling taste!' she muttered. 'All this strawberry colour. So morbid! Atrocious!'

I hurriedly led the way down the garden. Farther along the orchard was a bridge which led to the meadows, and thus to the main Cornford road, a hundred yards away.

'I cannot understand all this hurry,' she said breathlessly.

'No. Neither can I,' I said. I could see the Cornford bus just crossing the bridge. Obviously we could never catch it. Suddenly, also, I had remembered my bicycle. I couldn't leave it on Cookham Bridge.

'Mr Huntley,' said Miss Hargreaves, 'wait one moment, if you please. I wish to have a word with you.'

'Go on,' I said bitterly. 'I can bear it.'

'I should take it as a courtesy if you were to tell nobody about our - what can I call it? - mad frolic of last night. I blame you entirely, of course. But I dare say a little of the blame rests upon me. That is all. Where is this car you keep talking about?'

I couldn't stand any more of this. Could you have?

'You're insufferable!' I cried. 'I spend the whole night doing my damnedest to get you safely home - I trespass on other people's property - I behave generally like a madman - and then you treat me like this! It's absolutely shameful, Miss Hargreaves.'

Coldly, critically, she surveyed me through her lorgnettes. In a few hours she seemed to have lost all the affection she had once had for me. It was heart-breaking.

'Mr Huntley,' she said, 'you once came to my assistance at a critical moment in a bookshop. Do not suppose - do *not* suppose this gives you leave to address me as though you were my equal. A cat may *look* at a king. Oh, yes! There is little offence in that. But I have yet to learn that a cat may - to employ one of your own vulgar expressions - hob-*nob* with a king.'

'My *God*!' I said. For a moment I stared at her. I think there were almost tears in my eyes. Then I hurried on towards the bridge, far more hurt than angry.

My bicycle was still where I had left it.

'I hope,' she said, 'I am not expected to travel on the *step*.'

'No,' I said bitterly, 'you can find your own way home.'

'I would prefer it. Where is this car?'

'You can get it yourself. I didn't order it.'

'This is intolerable. I have never been so insulted. Leave me!'

'I'm going to. You can do what you like from now on. I've finished with you - finished with you.'

I swung my leg over the saddle.

'My bag!' she exclaimed. 'I have left it in that ridiculous house. Kindly run back and get it.'

'I'm damned if I will. I'm sick and tired of you. I never want to see you again.'

I rode off in such a state that I only just escaped being run down by a lorry. If I'd stayed on that bridge another second with her, I honestly believe I'd have picked her up and thrown her into the river.

*　　*　　*

I went straight to the Cathedral, played the organ desultorily, then returned home for breakfast. Nobody knew I had spent most of the night out. After Matins I saw the *Cornford Mercury* with Archie's picture of the swan in it. 'Coincidence,' I muttered, 'pure coincidence.' To this day I force myself to believe that.

So ends the first part of the history of Miss Hargreaves. I wish to God that were all; I wish to God there were no second part to write. But there is, and it's got to be done.

For more than a fortnight Cornford saw nothing at all of Miss Hargreaves. It was not a very happy fortnight for me. Not for one moment did I suppose that I had seen the last of her that September morning on Cookham Bridge. Instinctively I knew she would return. Even if I hadn't known that in myself, I had practical evidence of it. Where did she go in that fortnight? I don't know; I shall never know. All I knew was that she had left Mrs Beedle's, retaining her rooms for an indefinite period. Her luggage, her harp, Dr Pepusch - all were left behind. I never went to the house openly to make any inquiries for her; I got the news in a roundabout way - and you can always get news in a roundabout way in Cornford, if you've got an efficient spy-system. I used sometimes to scout up Canticle Alley after dark, thinking that perhaps I might see a familiar shadow against the blind of the downstairs sitting-room. But I saw nothing. Once I heard Dr Pepusch croaking away in a minor key; it was a sound that saddened me and filled me with apprehension. I slunk home, wondering how long it would be before she returned with renewed vigour.

Meanwhile, the most sinister development of all stared me day by day in the face. I mean Lessways. The house that had for so long stood empty and neglected was now the scene of tremendous activities. Ironically I used to think how glad I should have been to witness this in more ordinary circumstances, because I loved the place and could not bear to see it fall into decay. And yet - all those gallons of white paint, all those hods of cement, all those ladders - how could I rejoice over them as I should have liked? Gardeners with wheelbarrows, the sweep with his sack of soot, the sanitary experts, glaziers, the telephone men - all these swarmed to Lessways. Still there was no sign of Miss Hargreaves. Hour by hour I expected her to come and criticize the work that was going on, to walk round from room to room, from shrub to herbaceous border, tapping everything with her stick and making innumerable notes in her note-book. It seemed to me wrong that she didn't come. Often I felt like going over to Lessways myself in order to make certain that all the work was properly carried out.

*   *   *

The only person I ever told about our night on the riverside was Henry, and him I swore to secrecy. If that tale got round Cornford I knew it would be about the end of me.

'And now,' I said, 'I'm through with her. I'm finished. She can do what she damn well likes for all I care.'

Do what she likes. I paused and considered this sentence. Was it wise?

'What made you go up the river in search of her?' asked Henry. So then I had to tell him about the swan mystery. I fancied he'd already heard the first part of the tale from Marjorie, but he was nice enough to pretend it was new to him. He seemed, I thought, rather embarrassed by it.

'Of course,' I said, 'there's no *proof* I turned her into a swan. I don't say *I did*, Henry. I shall probably never know. But it does look funny, doesn't it?'

'Yes,' he agreed, 'it does look very funny.'

We were sitting by his fire in the half light, and I noticed he was looking at me rather anxiously, almost nervously. But I was getting used to that from everybody.

Slowly, endlessly, the days passed. I drilled myself to a firm resolution. Never again should I try to explain Miss Hargreaves to anybody; never again make up stories about her. If, in truth, she was subject to my will, my will must never more be exercised. I spent long evenings in my room, supposedly working for my examination in the spring, actually making a lot of notes which later I used in writing this book. Most carefully I wrote down what was supposed to be the truth about my friendship with Miss Hargreaves. How it had started in Blackwell's shop (in spite of the fact that I had told Marjorie this was a lie, it was pretty generally believed. I am afraid I never tried to deny it). How we had later met at the Albert Hall and had an amusing little adventure together on the Serpentine. I wrote down all the facts so as I shouldn't again get confused. I learnt the story like a book and almost convinced myself it was true. There was nothing to my discredit in thus commencing a friendship with an old lady. If I kept calm and stuck to it, people would get sick of talking to me about her; slowly she might drift completely out of my life. And, after all, she *might* never come back, in spite of the work that was going on at Lessways.

But she did come back. And - true to her perhaps unenviable fate - she came back accompanied by a distinction that I had unknowingly bestowed upon her.

*　　*　　*

October the tenth. I quote from my diary. 'Furniture at Lessways.' I don't think I need add much to that. It was pouring with rain. I watched from my window as the enormous van drew up on the other side of the road; for two hours I watched the men struggling up the wet drive. Grandfather clocks, tallboys, Chippendale chairs, a four-poster bed, crate after crate of crockery, bureaux, Sheraton cabinets, sideboards, pictures innumerable ...

That night smoke rose from the chimneys.

*   *   *

October the eleventh. I was walking back with Archie Tallents from the Cathedral. It was still miserably wet, but Archie was in his usual gay spirits, humming a tune from a rather absurd anthem we had sung at Matins - all about Aaron's beard and the ointment that ran down from it to the skirts of his clothing. Comic eighteenth-century stuff. Nares or Weldon.

As we went up the High Street - I on my way to the shop, Archie to his studio - Archie pointed to a magnificent Rolls-Royce waiting outside Truscott's, the drapery and furnishing store. It was a Rolls-Royce with more than the usual consciousness of pedigree; you almost heard the cogs and plugs (do Rolls-Royces have plugs?) and cylinders chatting to one another about their family trees.

'My friend the Duchess,' remarked Archie. 'I should recognize her crest anywhere.'

As we came nearer, the chauffeur - a smart, tall fellow, very brisk in all his movements - leapt from his seat. I immediately recognized him; he had been supervising the move yesterday afternoon at Lessways. Taking an umbrella, he opened the passenger door and stood waiting, the umbrella held out before him.

I began to feel a little sick.

'Take off your shirt, Norman,' said Archie. 'Lay it on the pavement and I'll believe you're a gentleman.'

I felt mesmerized. I made some sort of effort to move away, to cross the road, but there were a lot of people bustling about on the pavement; tweedy women all hot on elevenses, waterproofed women hot on Truscott's bargain basement. Both Archie and I were held up for a moment.

Slowly Miss Hargreaves emerged from the car. Hideously fascinated, as always, I watched her. She had changed; in a subtle way she had changed very greatly. Her expression was different; the old impish gaiety seemed to have left her. Her clothes were very much quieter; you could not imagine her now wearing a tall hat. Her little head was raised to a higher angle, pushed up, perhaps, by the high neck of her dress. Pausing for a moment, one foot on the running-board, one foot on the pavement, she sniffed fastidiously. Almost instinctively people moved to make way for her. Shivering a little, she drew her cape round her shoulders, adjusted a pair of dark horn spectacles (she no longer used lorgnettes) and addressed the chauffeur.

'You had better come in with me, Austen. There may be one or two things I shall want to take away.'

'Very good, your ladyship.'

I realized she was looking at me. Wrinkling her face into a peevish frown as though she were making an effort to remember me, she said in a cold, distant voice: 'Mr Huntley, is it not? What appalling weather!'

The chauffeur, lipping me superciliously, loomed above her, steering his umbrella over her head. They disappeared into Truscott's.

*　　*　　*

'My God!' I said to father, rushing into the shop. 'She's back!'

'Never did approve of women playing football.'

'I'm not talking about football. Miss Hargreaves, I mean; large as life in a Rolls-Royce. She's come into a title. Chauffeur called her her ladyship. What do you think of it?'

'Funny things, titles. No law of gravity about them. You can never be certain where or when they're going to fall. Take my Cousin Terence. He collected stamps. He'd never have found out otherwise that he was descended from Bonnie Prince Charlie. It was like this. We - '

I felt I couldn't stand father that morning. I went round to Beddow's to tell Henry the tremendous news. It was some days since I'd seen him.

'You'll never guess what's happened,' I said.

'Lady Hargreaves?'

'Oh, how the devil did you know? What a bore you are!'

'She's in the Court news,' he said. He went to the office and came back with a copy of the *Cornford Mercury*, which he showed to me. I read:

> 'Lady Hargreaves will shortly be in residence at Lessways, the fine old Queen Anne mansion in the London road. We take this opportunity of welcoming her ladyship to Cornford society. Many will be glad to know that Lessways - once the scene of so many distinguished gatherings - will again throw open its doors to the elect. Lady Hargreaves - a keen amateur musician and a poet of distinction - comes of an old Irish family and was, until recently, residing at Oakham.'

'You were a fool to give her that title,' said Henry.

I laughed uneasily. 'Oh, I wasn't serious about that,' I said. 'We were in rather an awkward fix. I told you. I thought Major Wynne would be impressed if I called her Lady Hargreaves.'

'Well, I hope you'll enjoy hobnobbing with a countess -
or whatever she is.'

'Do you know, Henry, the old devil looked at me as
though I were a tramp. It makes my blood boil.'

'Hers has boiled blue, old boy. That's the trouble. Yours
hasn't. Anyway, she might leave you alone now.'

'I don't care what she does,' I said lightly. But I was far
from feeling it.

'I hear she's been buying up half Truscott's. Carpets,
bedding, curtains. I expect we shall see quite a lot of life at
Lessways in a few days.'

*   *   *

'You can do what you like from now on. I've finished
with you.'

Bitterly did I remember those idle words, spoken in
anger on Cookham Bridge. Not only had I unwittingly
raised her rank; I had madly endowed her with autonomy.

Lessways was the seat of government. In a very short
while people forgot that the Lady Hargreaves who now
flung open her doors to the elect was the Miss Hargreaves
who had trespassed upon the sanctity of the Bishop's
Throne; who had worn a pantomime hat; questioned the
reputation of the Swan Hotel and, in a score of ways, been
the biggest joke of the town since old Canon Featherstone-
haugh married Miss Roma Noam, the novelist. (I'll tell you
about that one day.) Miss Hargreaves was no longer a joke.
From the moment when the Dean called and left his card
at Lessways, Lady Hargreaves' position as a fixed star in
the brilliant little firmament of Cornford was secured.
Archdeacon Cutler called. Canon Auty was reputed to
be going to call - and this was almost unprecedented, since
the old man never left the Close. Years ago he had been a

familiar figure in Truslove's, the barbers, where once a week he had gone to have his beard trimmed; but the opening of a department for ladies in the same establishment had greatly discouraged him: nowadays Mr Truslove himself, every Saturday morning, with scissors, tapers and combs, visited the Close to attend upon what was felt to be the best beard Cornford had known in this century.

Miss Linkinghorne, ever on the scent of Debrett and his offshoots, almost daily lingered by the gates of Lessways. Old Colonel Temperley was another early caller. And there were many more. Not a new visiting-card was printed in those days but it hoped for a day when it might repose upon the silver plate on the Tudor chest in the panelled hall of Lessways.

Let it not be thought that Lady Hargreaves kept herself within the doors of her new home. Oh, no! There was plenty to be done outside and she did it. She attended the chrysanthemum show in the Town Hall and had a terrific argument with old Countess Mumphry about the best method of raising the flowers. 'No coddling,' she was heard to say, rather critically. 'You must never coddle a chrysanthemum, my dear Countess.' Everybody said that they felt the Countess had spent her entire life misguidedly coddling chrysanthemums.

Towards the end of October the Choral Society gave their usual concert. Lady Hargreaves occupied a prominent position, following Verdi's *Requiem* from a splendidly bound full score (*full* score, mark you) embossed with the letter 'H' on the cover. Following this with a red pencil, she sat right below the doctor, whose beat suffered considerably in consequence. I'm not surprised. Even Beecham might have been intimidated.

She was asked to open a Conservative bazaar and she opened it damn well; I wandered in there after she had left and I had the strongest feeling that it was the best-opened bazaar I had ever been to. Not a bit of it was closed, you could see that.

Another matter brought her bang into the middle of Cornford, between the 'n' and the 'f' as you might say. For some time there had been a controversy waging upon the question of changing the time of closing the Cathedral. The Mayor, who had the impertinence to have a Roman Catholic daughter, had suggested to the Dean and Chapter that, in summer, the Cathedral ought to be kept open until sunset, instead of the usual hour, six-thirty. His idea was that shop people had too little opportunity of visiting the place. The idea was anathema to both Archdeacon Cutler and Canon Auty, particularly as the Mayor had used the expression 'the people's Church'. The Dean was for a compromise, but up to date the matter had not been settled. Letters poured into the *Mercury*, mostly supporting the Mayor. Almost at the same time there was a by-election and the Labour candidate, D. Howlsby-Skitt (who also wrote books on eagles which father sometimes put in the window), polled, according to the Nationalist supporters, a good two thousand more votes than he would have done, because he had used the Cathedral-closing-hour controversy in the course of his platform campaign. He didn't get in, but he was near the door, so to speak. They were critical days in Cornford, I can tell you. A nearly Roman Catholic mayor combined with a Labour member - I doubt whether the Cathedral could have stood up to it. In the height of the argument, Lady Hargreaves stepped in, writing to the editor of the *Mercury* a terse, crisp letter in which she poured fine and subtle scorn upon the attitude of trippers who treated the holy building as a super-museum piece. The Cathedral, she maintained, was the property of the Church, not of the 'people'. (And she wrote that word in inverted commas, too.) Coming down so firmly on the Close side of the fence, she so impressed Canon Auty that he declared for the tenth time to his wife that he would call at Lessways; he even went so far as to quote in a sermon two lines of a sonnet from Constance Lady Hargreaves' pen which appeared in the *Mercury*:

'Out, out bold Beauvais, thrust thy ancient sword
'Mongst those who never Magnify the Lord . . . '

(Nobody hated visitors to the Cathedral more than Canon Auty. He had once rudely turned out a gang of Colonials who wandered into the south transept just as the choir was lined up for Evensong. Amongst them was a retired bishop of the Windward Isles who, it is said, spent the rest of his windy life disputing in various papers the Canon's well-known and somewhat un-Anglican views upon the liturgies of the Eastern Church.)

I saw a good deal of Lady Hargreaves. But did she ever vouchsafe to me more than the flicker of a perfectly bred eyelid? The old devil did not. Upon one occasion when I happened to come across her making a sketch of the Norman font, there was not even a flicker. I was always running into her. Popping in and out of the Deanery; exercising Sarah along Meads (Sarah never yapped now, and not a tree did she sniff at); writing verses in unexpected corners of the Cathedral; soaring at thirty-five - never more - up and down the High Street in the Rolls-Royce. I did my best to avoid her. But even if I didn't see *her* I was constantly being tormented by the smoke that rose from the chimneys of Lessways. Once, when the wind blew a lot of soot over my music paper, I stood at the window and cursed her, shaking my fist at the house and watching the smoke, knowing I was powerless to do anything. You knew it was expensive smoke, fired from the very best household coal. I watched it in a gloomy reverie as it plumed away into the saffron evening sky and floated serenely round the Cathedral spire.

They were wretched days for me. When you make something, make it well as I had, endow it with a title and send it out into the best society, do you sleep easily in your bed when it spurns you and treats you like dust? Do you? If you do you're a stronger man than I am.

*　　*　　*

For some time at least I kept my vow not to have anything more to do with her. Of course, she helped me to keep that vow in a way. But I don't mind telling you it was torture - pure torture, made the more unbearable because everybody used to ask me why I wasn't friendly with her any more. Jim was particularly impossible in that way. It was a funny thing. Before, when she'd been merely Miss Hargreaves, mother and Jim had practically accused me of snobbery. Now, when she was Lady Hargreaves, Jim, at any rate, reproached me for not calling upon her.

'You *ought* to go and see her,' she kept saying. 'After all, she owes her life to you - she told us so herself.'

'Oh, she's far too grand for me now,' I said. 'I reckon I know where I'm not wanted. She's too high-up for me, Jim. I'm not in that Close set and never will be.'

'How stupid you are! She's probably offended because you haven't been to see her. It's your duty to go.'

'I agree with Norman,' said mother unexpectedly. 'I think he's quite right not to go there. If she wanted to see us she'd come here, but she doesn't want to. It's been a very unfortunate friendship for the boy, and the less he has to do with her the better. Personally I should hate to see him making up to her as everybody else does, just because she's a ladyship.'

'Thank you, mother,' I said. I thought it jolly sporting of her.

You'll want to know what the position was between me and Marjorie. Well, I'm sorry to tell you (or am I sorry?) that she'd quite given me up. She'd started to go round with Pat Howard. No, I can't honestly say I *was* sorry. There was a lack of imagination about that girl which had always worried me. She never quite came to life, somehow, though she looked pretty enough. I mean . . . Pat Howard! Greasy hair, padded shoulders, check plus-fours and a stinking little three-wheeler that belched blue smoke at you from an exhaust like a ship's siren . . . No! Pat Howard no doubt had his points. But I never liked him. I can't say I'd trust my money to the bank he works in.

And that brings me to the question of Connie's money. Where had she got it all from? She'd given five thousand for the house alone and a rumour had it that she'd paid Mr Carver, the agent, the entire sum in bank-notes. I knew in a roundabout way, via Pat Howard as a matter of fact, that she had no account at the Metropolitan and I'd never seen her going in or out of any of the other banks in the town. Had I (and this was only one of many such questions which I could never answer) made the bank-notes too? Suppose they turned out to be duds? A nice kettle of fish that would be - *my* kettle of fish as well as hers, for I hadn't the slightest doubt she would, in some ingenious way, plunge me directly into it. I should get boiled; not she.

On the other hand, imprisonment would at least mean the end of her in Cornford. It would be nice to visit her in jail and gently point out to her that I was still master of the situation. I toyed with the idea a good deal; perilously I approached a peak. It got possession of me. Whisperings round Cornford: Lady Hargreaves is a common crook: marked coldness from the Close: the Dean is twice out when she calls: discovery - by me - of a printing-press for turning out bank-notes in the vast cellars of Lessways: headline - 'Lay clerk discovers criminal plot in Cathedral City': the Trial: ten years: visits to Connie in prison: I appeal to the Governor to allow her to play the Chapel organ. Safely locked up I at last have her under strict control. No more high aristocratic jinks.

'My God!' I said, 'I'll scotch her!'

The plot thickened in my mind, in my room late at nights. She was climbing too damn high. Some rungs, if not all, must be wrenched from her ladder. Get the rumour round, get the tatty trotty tongues of Cornford wagging, and it would be the beginning of the end of her. She was not popular with the townsfolk after the Cathedral-closing incident, and the weather in the Close is as fickle as any April day can offer. I didn't suppose, of course, that the bank-notes *were* forged; I never carried the plot so far as trial and imprisonment. But it would be good enough if some such rumour got round.

It's no good your reading this and condemning me and saying I'm horribly malicious. I had to do something about it. I couldn't sit back for ever and watch Connie capering in her Cloud-Cuckoo-Land of Deans and Archdeacons. One kind word from her, one smile in her old fashion, one wink of recognition - and I would not have acted as I did.

It was easy enough. I sent an anonymous letter to Mr Carver the house-agent, choosing him because I knew that once a typed letter gets filed in a business house, it's as good as placarded on the town walls. And I wanted the story to buzz from the town, not from the Close. Nobody believes stories that start in the Close, everybody believes what they hear in the barber's shop, over the counter of the Happy Union, or what the office boy tells the messenger boy from the bank.

I was very careful about it all. If you're going to be Anon you've got to do it well; otherwise you'll end up by merely being incognito. I went to town one plain day and spent half a crown in a typewriting office in St Martin's Lane. This is what I wrote:

> 'Sir. This is a warning to you. *Do not trust* the woman who calls herself "Lady Hargreaves". Neither her title nor her money are genuine. She is a dangerous member of the I.R.A. If you value Cornford Cathedral, keep an eye on her.'

I signed it 'Ulsterman'.

How well I remember that afternoon. I was standing in Charing Cross post office with crowds of busy people buzzing about me. The letter had just been dropped into the country box. I stood there, biting my fingers and wondering how I could get it out again. I knew at once that I had done a mad thing. But the whole trouble with me, as you'll have found out, is that I never realize I've done a mad thing until I *have* done it.

*　　　*　　　*

The evening after that I was in the Happy Union, sitting alone in the corner by the fire. The wind was wailing outside, the rain pouring. I was sad. Bitterly I regretted sending that letter, the first and the last anonymous letter of my life. I don't know whether you've ever tried it, but sending anonymous letters gives you a kind of thin, mean feeling inside, as though in trying to hide your own personality, you'd only succeeded in giving birth to a new and detestable one. I've always hated that fellow Anon whose poems appear in so many anthologies; now, sneaking into the seclusion of the Happy Union under his name, I hated myself.

The swing-door opened suddenly, and I heard Henry's voice, talking to somebody with him. I was in the public bar (father and I hate the saloon lounge) and I was expecting Henry to come in. But he didn't. I heard him go through to the saloon, and then I heard Pat Howard's voice. I sighed. If Henry went into the saloon with Pat Howard, we might just as well not be friends any more, I thought.

Well, I eavesdropped. Anon would; it's in character. Anyhow, I couldn't very well help overhearing what they said - which is the typical sort of excuse Anon would make.

'What's the matter with Huntley, these days?' I could hear Pat saying. I guessed they were drinking pink gins.

'God knows!' So Henry. And I could hear his shoulders shrugging. 'He's miserable to death over this Hargreaves woman.'

'Most extraordinary yarns are going round. Marjorie thinks he's quite dotty, you know.'

'Oh, he's not *dotty*,' said Henry. (I *knew* Henry felt uncomfortable.) 'Of course, it's been a frightful blow to him the way the Hargreaves has cut him dead.'

'There always was something a bit odd about Huntley,' said Pat, 'even as a kid. Too damned introspective, you know. As for the old man, well, of course, he's quite mad.'

I got up. I couldn't stand that. No. That was too much.

I went into the saloon and walked up to the bar. Henry and Pat were the only people there.

Henry went a flaming red when he saw me; and he does go very red, Henry does, right up to the roots of the hair. I felt sorry for him in a way.

'Look here,' I said to Pat, 'you may say what you like about me and we shan't quarrel. But if you say anything more about my father, Pat Howard, I'll wipe your nose on the floor.'

'Oh, I didn't mean anything,' he began quickly. 'Have a drink, old man. I - '

'Of course Pat didn't mean anything,' said Henry. 'Have something to drink and be nice to us, old boy.'

'No,' I said. 'I won't drink with you. As for you, Henry, I hope that bath will stick in your throat and choke you. You can drown yourself in it - '

'Here, old boy, don't go on like this.'

'I will go on like this.'

But instead of going on like that, I turned suddenly and went out of the bar. In the street I hunched up my coat miserably from the driving rain. I felt suicidal. I'm very fond of old Henry, and it did seem to me that he'd let me down terribly. The whole of the Hargreaves business suddenly mounted up like a cloud over me. I felt I couldn't breathe.

While I stood there the side door of the Happy Union opened and a man came out, fumbling with the catch of his umbrella. 'Now,' I heard him saying, 'I shall really expect to see you at Mass on Sunday, Mrs Paton. I know it's very difficult for you, but you must try to come. Good night.'

'Good night, Father.'

It was Father Toule. I remembered that Mrs Paton, who runs the Happy Union, was a Roman Catholic. For a moment I stood lost in thought, watching him walk up the hill towards the presbytery in Bethany Lane. Then I ran after him.

'Father Toule!' I called, a few yards behind him. He turned.

'Yes? Who is that, please?'

'It's me. Norman Huntley. Huntley's bookshop. You remember - '

'Of course. How are you, Mr Huntley? And how is your father? Very wintry, isn't it?'

'Yes,' I said. 'I'm all right, thank you. At least, I'm not - not really. I awfully want to have a talk with you, that is, if you've got time.'

'Oh? Certainly. Come and have a cup of cocoa with me at the presbytery. Dear me! What a night!'

So it was a night. We struggled against the wind, up to the top of Candole Street, round the corner by the Northgate, and eventually down into Bethany Lane, by the recreation park. It was impossible to talk in the driving wind and rain. Father Toule insisted on my sharing his umbrella, which I thought kind but silly of him, as I only got the drips from it down my neck.

We went into the presbytery and he lit a small gas-stove in the parlour. I had been in once before to bring some books round. It was, I thought, a terribly dreary room, with much the same atmosphere as a dentist's waiting-room. It was full of sacred pictures and dried flowers, with a lot of blotting-pads and penny pamphlets on the walnut oval table in the middle. It seemed a little more cheerful that evening with the gas-fire alight. Father Toule kept skimming round me, making me comfortable, offering me cigarettes and going in and out of the room to some mysterious kitchen down a dark staircase to see about the cocoa. There was an awful draught from one of the opened windows, but I didn't like to tell him. After some time the cocoa was ready and I sat with the steaming cup before me, stirring it vigorously and wondering how on earth I was going to say what I wanted to say. It was getting on for ten.

Father Toule didn't try to make me talk; just said a few things about the weather and books. He's a very small man, quite young, with the most extraordinarily innocent expression and grave blue eyes. He's got rather a comic little laugh and he tries so hard to make you comfortable that you can't help feeling uncomfortable.

'Well - ' I choked over the boiling cocoa. How much easier it would all have been if he'd offered me sherry! 'The fact is - ' There was no sugar in the cocoa. I wondered whether to tell him.

'Yes?'

'Father Toule,' I said, putting the cocoa on the table and determining to plunge into my story, 'Father Toule, suppose I told you something fantastic, such as that I'd been swallowed by a whale? If I swore it was the truth, you wouldn't laugh at me, would you?'

He did laugh. But not at me, which was kind.

'I expect everybody laughed at poor Jonah, don't you? And he must have found it hard to put up with. No, Mr Huntley, I'll try not to laugh. What is the matter?'

'I'd better get it out at once. I'm terribly worried. I've created something. I've created a woman. She's alive now in this town. Her name is - Lady Hargreaves.'

There was a long silence. Not a shadow of a smile crossed his face. It was quite expressionless. Then - 'Would it be better for you to tell me all about it, Mr Huntley?'

I told him everything, right up to the swan affair. The only thing I left out was about our night on the river. I couldn't bear the idea of that getting round, and even presbyteries have ears.

'Do you believe me?' I asked.

'I believe,' he said, 'that you believe you are telling a true story. Nobody could come and make up a story like that.'

'I could,' I said.

'Ah!' he smiled. 'Yes. You could. But I don't think you'd walk up Candole Street all the way to Bethany Lane on a wild night just to pull my leg, would you, Mr Huntley?'

I shook my head. 'You believe me, then?'

'I said I believed you believed you were telling a true story. But whether you have the true explanation - ah! That's another matter.'

'I'm positive!' I cried. 'I feel it in my bones. There *can't* be any other explanation, there can't be. Everything fits in with what I made up from the first.'

'Well, if you are certain you have - made this woman, Mr Huntley, why do you come to me?'

'Because - because - Well, I haven't got *proof*, have I? And I don't know what to do about her.'

'Ah. You haven't got proof. Then you are not quite certain?'

'I see. You're another one who doesn't believe me,' I said bitterly. The rain beat against the windows; a calendar was flapping on the wall from a partly opened window.

'No, no!' he said quickly. 'After all, none of us can know what is in the mind of God, can we, and - '

'That's it!' I cried. 'That's just it! I felt you'd - there was that saint you were interested in. That's what made me come to you. The saint who flew.'

'Oh, you mean St Joseph of Cupertino? Yes. You must not take such stories too seriously. There is very little evidence - but do have another cigarette - that he actually *flew*. He was supposed to be suspended above the ground. But even that is not known for certain.'

'Can *anything* be proved?' I said. And I remembered father saying that the only thing he certainly knew was that he knew nothing.

'Supernatural phenomena cannot be proved by natural evidences, Mr Huntley.'

'But I *know* I made Miss Hargreaves. I know it, Father. I - '

'Wait a minute. Wait a minute. I would like to suggest to you that it is no more certain you created Miss Hargreaves than that St Joseph flew about his church. God *may*, of course, in His own inscrutable way, have used you for the demonstration of a marvel that we cannot at present understand. He *may* have done that.'

'That's it. That's what I mean.'

'And there *may*, of course, be a perfectly natural explanation, overlooked at present.'

'I don't *want* natural explanations!' I cried.

'Really, Mr Huntley - don't you?' He smiled.

'Suppose,' I went on, 'that it turns out beyond doubt that nobody in the world had ever seen or heard of Miss Hargreaves before that day I first spoke her name - that she suddenly appeared in the world at that moment? Why then, Father Toule, it means that I *must* have created her.'

'No, Mr Huntley. It means that there must be a supernatural explanation.'

'But that is the only supernatural explanation.'

'Oh, no! Since we really know nothing of the supernatural, there might be a million supernatural explanations. There is one quite obvious possibility. I merely put it to you. There *is* precedent for our believing that it is possible to raise a dead body from the grave. But no doubt you have thought of that and dismissed it.'

I was silent. 'I don't - like that,' I said slowly.

'Ah. You prefer the other? Yes. I can quite understand. I wonder - ' He was silent. 'I was going to say,' he suggested, 'that it might ease your mind a little if you could go to Lusk some time and see if by any chance there is a tombstone in the graveyard which bears this lady's name - or a plate, perhaps, in the church itself. What I am trying to suggest to you is that you might have subconsciously noticed the name on your way into the church and brought it out later, not realizing you had seen it.'

'But - you don't mean - that - I raised her from the dead - the cockatoo - *everything* - no, I - '

'Oh, please do not let it add to your worries. It is only another possible supernatural explanation. In any case, I feel that a visit to Lusk church might help you to get a clearer perspective of the matter. How very, very interesting it all is! I think you ought to tell this sexton that you were playing a joke on him. Forgive my putting that point of view before you, but it was perhaps rather an unkind thing to do. Unintentional, of course, Mr Huntley.'

'Do you know, that never once occurred to me.'

'He, you see, firmly believes in her existence, though he has never seen her. Whether you have created her in the flesh, you have certainly created her in the mind of that one man. You have, in fact, planted in that mind what may be a lie.'

'Unless - I raised her from the dead.'

'Yes. But I would not dwell too much upon that. It was perhaps silly of me to lay it before you.'

'It's so awful, Father Toule. Not a soul will believe me. And I can't help feeling I want to tell everybody, *make* them believe me, do something that'll compel them to believe me. That swan, for example - '

For the first time that evening he frowned.

'I would be very, very careful,' he said, 'if you really believe you are endowed with some strange supernatural power, then you must walk very carefully indeed. You must learn to be very humble. Say your prayers about it and accept God's will. I would not try to probe too deeply into the matter. I am very honoured that you should have come to me, Mr Huntley. I shall accept all that you have told me as if it were under the seal of the Confessional - '

'I don't mind who you tell,' I said.

'I would prefer to tell nobody, Mr Huntley.'

'You're awfully kind,' I mumbled. For some moments I sat there staring into the gas-fire. Father Toule stifled a yawn. I rose hastily.

We went to the door. 'Come and see me at any time,' he said.

'Yes. Thank you. I'll - be quiet about it. Do as you suggest.'

'I wonder,' he murmured, 'whether she has been baptized?'

'Why?' I asked.

'Never mind. It is a vast problem, Mr Huntley. Too big for our small minds, I fear. I hope, for your own peace, that you discover some perfectly straightforward explanation of the whole mystery.'

But the trouble was, *that I didn't hope that.* As I walked home through the rain, pondering over our talk, I knew that I preferred a supernatural explanation. I stood outside Lessways for fully five minutes, thinking that, inside there, going now to her bed perhaps, was the woman that I had created; or, the woman I had - raised from the dead.

*   *   *

A letter was waiting for me on the hall-stand. I snatched it up quickly, immediately recognizing the large, flowery handwriting.

'Is that you, Norman?' called mother from the drawing-room. 'We've got those new records of the *Mikado*; come and hear them.'

'Not now, mother,' I said.

I ran upstairs, past father's room, up to the next floor to my room at the top of the house. It was cold. I switched on the electric heater, drew the blinds, put on my dressing-gown, one that an uncle of Henry's had brought back from Persia, rather a gay affair, a reassuring sort of garment. Lighting a cigarette, I took off my shoes. I realized to my annoyance that my hands were shaking. 'Nervous fool!' I muttered. Then I tore open Connie's letter. A minute later I sank back into my chair, Anon with the mask off, beaten, reduced to jelly.

This is what the letter said:

'Lessways.

'*October the 24th.*

'An anonymous letter containing a scandalous libel against Lady Hargreaves has just been put into her hands by Mr Carver, who had intended taking it directly to the police. Lady Hargreaves would like Mr Norman Huntley to know that she is well aware of the identity of the cowardly villain who, from his infamous shelter of anonymity, hurls such calumnies against her. Were it not for the fact that she remembers an occasion in Blackwell's bookshop in Oxford, she would do nothing to prevent Mr Carver from calling in the assistance of the law. As it is, because of an old courtesy, she has decided not to divulge the truth.

'Lady Hargreaves is prepared to overlook, even to *forget*, this most shameful attack upon her integrity. She will defend herself, if necessary, in her own way and in her own time. Let it not be thought, however, that Mr Norman Huntley will escape a second time, should he be led to perpetrate further outrages upon her.'

An overwhelming penitence seized hold of me; the most bitter regrets for what I had so shamefully done. Bleakly I looked into the future. All that Father Toule had said came back to me. I went to bed, but I was haunted by her and could not sleep. The window was open a little and, from the other side of the road, through another open window, I could very faintly hear the playing of a harp. What was the tune? I listened, lost it for a moment as a late bus passed, then caught more of it. It was 'Over the sea to Skye'. A lovely tune. Were they ghostly fingers that plucked the strings? Were they ghostly strings? Was Father Toule right? Were I to return to Lusk should I find a tomb with the words 'Constance Hargreaves' engraved on it in beautiful eighteenth-century lettering? And would she ever rest in peace? Was she, perhaps, haunted now by me as I was by her? Who was the haunter, who the haunted?

If I could undo, if I could only undo what I had done in Lusk church, I moaned to myself, I'd give ten years of my life. Suppose I went back to Lusk, told the sexton it was all a great lie, stood there again by that awful lectern, disclaimed all knowledge of 'dear Mr Archer', and, with all the power that my will is capable of, willed her back to her proper place - wherever that might be?

*　　　*　　　*

Father's room is directly below mine. While I lay on my bed I heard his violin. I pricked up my ears. Was it true? Yes. He, also, was playing 'Over the sea to Skye'. As I had, he must have heard Connie's harp and, consciously or unconsciously, drifted into the same tune himself. The harp stopped now. When he came to the end of the tune, father stopped. The harp started to play again. This time it was 'The Wearing of the Green'. Half-way through, father took up the tune; for a few moments harp and violin sounded together, the harp almost lost, just audible.

I got up and went to the window. It was entrancing; other-worldly; I wanted it to go on for ever. Go on, Connie, I said; go on, don't stop. But she wouldn't go on. I saw someone coming down the path of Lessways, to the gate, to the road, crossing the road, waiting by a lamp-post, right under father's window. It was Connie. And, something told me, it was the old Connie, the Connie who had sat in the organ-loft with me and played Handel's Largo. She was wearing a black coat; no hat. Father was playing 'Greensleeves', very slowly and sadly; Connie stood below, her head turned down to the pavement, one hand holding her stick, the other waving gently to the beat of the music. 'Oh, bravo, bravo!' I heard her say to herself when father had stopped playing.

I opened the window a little wider and leant out. Surely, I thought, music must for ever reconcile us?

'Miss Hargreaves - ' I called softly. 'Miss Hargreaves - '

She did not hear me. I called again, a little louder. This time she looked up sharply. I had no chance to say any more. As quick as lightning, she crossed the road and disappeared up the drive of Lessways. I heard the slamming of the front door, and though the width of the road and the two gardens was between us, I felt as though it had been slammed straight in my face.

*   *   *

It was the next evening, or a day or so after - I can't remember now and my diary got muddled during those queer days - anyhow, it was very soon after that I sat in the Happy Union with father and had one of the most strange and interesting talks with him in my life. He was the smallest bit drunk, to tell you the truth. He'd lost his match in the skittles championship, and losing a match always makes him drink more than he should. Not that my father is a drunkard; don't go running away with that idea. Only once or twice have I known him like he was that night; another occasion was when Horace scratched the varnish of his violin.

I came into the bar about half-past nine and found him, for once, sitting alone in my favourite corner, under the framed photograph of all the kings of Europe, taken about 1912 when there were enough kings to make a passable group. Somebody, years ago, had stuck a halfpenny stamp over the Kaiser and it was still there.

There was a grand fire going and not many chaps in the bar.

'You look glum, Dad,' I said.

'Fill up,' was all he said. I ordered a pint of old and mild. Father looked rather glazedly at the row of empty glasses on the table. 'Janus lost the three-thirty,' he said. 'Backed him both ways, my boy. Had to with a name like that. What did Janus have - two ears or two elbows, something; anyway, he doubled himself. Put some rum in that. Talk to me. Tell me everything.'

I took his half-empty beer glass over to the bar and engaged it with a noggin of rum. 'Talk to me,' he said again, when I returned.

'Are you in a serious mood, Dad?'

'Never more serious in my life, boy.'

'Well, tell me this. Do you believe you can - raise the dead?'

'Never tried. Dare say' - he drank - 'you might.'

I drew my chair closer to him. I didn't want the whole bar to hear. I told him about my talk with Father Toule. For a long time father was silent; he didn't even drink.

'A ghost couldn't play a harp as well as she does,' he said.

'Did you know she came over the road and listened to you last night, Dad?'

'She's a fine woman. I like her. I shouldn't like to think she was a ghost.'

'I don't like to, either. Not a bit. But - I'm getting scared, Dad.' Should I tell him about the anonymous letter and her answer to it? No. Not yet. 'She may be a fine woman,' I said, 'but - she's getting sinister, these days. The way she slammed that door! I can tell you, she's properly got her knife into me. And it isn't an ordinary sort of knife, either.'

'I'm a bit muddled, boy. This is the woman you made up?'

'Well, do you really *believe* I made her up? Do you?'

He leant low over the table, looked at me with his impossibly ambiguous eyes, and caught hold of my sleeve with his fingers. 'Look, Norman, my boy, I believe you. I believe in anything. I don't believe a damn thing's impossible.'

For once I knew he was speaking seriously. Whenever father uses the word 'I' a good deal, it means he means what he's saying.

'Go on,' I said. 'Talk, Dad.'

'When I was a boy I wanted a lizard, pined for a lizard. In South America it was and everybody had lizards, all the boys had lizards, except me. I sat under a yan-tan tree and said, "I've got a beautiful new lizard, the best lizard ever hatched from a lizard egg." There was a pain in my hand; couldn't make out what it was. Went on saying that about the lizard over and over again. Presently the pain in my hand got worse and I looked at it; a lizard as long as my violin was biting my little finger. Well, there you are. Did I ever tell you about those elephants? I - '

'Yes. You told me that. But damn it, father! That was just a lizard crawling over the ground in the ordinary way. I mean - '

'Live lizard.' He banged his fist on the table. 'Lizard plague that year and every lizard in the country had been killed by lizard poison except the tame ones the boys had. Tell you this lizard was *trained* to come to me; tell you I made that reptile. In the Zoo now. I presented him. Got too much for me.'

'Yes, but - ' I wiped the sweat off my brow; I felt uneasy. 'That's got nothing to do with Miss Hargreaves.'

'Matter of degree,' he said. He looked at me solemnly and stroked his moustache with the rim of his glass. 'I could put the whole thing in a nutshell for you. Three words - '

'*Don't* tell me about Tennyson. I shall scream.'

'Well, damn it!' Again he thumped the table. 'It *was* Lord Tennyson! I remember those words now. Skulking behind a pillar he was and he dropped this bit of paper. Three words on it. I read them.'

'Well, what the devil *were* they?'

'*Creative thought creates.*'

'That all?' It didn't seem much to me at the moment.

Father glared at me. 'Enough, isn't it? There's the key to the whole mystery and you say "is that all"? That's not the way to treat your father, my lad; not the way at all.'

'I'm sorry, Dad.'

'So you ought to be. I'm trying to help you. I've seen what's going on. I know. She's no ghost. Creative thought creates. More people in the world than you know started life in that way. Do you realize that millions of people every year are writing letters to Sherlock Holmes? They're still digging about in the Gray's Inn Road - '

'Baker Street - '

'Well, wherever the devil lived - still digging about trying to find him. He's got the biggest mail of anyone, barring Santa Claus and a bambino they put out in some church in Italy on Palm Sunday, or is it Ascension? Your Miss Holway's another. I'm proud of you, my boy. Proud of you!' He drank and shook his head several times at me.

'Well,' I said, 'I'm glad somebody's proud of me, any-way. I don't like it, Dad; I don't like it, whichever way you look at it I'd give anything never to have started it. I'm miserable. Everybody's fed up with me. Even Henry keeps out of my way nowadays. They all think I'm dotty, and they're sick to death of me talking about her. I've never been so miserable. She's ruining my life.'

'Of course,' said father slowly, 'you *were* a fool.'

'How?'

'My boy, I warned you years ago. I knew you'd got this gift. I've got it too. I don't use it. You can't go tampering with spiritual things and not expect trouble. Look at that Bitch of Endor.'

'Miss Hargreaves isn't like that at all.'

'H'm.' He shook his head slowly from side to side and kicked the coals in the fire with his foot. 'She's going to be.'

'Going to be - ' I stared at him and he looked at me very seriously. I got up. I felt hot and heady. 'My God!' I said. 'I must finish this somehow.'

'Be careful,' he said. 'Be damn careful. They turn and bite you, boy. I got so worried I nearly took to opium. It was just about then I married your mother. Keep off drugs, boy, whatever you do.'

'It makes you feel like trying anything, doesn't it?'

'They say Raleigh smoked opium in the Tower. Ever been to the Tower, by the way?'

'I do wish you'd keep to the point, Dad.'

But father wasn't interested in the point any more.

'Extraordinary thing, chopping off all those heads. Took your mother there once, but it was closed for repairs.'

Dreamily his hand curled round the tankard. I could see a story coming.

'*Shall* I go to Lusk,' I said, 'and do my damnedest?'

'Of course,' murmured father, 'I was never an admirer of Raleigh. Take that cloak affair. Too ostentatious. Then there was Blenheim. Who lost Blenheim? The whole campaign was sheer folly! He had no powder. Take this beer mug: that's Austerlitz. This vase is Wellington; this ashtray, Nelson. Hey, miss, bring me a pint of eight! Well, you *see?* Can't be done. Tolstoy demonstrates that in - what's that hellishly long book about peace and war?'

I left him; I knew I should get nothing more out of him that night.

* * *

'Creative thought Creates', I muttered over and over again to myself. I went to sleep with those words on my mind. At three o'clock I woke in a sweat from a nightmare. I won't tell you the nightmare because other people's dreams are always boring and, if it terrified me, I can't expect it to terrify anyone else. The point is, when I woke out of that 'mare, I found myself muttering three words over and over again. And those words were 'Destructive thought Destroys'.

* * *

Next morning I was in the shop, upstairs, trying to locate a Liddell and Scott for a customer. I heard the door open downstairs, someone coming in. I heard the tapping of a stick. Quickly I went to the head of the stairs and listened.

'Ah, Mr Huntley. I imagine we have met?'

'Dare say. Hand me that pawn, will you? There, by your foot.'

'I am Lady Hargreaves, Mr Huntley.'

'Oh, yes. Play chess?'

'Tolerably. But I came to talk of music.'

'Ah, Music. Yes. H'm. Ah. Music? You like music?'

'I could not say I *like* music, Mr Huntley. Music is air to me. Without it, I could not live.'

'H'm. I feel just the same about food, so we've something in common. Oh, damn! I'm checking the wrong king again!'

'The harp is my instrument.'

'Oh? You're the harper? Yes, I remember. Or do you call yourself a harpie? Fine! Heard you last night.'

'And I heard you, Mr Huntley. Allow me to congratulate you on your playing. I am no mean judge.'

'Thanks. Take a seat if you can find one. People generally use books. There's the *Britannica*. You gave a recital in Bath, didn't you. Or was it Wales?'

'I have hardly reached the standard of a public recital, my dear Mr Huntley.'

'Private one, perhaps?'

'That is precisely what I have come to see you about. I am thinking of giving a small musical party at Lessways. I should very much like you to play the violin.'

I could hardly believe my ears. After that letter to me - and everything. Music, then, *had* reconciled us. Was I glad? I didn't know.

'Good idea,' said father. 'We can do the Bach double D minor. You'd better practise it.'

'But I play the *harp*.'

'Oh, the harp. H'm. Yes.'

'I had in mind a group of solos from you, Mr Huntley - to include a little composition of my own which I think you would interpret well. A *Canzona* inspired by a willow-wren.'

'Queer birds. I remember one once that had hiccups. Yes - certainly. I'll play my tune on the G string. Norman can accompany. Squeen, order a new G at once, you devil! Funny, Lady Harton, Squeen plays the fiddle too. Think it'd be the flute, wouldn't you?'

'Oh? Why?'

'All that looking sideways. Suits Squeen more.'

'Well, then, I shall play some harp solos. As for the accompaniments to your pieces, including my *Canzona*, I will be responsible for those myself.'

'Oh, no!' said father promptly. 'Norman must play. Hi, Norman!' He called out. 'You there? Come down. Lady Harton wants you to play for her concert. We're doing my tune. Where are you?'

I sat tight and didn't answer. I suppose it was eavesdropping, but what I always say is, if eaves are worth dropping you're a fool if you don't pick them up.

'Unreliable fellow, my son,' said father. 'Never know where he is. Still, he's a good musician. That'll be all right. I'll settle him for you.'

There was a pause. I heard father murmur 'check'. Then:

'Mr Huntley,' she said, 'let me be quite frank with you. I do not wish your son to play.'

'Oh? Why? Thought you and he were as thick as thieves?'

'By no means! It is all a most painful subject. I had not wished to refer to it. But you compel me to.'

'Go on. I'm listening. Check.'

'As you know, Mr Huntley, your son had the good fortune to save my life. He was - I dislike saying it - grossly incompetent; I have no doubt I should have been out of hospital weeks earlier had he sent immediately for a skilled nurse. Still, it was kindly meant; we must not deny that. But a life saved, Mr Huntley, does not become the property of the saver! *Oh*, no!'

'Certainly not,' agreed father. 'Quite right.'

'I am very much afraid your son's head was turned. Not content with pestering me in hospital, he actually invited me to stay at your house. *Most* foolishly, I accepted. I am a poet, as you no doubt know, Mr Huntley, and believing as I do that the seed of poesy cannot bear fruit in one soil alone, I have always endeavoured to vary my range of experience.'

'Of course, you get the best fruit by sticking to the same soil. What fee are you offering, by the way?'

Ignoring this, she continued, her voice rising passionately.

'I come to Cornford. What do I find? *What* do I find? A welcome? By no means! A succession of insults? Precisely. Not from *you*! Oh, no! Or Mrs Huntley. I have no doubt we could all have been good friends - or, at any rate, friends. But your son's - ' Her voice broke in an angry sob. 'I will not speak of it. I have no desire to speak ill of him.'

'Let's talk about something else,' said father, which must have been very disappointing for her.

But she went on. 'One goes far afield for one's inspirations, Mr Huntley. The true fount rarely springs from the hearth. The waters of Lethe, I should suppose, run more freely in the Thames than in a teacup.'

'Have you seen our new teapot, by the way? It's a new sort.'

'Yet - even there - he sees fit to intrude, interrupting me with a crude call just as I am about to enter upon the fourth stanza of a poem that I was actually foolish enough to give to him. What has *since* happened I *cannot* talk about. It is too painful. It is, indeed, pitiful that a young and intelligent man should sink so low as he has. I hope I have said enough to make it quite clear to you that, with the best will in the world, it would be difficult for me to invite him to my home. I hope you understand, by the way, that I am inviting you to play in a professional capacity?'

There was a long pause.

Then: 'What were you saying?' asked father. 'Oh - your concert. Oh, yes. When is it?'

'A week to-day - if that allows you sufficient time. Perhaps you would care to call in this evening, when I will show you my *Canzona* and we can go through it. Come in to coffee at nine.'

'All right. I'll arrange a programme with Norman. You'll like my tune. What fee did you say?'

'Oh, I do not *offer* fees, Mr Huntley. If you will send in your account after the recital, I will see that it is dealt with.'

'All right. I'll send in Norman's bill too.'

('Bravo, father!' I muttered to myself.)

'Mr Huntley,' said Lady Hargreaves coldly, 'have I not made the position clear regarding your son?'

'Oh, well, we'll see about that later. You'd better let me have a copy of this Peacock Canon you keep talking about Norman and I can go through it. By the way, do you want a nice clean set of Beaumont and Fletcher, unbowdlerized? Go well in your shelves. I'll read you a bit. It's spicy stuff and - '

'Good afternoon, Mr Huntley. *Good* afternoon. I shall expect you at nine.'

The door closed; she had gone. I went downstairs.

'That was good of you, Dad,' I said. 'But I'm damned if I'll play for the old bitch.'

'Oh. There you are. Did you find that Beardsley *Morte d'Arthur?*'

'You don't believe what she said about me, do you?'

'Who? Oh, Lady Hurley. What did she say? I didn't quite catch it all. We're to go in for tea to-night at nine. Pity. I've got a skittle appointment.'

'She doesn't want me. Can't you listen?'

'We must get up a good programme,' said father. 'Might manage that Delius sonata. And I'll play that thing of Svendsen's. Old-fashioned, but I like it.'

'Idecide to have it out once and for all with C. H. "O Thou, the central orb." Destructive thought destroys.'

How vividly that entry from my diary recalls the afternoon of October the 26th! Lady Hargreaves sat in her usual place in the Close stalls. Archie Tallents had a solo in Gibbons' anthem, 'O Thou, the central orb'. I see him now, opening his large mouth and warbling his dulcet tones directly to her. It was always Archie's habit to pick upon one particular member of the congregation to sing to. He used to call it 'the personal touch'. A shadow of a smile passed over Connie's face. Yes, I reflected bitterly, if *I* were to sing to you like that you'd frown and report me to the Dean for irreverent behaviour. The conversation she had had with my father that morning seethed in my mind. It was the turning-point in my relations with her. Was it *fair* that she should attack me in this way? If father could play at her concert, why shouldn't I? Could I go on for the rest of my life, or the rest of hers, silently suffering her insults? Destructive thought destroys ... destructive thought destroys. To-day, I swore, we should see what destructive thought could really do. The moment had come to end it all. After Evensong I would go to Lessways and, once and for all, prove to her that I was still master. While Archie drooled blithely on and, outside, the west wind battered against the Cathedral walls, thoughts such as these surged madly in my mind.

Evensong over, I tore off my cassock and walked quickly down the south aisle. Far ahead of me I saw her going out of the west door. I ran; I actually ran. It came back to me how, a short while ago, in this same building, she had been the pursuer, I the pursued; I began to understand what the psalmist meant when he complained about the iron entering into his soul. I don't know whether iron's ever entered into your soul, but I can tell you it's pretty grisly.

Her car drove off just as I went out of the west door. Hot on the scent I leapt on my bicycle and pedalled furiously to Lessways. She had arrived only a few moments ahead of me; the car was still standing outside the door. I rapped peremptorily on the door-knocker. Almost immediately a curtain to a small side-window in the porch was drawn aside. Lady Hargreaves looked out. For one second I met her eyes. Then the curtain was pulled back; I heard her steps receding to the back of the house. I waited. I knocked again.

Austen, the chauffeur, came round the side of the house from the garage. I swung round, hearing his footsteps on the gravel.

'Anything you want?' he asked. He looked large and determined. Whatever I wanted, I could see I shouldn't get it from that fellow.

'I want Miss Hargreaves,' I said. 'At once.' I tried to make my voice sound important.

'There's no such person as "Miss Hargreaves" here. Try farther down the road. And that's a door-knocker, not a coal-hammer.'

'Lady Hargreaves, then.'

'Her ladyship is 'aving tea. In case you're selling anything, we don't want it. But her ladyship, with her customary kindness of 'eart, asked me to give you - '

Furiously angry I dashed the half-crown out of his hand. For a moment Austen looked at me curiously, pursing up his lips as though he were considering the best thing to do.

'I don't want to 'it you,' he said, 'not a little fellow like you, I don't. It isn't in me to do it.'

Now that made me really furious, because I'm not little. I'm five foot ten and a half if I'm an inch.

'I won't have any of your insolence,' I snapped. 'I'm here to see Lady Hargreaves, and if she won't open the door I shall bang it down.'

'Ho! So you're going to be like that, are you? All right. I'll go and phone for the police.'

He turned and disappeared the way he had come. 'Coward - ' I cried. 'Coward - ' I ran after him a few steps. Then I stopped. If he did call the police I shouldn't stand a ghostly chance.

All right, I thought; all right. We'll find another way. I went down the drive to my bicycle, propped up against the gate.

Under the rhododendrons, glinting in the earth, I saw silver. I took my bike, wheeled it out into the road, hesitated, then came back. I didn't see why I shouldn't have the half-crown. After all, it was more mine than hers.

* * *

Janie had laid tea. I sat down and cut myself some cake. An idea was simmering in my mind; rather a big idea, undeveloped as yet. As usual, it turned out to be quite mad, but I didn't see that then. Ideas, as I dare say you've noticed, are very like eruptions with me; before I know where I am I'm wallowing in my own lava.

So it was then. Gulping down some tea, I flew to the telephone and called Cornford 4277, the Lessways number. Another Spur of another perilous Moment.

A maid answered, and I asked to speak to Lady Hargreaves. Who would it be speaking? For a moment I hesitated. Who would it be? Certainly not Norman Huntley. Then, plunging down from the Spur, I said in my most plangent voice, 'This is the Dean.' Would the Dean hold the line? He would. He did.

A second later Connie's voice floated cordially to my ears.

'How nice of you to ring, my dear Dean! I was just sending you an invitation to a little musical party next week. I hope you will be able to come. Yes?'

'Delighted,' I murmured.

'I have engaged a local musician for the occasion. A somewhat interesting - though eccentric - creature.'

'Oh? Who is that, pray?'

'One Huntley. A bookseller. I have always believed in encouraging the gifted amateur.'

'Oh, quite, quite!'

'I understand he has a touch with the violin. By the way, Dean, now that I am talking of this man Huntley, I wonder if I may bother you with a matter that has given me considerable anxiety of late?'

I paused. Should she bother the Dean?

'By all means,' I said. Janie came out from the kitchen with a plate of bread and butter. I waved her aside impatiently.

'It is about' - continued Lady Hargreaves - 'this man's son. He is being a very great nuisance to me, claiming a friendship with me solely because of an unfortunate accident which threw him across my path. What is one to *do* about such people, Dean?'

(*What* was one to do?)

'Shall I - ' I paused and coughed. 'Shall I have a word with him?'

'A most capital suggestion! But I would like to talk to you first. There is another matter, as well, rather more serious. May I look in to-morrow morning, after Matins?'

Again I hesitated. Did I want her to come in after Matins? No! I saw at once what to do. The pit that she was digging for others she should fall into herself; bang down to the bottom.

I said, 'I was just about to call on you, as a matter of fact. That is why I rang. Would it be convenient? I wanted to discuss confidentially this difficult question of the hour for closing the Cathedral.'

Beautiful bait. She took it almost ravenously.

'Oh, splendid! By all means. Do come. Incidentally, this man Cornelius Huntley is coming in at nine. Perhaps we might talk to him about his son. We must be tactful. I abominate fuss.'

'Oh, quite, quite!'

'*Good*-bye, then. Good-bye.'

I rang off. For the first time I noticed Jim who was standing in the passage.

'What on earth's the matter with you?' she asked. 'You sound like a rural dean with adenoids.'

'Oh, quite, quite!' I muttered gloomily. Going upstairs, I shut myself in my room to think it all out.

*   *   *

As usual, it was the sort of idea that on paper looked well; but when it came to actuality - no! I might manage to impersonate the Dean on the phone; I've always been good at altering my tones of voice. Anyway, a phone gives you confidence. But could I ever make myself up to look like him? It was possible. If I put a collar on back to front, wore some horn spectacles and a black hat, the maid who opened the door would probably admit me, at any rate. Once inside I could beard Connie, lock the doors if need be, and spend the whole evening hammering home the truth.

Beard Connie? *Beard* her?

I laughed. A more attractive, more dramatic idea came to me. A beard, even a false one, gets you anywhere; it might even get you past Austen, particularly if it was submitted to him that this was Canon Auty's beard. In spite of the Canon's well-known admiration for Lady Hargreaves, he had not yet made his call to Lessways. Lady Hargreaves, it was said, was waiting keenly for this occasion. Very good. Very good indeed. He should call that evening.

I rushed to the theatrical chest on the landing. We're mad on charades at number 38, and we store everything in this chest that might come in useful. A year ago I had acted Father Time in a New Year's Eve sketch at a choristers' party. Here was the cardboard scythe; the hour-glass. I shouldn't want those; impatiently I rummaged down farther. At last the beard - tucked away in a black felt hat which might almost have belonged to Canon Auty. I returned to my room, put on the beard and looked in the mirror. Hat, thick wool scarf, old dark overcoat of father's. Magnificent - so long as I kept my hat on. Skull-cap? Yes! We had used them in a performance of the *Boy Bishop*. I rummaged again in the chest and found a purple one. Why not a cassock under overcoat? Yes! Canon Auty was known to have High Church leanings, and when you lean that way you always wear your cassock in the street. I went back to my room, locked myself in, found some grease-paint, and began to get under the skin of the noble canon.

There was a knock at the door. Mother called.

'We're going to the pictures, Norman. It's Greta Garbo. Are you coming?'

I adore Greta Garbo. It was a pity to miss her. Still -

'Not to-night, mother.'

'Whatever have you locked yourself in for?'

'I've got a frightfully difficult bit of counterpoint to do for the doctor. I don't want father interrupting.'

'That's a good boy. Don't get cold. Put on the heater.'

'All right, mother.'

She went down. Ten minutes later I heard the front door close, saw from my window mother and Jim walking along the street. It was nearly eight now. The moment had come. Limping a little and bowing my shoulders I left the house, crossed the road, walked up the drive to Lessways, and tapped in an Autyish manner on the door. A pretty little Irish maid came. Seized with a fit of asthmatic coughing, I asked to see Lady Hargreaves. 'What name would it be, sir?' I fumbled impatiently for a card. Then, 'Canon Auty,' I said gruffly.

*   *   *

'Will you wait a minute, sir? I'll tell her ladyship you're here.'

I nodded without speaking and the maid went upstairs. I was sitting in an oak armchair, holding out my hands to the fire and coughing hoarsely. Curiously I studied the furnishing. It was all antique, mostly Jacobean, beautifully polished. Firelight glowed in a grandfather clock. There were samplers, glass paintings and old prints on the walls. A lantern clock struck eight. Behind me, a wide staircase rose to the second floor and doors opened on to the other rooms. The stair-carpet was of pale gold; so were the curtains. On a table, under a gigantic chrysanthemum embedded in a brass pot, I saw several copies of the *Cornford Mercury* and two volumes of *Wayside Bundle*.

Some minutes passed. Nobody came. I grew more and more uneasy. Was she suspicious? Was that devil Austen spying on me somewhere? Were they sending for the police? Could I ever hope to claim the owner of this house - a house branded by so many years of impeccable taste - as *my* Connie Hargreaves?

The maid came down the stairs.

'Her ladyship won't be a minute, sir,' she said. 'And won't your reverence let me take your hat and overcoat?'

'No, no - ' I mumbled crossly.

She was a darling girl. Black hair and rosy cheeks; simply topping in the firelight. I was getting more and more sick of my beard. There aren't many pretty girls about and when you meet one you don't want to be whiskered. It was damned hot too.

Suddenly a voice called from an open door upstairs.

'Mollie - Mollie - '

The girl hurried away, and I heard voices on the landing.

'Have they covered up Dr Pepusch, Mollie?'

'I'll go and see, your ladyship.'

'Do. He must always be covered when we have visitors. Remind cook.'

'Yes, your ladyship.'

'That is all, then. I shall not need you any more. I hope you are not forgetting your prayers, Mollie?'

'Oh, no, your ladyship.'

'Whenever you wish to go to this Mass, you must tell me. I do not approve of the Roman Catholic religion, but since you *are* one I expect you to fulfil your obligations. I believe you are *obliged* to go to this Mass?'

'That's right, your ladyship.'

'Quite wrong - quite wrong - still - by the way, is the Dean arrived yet?'

'No, your ladyship. Canon Hauty - he's waiting downstairs.'

'Dear - dear! How stupid of me! I quite forgot. Tell him I am just coming. Offer him *Wayside Bundle* to read.'

* * *

'Oh, my *dear* Canon! *Too* bad of me to have kept you waiting. But why do you not take off your greatcoat? Are you cold?'

'No,' I said. 'I'm hot.'

I took off my beard.

* * *

'How dare you! *How* dare you!'

She moved towards a bell-rope that was hanging by the side of the great open fireplace. With a sudden wild vehemence Dr Pepusch screamed from somewhere in the back of the house. 'Avaunt! Avaunt!' A door slammed. I ran to the bell-rope and caught her by the arm.

'Oh, no, you don't!' I said. I stood with my back to it. I felt my power rising. I fixed her with both my eyes. 'Sit down,' I commanded.

Panting a little, wringing her hands, she began to speak. 'I - I - ' But she could not go on. She was weakening. I knew I was winning the first round. Brutally, I determined to deliver a knock-out blow, now, at once, while my power was on me.

'You're a naughty old woman!' I said sternly. I hated it; I loathed calling her that. But it was no use showing any mercy now.

Amazed, speechless, she fell back into a chair as though I had struck her. Quickly I continued. 'I've got a bone to pick with you. A *lot* of bones. And when I pick bones I don't like an audience. You leave that bell alone.'

Her head fell forward on her chest; she was breathing heavily. I suppose it must have been a terrible shock to her, particularly as she'd put on a puce-coloured velvet dress with a high lace collar brooched by a handsome cameo. All done in honour of Canon Auty, of course; you could see that. I believe, though I won't swear to it, there was a dash of rouge on her cheeks.

'I've given you every chance,' I said. I spoke hurriedly and tried to avoid looking at her. There was something so terribly pathetic about her; it was hard to speak sternly.

'You forced me to this,' I went on. 'I don't like getting into your house in this way. It's beastly; I hate it. But when you go round telling vile lies about me - when you turn your horrible chauffeur on to me with half a crown - '

'Which you took!' she snapped, with sudden spirit. 'Contemptible!' Her eyes glittered angrily.

'And why not?' I cried, her anger infecting me. 'Who are you, I should like to know? You think you're Lady Hargreaves, don't you? Well, you're not. You're a thought, that's all you are; a mere thought. Uncle Grosvenor! I'll Uncle Grosvenor you! You reckon you can do what you like ever since I gave you that title, don't you? Well, you can't! You're going to do what *I* like. Suppose I had turned you into a mouse, eh? A *small*, underfed mouse; a *church* mouse. And then set our ginger Tom on you? I might have done that if I'd had a spiteful mind. But I didn't. I made you Lady Hargreaves. And this is the thanks I get - half a crown flung at me by an illiterate chauffeur. You ought to be downright ashamed of yourself, downright ashamed - '

I stopped. It was like the scene I had had with her in the lay-clerks' vestry over again. She was holding her handkerchief to her eyes; her shoulders were shaking. A most unaccountable anguish came over me. I could not *bear* to see her cry. It was no good. Minute by minute I was losing my ground. And - minute by minute - I knew with a fatal certainty, she would gain the strength that I was losing. Power ebbed from me and rose in her. It would always be so; always. If I relinquished my power over her, she would seize it and exert it over me. What I had made was becoming too strong for me.

There was a long silence. I made a last valiant effort.

'Well, what have you to say?' I demanded.

'What - can - I say, dear?'

'Eh?' I sat up and took notice. 'Did you call me - dear?'

'Yes, dear. I did, dear.'

Had I then won? Had I for ever driven away her assumed independence?

'Oh,' I grunted. 'So you're sorry, are you?'

'My *dear* boy - I - ' She burst into floods of tears. With an immense effort I bit the tender, consoling words from my tongue. But they were in my heart.

'What can I say?' she sobbed. 'I am but human.'

'I'm not so sure,' I muttered uneasily.

She looked up at me with tearful eyes. 'I have wronged you - yes! I confess it. I have treated an old friend badly. And yet - am I entirely to blame?'

'What do you mean?' I felt my bones turning to water.

'Did you,' she cried with sudden passion, 'welcome me to Cornford as an old friend deserves to be welcomed? Have I once been able to recapture with you the happiness of that sunny day we spent together upon the Serpentine, when all your youth and - '

My voice rose wildly. 'You've got to come right off that stuff once and for all. You know as well as I do that we never went on the Serpentine. The whole story is a pack of lies. Lies - Miss Hargreaves! *You are my lie!*'

It was my last bolt. She stared at me - half frightened - half frightening.

'Norman' - and her tone was almost pitying - 'there can be no doubt. No further doubt. Your brain is rapidly becoming affected. My *dear*, I am so sorry. For a long time I have been fearing something like this. I should have faced up to the matter sooner. I am afraid that you are not - quite as you should be, dear. *Try* to realize it. Hold *on* to yourself. Get *grip*. Grip is essential in such cases. My poor Agatha suffered in much the same way. You would not care to end as she did.'

'No,' I muttered. 'I wouldn't care to end as - she did.' And, in my mind, I conceived a hundred different deaths for Agatha, each one more horrible than the last.

She rose slowly from her chair.

'Stay - where - you - are,' I hissed malignantly. But it was a half-hearted hiss, I knew that.

'Sit down!' she snapped suddenly. I stared at her. Was I crazy, or was she actually growing larger, seeming to tower above me? Her eyes blazed out at me from her powerful little head; her fingers clutched an ivory paper-knife on a console table.

'I warn you - ' I began weakly.

'SIT DOWN!' The words were like iron. I fell back into a chair. My God, I thought, this is the end; this is the terrible end. She is beginning to control *me*. In a week or so I should be powerless to do anything except what she desired. Already my will was impotent; I could do nothing but stare at her feebly, as a rabbit must stare at a snake. They say the rabbit enjoys being hypnotized by the snake; I can believe it because, in spite of my wretchedness, I could not be otherwise than wholly fascinated by her. It was terrible to realize that I had given her this power; that I had, from the depths of my misguided compassion for her, silently willed strength into her mysterious being.

'You witch,' I murmured. 'You absolute old witch!'

'That is enough!' she rapped out. Then she let me have it, true and proper. In blazing anger she told me exactly where I got off. And I *got* off; meek as a lamb.

'I have tolerated too much - far too much. No doubt but you are suffering from an aberration of the mind - but is that any reason why I should be inconvenienced? You have insulted my family, you have dogged my footsteps from place to place, you have written a scandalous letter about me - you have, most seriously, imperilled my name in this town. And now you have the impertinence to come before me, wearing a *beard*, abusing me in language that would be *criminal* did I not mercifully assume it to be insane. It is an outrage, Mr Huntley; it is an outrage. Only one of two courses is now open to me. Either to invoke the power of the law upon you or have you sent away to a mental home. You have gone too far, Mr Huntley; I do not know whether anybody could go farther.'

It was true. It was horribly true.

'Yes,' I muttered. 'I have gone too far. I know that.'

'Then you must be prepared to pay for your foolishness. I cannot any longer allow the twilight of my days to be clouded by the menace of a criminal lay-clerk who happened to cross my path because of an accident.'

'I - do wish you wouldn't keep saying I crossed *your* path,' I said weakly.

She held up an imperious hand. 'Cease!'

I ceased. I watched her wonderingly as she swept across to a bureau on the other side of the room. Finding paper, ink and a quill pen, she sat down. After a little thought she began to write.

'What are you doing, Miss Hargreaves - please?' I asked. I started to rise.

'Stay where you are!' she snapped immediately. 'I am writing to my solicitor. There shall be no more anonymous letters, Mr Huntley.'

'But - ' A ruined career stared me in the face. I didn't like the look of it. 'Please don't do that,' I cried. 'Please don't.'

'And why should I not?'

Why should she not, indeed? I racked my brains in search of an argument that would touch her. 'You couldn't do it,' I said. 'Not after - not after the wonderful times we've had together. Look at that morning in the Cathedral! The person who played the organ as you did, couldn't write the sort of letter you're going to write now, Miss Hargreaves - '

'*Lady* Hargreaves, if you please!'

'Lady Hargreaves, I mean. Please don't give me away - *by all that we have in common* - please don't give me away. I won't bother you any more, I swear I won't. I was mad. I don't know why I did it.'

I was almost down on my knees before her. It was ghastly.

She put down her pen and slowly came over towards me.

'Norman,' she said in a gentle voice, 'because of what we have in common - yes, I will once more overlook your conduct. But it must not happen again. It must never happen again.'

'I promise it shan't.'

She rang the bell suddenly.

'James Burley,' she said briskly, 'would, I know, give you special attention if I write to him. I imagine he is still in

Harley Street. Yes, I will write to-night. Expense? Tut! You must have the best advice. Obviously it is a very complicated case.'

Mollie came in, stopping and staring at me in bewilderment.

'Oh, Mollie,' said Lady Hargreaves, now completely herself, 'bring a carafe of water and some sal volatile. Mr Huntley is unwell. Is Sarah fed?'

'Y-yes - your ladyship.'

'Go along, child - go along. Don't stand staring at Mr Huntley like that.'

Mollie went out, still looking back at me over her shoulder. Lady Hargreaves settled herself in an armchair, crossed one leg over the other, played with a golden chain round her neck, and looked at me with a patronizing smile.

'Yes. James Burley's little establishment on Exmoor would, I think, be the place for you. Poor Norman! No matter for the moment. Let us put aside the tragedies of life. You told me, I think, some time ago that your mother was similarly affected? Yes? Rest, I beg you. Relax. Close your eyes.'

I felt drowsy, numbed of all movement. Like a shadow in a dream I was aware of Mollie coming in. I heard Lady Hargreaves speaking.

'Thank you, Mollie. That will do. Oh - take Mr Huntley's beard and skull-cap and hang them in the coat-cupboard. I abominate untidiness. Yes, yes, child - the beard.'

Mollie took them gingerly. I stared at a glass of sal volatile Lady Hargreaves was holding out before me. I shuddered. I loathe sal volatile.

'I don't *want* it,' I protested feebly.

'Naughty! Tch! Come now - you mustn't excite yourself again. I abominate scenes! Let me put a cushion behind your head. There - there!'

CHAPTER EIGHT

Vaguely I realized that somebody was knocking at the front door.

*   *   *

Mollie showed father in.

'Hullo,' he said. 'Am I interrupting? You said something about coffee.'

'Come in, my dear Mr Huntley. Mollie, take Mr Huntley's coat; and beard - Oh! he has no beard. Then bring some coffee and a bottle of cognac. Sit down, Mr Huntley. Your son and I were having a little tête-à-tête. I was about to read him my sonnet sequence, "The Nine Owls".'

'Owls, eh? H'm.' Father wandered about in his usual large manner, picking up things and looking at pictures. 'Nice place you've got here,' he said. 'Oliver Goldsmith used to live here, you know. Or was it Grinling Gibbons? Never can remember. Their style's very alike.'

He sat down. 'I suppose you two have settled everything about the concert?' he said.

'Well - ' began Connie.

Father nodded. 'Good. Now we can have a nice little chat about books and things. One or two stories I should like to tell you. Ever met Conrad?'

Lady Hargreaves screwed up her face. 'I cannot *quite* remember,' she said.

'I didn't,' said father. He lapsed into an unusual silence.

'*Such* an age - *such* writers - ' began Connie.

'You remember Henry James' story about the owl?' asked father.

'I think not.'

'Never can be sure of it myself. But it seems he kept an owl - an albino bird it was - in his bathroom. Well, one evening he took up the sponge, see - and it bit him and said,

243

"Lovely-lovely-lovely". Like that. Of course, he'd picked up the owl by mistake. But this is the interesting part. The owl saying "lovely" gave him the idea for one of his best lines. Dare say you know it. "Lovely are the curves of the white owl sweeping, wavy in the dusk lit by one large star." Beautiful poetry, Lady Marston. You and I couldn't write like that, not even if we kept ten white owls in our bathrooms.'

'But surely, Mr Huntley, George Meredith wrote those lines?'

Father nodded. 'So everybody thinks. Actually he stole them from Henry James. Happened to be lighting his pipe outside the bathroom. They had a cottage at Winchelsea. My aunt lived there later. Funny, really.'

Mollie came in with the coffee, cognac, and three balloon glasses.

'Ah!' Father rubbed his hands together. 'I like brandy. My father was a smuggler, y' know. Practically lived on brandy. Nice life, really. Thanks.'

I waited, wondering whether I should be offered any. But I was not. Father pushed his coffee aside and closed his palms round his glass. He looked over to me. 'Put it to your nose, boy,' he said. 'Get the bouquet.'

I looked down at my empty hands and shook my head slowly.

'Norman is a little unwell,' explained Lady Hargreaves. 'It would be most unwise for him to take brandy.'

'Unwell? How do you expect the boy to be well without brandy? Here, boy - ' He poured out a stiff glass for me and passed it over. I took it. Lady Hargreaves frowned and tapped her stick on the floor. I drank quickly before she should snatch it away from me. 'Here,' cried father, 'you mustn't drink brandy at that speed. What's the matter with you?'

'I told you,' Lady Hargreaves said coldly, 'he is unwell.'

'H'm,' said father. 'H'm.' He drank, and we were all silent for a little while.

'I've brought my tune,' remarked father presently. 'Here it is.' He drew a postcard from his pocket. 'Doesn't look very long, but I always add bits as I go along. Norman'll have to write out the accompaniment.'

Lady Hargreaves, glancing at the tune briefly, rose and went over to a Sheraton cabinet in a small boudoir adjoining the hall. She returned with some manuscript paper which she gave to father.

'This is the *Canzona* I spoke of,' she said. Father glanced at it cursorily.

'The great thing about my tune,' he said, 'is *cantabile*. I'll run over and get my fiddle and play it for you.'

'You see,' Lady Hargreaves was saying, leaning over father's shoulder and pointing to a bar in the manuscript on his lap, 'you see how skilfully the tune leads into the variation, without a break. I hope you will bring that out, Mr Huntley. This *appoggiatura* here is, of course, the willow-wren. You must bring that out too.'

'H'm. Yes. Like that bit,' said father vaguely. He sipped his cognac and casually dropped the manuscript on a chair by his side.

Stifled by the great fire, feeling almost incapable of speech or movement, I struggled up from my chair.

'I'll leave you to discuss the concert,' I said wearily.

'Yes. It would be as well for you to retire early,' said Lady Hargreaves. 'By the way, before you go - what was the name of that most interesting young man - a friend of yours who came to the station with you? Henry - something. I cannot remember.'

'Henry Beddow,' I said.

'Beddow. Ah, yes! I must make a note of it.' She turned to father again, taking her manuscript from the chair and holding it out before him. I wandered out to the coat-cupboard.

'*This* bar,' I heard her saying, 'is very subtle. Observe how the theme, now inverted and accelerated, creeps in to -'

'And it ends *niente*, you see,' said father. 'And by *niente* I mean *niente*. Want you to notice how -'

I took the beard, the hat, skull-cap and coat, closed the door behind me, crossed the road and wearily went home to bed. I felt that years had been added to me.

*   *   *

Destructive thought destroys. But it had failed to destroy. What I realized was this; it is a thousand times more difficult to destroy than to create. You will laugh and say I am mad; that destroying is far easier. But it isn't so. Try to destroy anything - try to annihilate it. Burn it and consider the ashes. Then consider how easily you create. Every time you open your mouth you create something. The chord of D flat major sounding to infinity from father's little Bord. How do you destroy that? What was Miss Hargreaves? She was the embodiment of my lie. It was no good my just trying to will that lie away. It was, that lie; it absolutely *was*. Some formula had to be found; something that would cancel the lie from the very beginning. Could it be done in Lusk church? Could it? And what was the formula?

Those were my thoughts as I lay on my bed that night.

About midnight father came in without knocking. Father never knocks.

'My God!' he said, 'she's a grand woman! Congratulations, my boy! If I had my time over again, I'd - I'd be damned if I'd stop at lizards.' (I wondered how much of that cognac was left.) 'What the devil do you mean,' he snapped suddenly, 'wearing beards and skull-caps? She says she's going to put a specialist on to you. Better wait till after the concert. She's agreed to let you play. We've got to practise this damned fugue of hers. Funny. Found we'd both known Hardy quite well. She says she comes in one of the novels and, of course, as anybody knows he put me in "Far from the Trumpet Major". Must read the others and see where she comes in. Hope she's not Tess. Don't want to see her hanged. Good night, my boy. Congratulations. She's no ghost.'

$$* \qquad * \qquad *$$

Over the tankards in the Happy Union:

'I 'ear tell as 'ow th' 'ole bitch've bin sent 'ere by those I.R.A. devils . . . '

'She'm no woman at all. All that 'obbling about on sticks never did take me in . . . '

'Serve the old Dean bloody well right if the Cathedral was blown sky 'igh. . . . '

Over the teacups in the Close:

'My *dear* Mrs Auty, I wouldn't say a word against her. But the most extraordinary story is . . . '

'Of course, Miss Linkinghorne, these Irish titles are *most* remote and . . . '

'Nonsense, my dear! Women of that age don't carry bombs about . . . '

'But, my dear Mr Dean, I saw her *myself*, making *plans* of the Cathedral and . . . '

In the lay-clerks' vestry:

'Always knew she was a bloody Guy Fawkes ever since I saw that 'at . . . '

And in the choir school:

'Say, chaps, have you heard? Old Hargy's an anarchist. Fact!'

'Go on! How do you know? ... '

'What's an anarchist, anyway? ... '

'Old Meaks says he saw her trying to get down into the crypt with a black bag. It was ticking too, he swears to it ... '

So the tale flickered, from a spark to a cinder, from a cinder to a flame. Within a week, whenever Connie went abroad, she was the victim of curious and resentful eyes. God - how I suffered! More, I swear, than she did. Innocently sketching the Cathedral from Meads one fine autumn afternoon, a lout from the town threw a clod of earth at her and quickly disappeared. With great dignity, Connie brushed her clothes, gathered up her sketching materials and returned home. For three days she did not leave the house. The flame of rumour grew to a bonfire of fact. There was an Irish maid at Lessways. Yes, that settled it. Hargreaves must go. The town spoke as one man.

On the fourth day she dropped her bomb. It appeared in the form of a letter in the *Cornford Mercury*.

'To the Editor.

'SIR, - Recently you were good enough in your columns to welcome me to the ancient Cathedral town of Cornford whither I had come to reside. I was proud to become a resident of Cornford and I looked forward to many happy years here. But what has happened? You, sir, must know only too well. I have become the victim of a cruel and malicious rumour which threatens to undermine my very existence here. I am not deaf. I have heard what is being said about me. I am, I understand, associated with bombs. Ridiculous as I regard this, there are apparently some people who believe it. I can no longer, therefore, be expected to remain silent.

'I know full well how this wicked rumour arose. I am able to refute it and I shall take immediate steps to do so. Let the lying tongues cease before hot burning coals fall upon them.

'Meanwhile, the honour of Cornford is at stake. Is it to be said that she drove an old lady beyond her ancient walls because of the wickedness of a deceitful pen?

'The poison of asps is under her lips, sir. The poison of asps is under her lips.

'HARGREAVES.'

Mother ran up to father's room early one evening with the paper in her hand. We were rehearsing for the concert, only a few days ahead now.

'Look at this!' she cried. 'It's all round the town. Nobody's talking of anything else.'

We read the letter. 'H'm,' said father. 'Can't understand why towns are always female.'

I said nothing. She'd attack now, I told myself; she'd attack.

'I must say,' said mother, 'I think it's rather splendid of her. Don't you, Norman?'

'Yes. Fine,' I said uncomfortably.

'Whatever she is, whoever started that story ought to be horsewhipped. Horsewhipped! I can't bear that sort of thing. Of course, I never did believe it.'

'A few days ago, mother,' I said, 'you said you wouldn't put anything beyond her.'

'Of course, I never meant it.'

'You go along now, Dorothy,' said father, 'we're busy'.

'I do think you ought to go and see her, Norman,' said mother. 'Ask her to come to tea if you think she'd like to. It would show people that we don't believe this absurd tale.

I hear Mrs Auty's been spreading the most *awful* stories. How I do hate those Close people!'

'Honestly, mother, I think she'd prefer it if I left her alone.'

'I do think she might have asked Jim and me to come to her concert. If you went over now, Norman, and asked her in to tea, and said how sorry you were about this awful gossip, she'd probably give us invitations to her concert. It would serve Mrs Auty right to find us all there. Anyway, I should like to hear father play properly for a change.'

'Always play properly,' said father. 'Norman, there's a bar you haven't filled in here, you devil.'

'No, mother, if you don't mind. I won't go just now.'

'Well, you are a queer boy. I shall never understand you.'

Mother turned and went out. Father shouted after her, 'See my dinner-jacket thing is pressed, Dorothy; and sew up the moth-holes.'

Father and I went on with Connie's *Canzona*. It was a rather sticky composition - Spohr at his jammiest - full of pretty work in six sharps and a good many double ones. You had to cross the hands. As I crossed mine I looked at them gloomily and wondered how long it would be before they were hand-cuffed. Sure as nuts, Connie would attack now. I knew it.

*   *   *

Cathedral towns are funny, fickle places. The day after Connie's letter had appeared in the *Mercury*, she drove up the High Street. It was four days since she had been seen abroad. Stopping in the market, she got out and, with Austen's help, purchased a number of potted cinerarias from a stall in Disraeli Square.

Connie was news, of course; more news than ever since the publication of her letter. At her appearance in the centre of the town at the busiest hour of the week, tongues which had been wagging for days - some in support of her, many more against her - suddenly stopped wagging. You almost felt that the drivers of buses and cars would stop their engines.

I had just come out of the bar of the Swan and I stopped, watching her as with minute care she examined the cinerarias, handing some over to Austen, dismissing others. She did not see me. Finally she handed a ten-shilling note to the woman at the stall and, refusing the change, turned slowly back towards her car.

All this time she had behaved as though the people of Cornford didn't exist, although she must have been acutely aware that everybody was looking at her. Suddenly, as she stepped up into the car, somebody - they said it was young Sanderson, son of the old man who was now head-gardener at Lessways - sang out at the top of his voice:

'Three cheers for her ladyship!'

There was a second's silence. My heart beat wildly. Which way would Cornford turn? Then there was a roar of cheering. Bowing graciously, she paused on the step of the car and raised her hand. A mighty silence fell. She might have been Queen Mary.

'Thank you, my friends,' was all she said. Still bowing a little, still smiling, she got back into the car and Austen slowly accelerated to the usual thirty-five.

From that moment Constance Lady Hargreaves could do no wrong.

*　　*　　*

I never expected she would spare me. She didn't. This is what happened.

That afternoon father was out and Squeen and I were in charge of the shop. I had a vile headache, and I don't wonder.

About three o'clock the Dean came in. My heart fell. I'd never been easy in the Dean's presence; I was less easy now.

Squeen buzzed busily round him, of course.

'Would Mr Dean like to see a very nice clean set of Jeremy Taylor's Discourses? And would it please Mr Dean to know that his little monograph on the Cathedral glass was selling very well?'

The Dean turned to me. 'Huntley, put aside these Bampton Lectures of Hutton's, will you? I'll take those. Oh - what have we here? An early edition, eh - '

He murmured away to some back shelves. He was in a very buying mood. After twenty minutes he'd selected a pile of a dozen or so books.

'I'll have them sent round, Mr Dean,' I said, edging him nervously to the door. Sure as a bee smells honey I smelt trouble.

'Oh, no.' He smiled amiably. 'Let us take them round to the Deanery now. Squeen can look after the shop, can't he? You can help me carry them.'

'Oh, no - no - ' I protested. 'I couldn't dream of your carrying them, Mr Dean. I - '

But he hitched three volumes under his arms and was piling the rest upon me. 'Come along,' he said. And from the tone of his voice I knew I should have to go along.

We walked slowly up Canticle Alley (not a favourite place of mine nowadays) and out into the Close.

'And how are you getting on with your music?' he asked, as we came within sight of the Deanery arches.

'Oh, not so bad, thank you, Mr Dean.'

'Have you taken your diplomas yet? The Royal College, isn't it?'

'No. Not yet, I'm afraid.'

'Really? I quite thought you had. Oh, come in - bring the books in. Yes, put them on the table. Have you seen my dahlias, Huntley? I have quite a show. Come along.'

It was a superb autumn day and the splendid garden, stretching away its long smooth lawns to the two great walnut trees at the bottom by the stream, had never looked more attractive. Slowly we walked down, the Dean waving his silk handkerchief at various shrubs and flowers and naming them in Latin for my benefit. I grew more and more uncomfortable. After all, I *do* like the Dean. I didn't want to quarrel with him.

We paused on a rustic bridge at the bottom and leant over, looking at the clear, thin stream where trout were darting from weeds to stones. The Cathedral clock chimed the half-hour. Thank heaven, at any rate, that I should soon have to get away for Evensong.

'I wanted to have a talk with you,' said the Dean suddenly, smiling still and blowing his nose. 'I suppose you're quite free now? I don't wish to keep you from your work.'

'Oh, yes, Mr Dean. That is - until Evensong.'

'I can dispense you from that, can't I, if I wish?' He smiled at me almost warmly.

I laughed feebly. 'Yes, that's right. So you can.'

'Well, let us take the books up to the library. It is a little chilly, isn't it? Dear me! I wish the Bishop would learn how to prune his plum trees! He is for ever complaining that he cannot grow fruit against that wall, and it is entirely his own fault. There are my dahlias. Fine, are they not?'

My mind wandered. 'Oh, quite, quite!' I said, both absently and inadvisedly.

He frowned. He blew his nose. He smiled.

'You are quite a good mimic, aren't you?' he remarked gently. 'But' - and suddenly his voice was as sharp as an east wind - 'let me remind you, Huntley, that mimicry has got people into very serious trouble. So have' - he looked at the Cathedral spire and paused before the next two words. Then he glared at me and added - 'an-on-y-mous let-ters.'

Again he blew his nose. My heart sank to the bottom of my shoes. I said nothing. I couldn't.

We went into the hall. Carrying the books, we proceeded slowly and silently up to the library.

It is a long, splendid room with a great Gothic window at the end, lit by coats-of-arms of former Deans, and framed by a long view of the garden with the Cathedral and the Thames meadows beyond. Lined along the walls are bookshelves, stacked with ancient books. A first-folio Shakespeare has a place of honour. Against the shelves are bureaux, cabinets, side-tables groaning under masses of papers. In the window-sills framed photographs of distinguished friends and many jars of flowers - that day, golden rod, michaelmas daisies, dahlias, roses. A lovely room. It broke my heart to have to face trouble in it. I wished he could have taken me to the kitchen.

'Now, sit down,' said the Dean. He spoke kindly. 'I think,' he continued, standing in the middle of the floor as clergymen always do on such occasions, 'I think you understand what I was referring to just now. Don't misunderstand me, Huntley. I suppose a Dean can appreciate a joke against himself as well as any reasonably minded man. But when' - he paused, his voice rose - 'that joke - is directed against a lady, moreover a newcomer to Cornford, and a very honoured member of our Cathedral society - then it goes beyond the bounds of a joke and becomes what I can only describe as' - (business with handkerchief) - 'im-per-tin-ent and' - (approach of handkerchief to nose) - 'of-fen-sive!' (Nose-blowing.)

I bit my lip and said nothing. I fumbled with some keys in my pocket. The Dean continued:

'I suppose you must be aware of the terrible things that have been said about Lady Hargreaves in this town in the last few days?'

'Yes,' I muttered.

'She, very rightly, came to me about the matter. Most reluctantly she told me that all these dreadful rumours had their foundation in an anonymous letter which you sent to Mr Carver. I was most unwilling to believe this. But I promised her I would at least see you about it. I hope, Huntley - I hope with all my heart that Lady Hargreaves is mistaken.'

He waited. 'Well?' he said.

'It *is* true,' I said.

The Dean stared at me, pursing up his lips thoughtfully. 'I also hear,' he said, 'that you actually' - the shadow of a smile crossed his face - 'impersonated' - here he frowned again - 'Canon Auty.'

'Yes. That's true too. I didn't look much like him, though.'

He walked abruptly to the window; then came back again to the centre of the room.

'Huntley, are you - out of your senses?' he asked. 'I might as well tell you that Lady Hargreaves is convinced there is really something wrong with your mind. I - '

'Yes,' I said, 'I'm dotty. That's the truth, Mr Dean. Something's gone wrong with me.'

But he didn't seem to approve of this idea.

'Rubbish!' he snapped. 'I refuse to believe it. I have no desire to be hard on you, Huntley. I very willingly give you credit for the way you came to Lady Hargreaves' assistance when you first had the privilege of encountering her at Oxford - '

'Yes,' I blurted out, 'and what does she say about that? She says I bungled it. There's gratitude for you! The old devil actually - '

'Stop, Huntley! Stop!'

Again the Dean walked to the window. This time he spoke from there, with his back turned to me. He spoke quietly and gravely.

'We - you and I, Huntley - are both servants of this great Cathedral. I want you to remember that. It is our paramount duty to preserve it from even a breath of scandal.'

There was a long silence. 'Well, have you nothing to say?' he snapped.

'It's - it's like this, Mr Dean. She - I - that is - well-'

I could not go on. What was the good of *trying* to tell him the truth? I suddenly wished to God Father Toule had been the Dean.

He left the window, sat at a bureau and slowly polished his spectacles with his silk handkerchief.

'I will be quite frank with you,' he said. 'Lady Hargreaves is not a poor woman. You, it is well known, are in debt. Oh, yes - Huntley! I have to keep my eye on such matters, you know.'

'I've never asked her for a penny!' I cried. 'If she says things like that I'll - I'll have her up for slander.'

'Come, sir - come! Surely the boot is on the other foot? What do these foolish pranks mean? I will not believe they are merely prompted by malice. I have always had an interest in your future, Huntley. It is still my desire to help you.'

'If I were to tell you the truth about Miss Hargreaves - '

Instantly his hand shot up.

'Why do you insist upon addressing her as Miss Hargreaves? That alone is unnecessarily offensive.'

'But, Mr Dean,' I pleaded, 'you don't *know*. It's all something I can't understand. My whole life's gone to pieces over this Miss Hargreaves affair - '

'*Lady* Hargreaves!'

'Lady Hargreaves, that is.' I swallowed. 'She's not real, that's all I can say.' I felt myself working up to the truth, whether he liked it or not. 'You ask my friend, Henry Beddow. We made her up - we made everything up - even the Duke of Grosvenor - '

'Stop! Stop!'

'I'm not - myself,' I muttered. 'She's quite right. I expect I'm going potty. If I could go away for a bit - things have got on top of me - if you'd give me leave, Mr Dean - I can't help feeling once I got away from Cornford - I don't know - '

He sighed as my idiotic babblings ceased. 'You completely bewilder me. Go away, by all means, if it is going to drive any sense into your head. You may *have* to go away if you persist in this extraordinary behaviour. I must confess I am deeply disappointed that you can't be frank with me. I am your friend, not your enemy.'

The two bells started to chime for Evensong.

'I *can't* be frank,' I said. 'It's no good, Mr Dean. You wouldn't understand. Nobody can, except Father Toule.'

'*Father Toule?*' The Dean stared at me. I wished to God I hadn't mentioned the name.

'Yes,' I said. 'He - well, he knows all about it.'

'I see,' said the Dean coldly. 'You prefer to place your confidences in Roman Catholic hands. The Cathedral clergy are not - imaginative enough for you. I quite understand.'

There was a pause. I wondered whether I might edge to the door. I was longing above everything for a cigarette.

'What *you* must understand,' snapped the Dean suddenly, bringing out his handkerchief again, 'is this. If there are any more complaints of you from Lady Hargreaves - or anyone else - you lose your position here. I am not a hard man. But I will not tolerate this pantomime behaviour. You may go. It is time for Evensong.'

As I walked slowly and heavily of heart down the great staircase, past portraits of older Deans sulking in oils and elaborate gilt frames, I heard him savagely blowing his nose up in the library.

*   *   *

That evening, in an agony of misery and fear, I went to see Father Toule again. I told him everything - the anonymous letter, my last meeting with Connie, my interview with the Dean. He didn't seem at all surprised. He had a wonderfully simple way, that man, of taking everything for granted. I suppose hearing all those confessions makes them used to anything.

'Of course, Mr Huntley,' he said, 'it was very unwise of you to do what you did. But it doesn't help you to hear me say that. Still, I do wish now you would make a firm resolution to leave the matter entirely alone - '

'I can't, Father Toule. I've got one idea into my head - and one only. It was your idea. I'm going to Lusk.'

'Indeed? H'm. Yes. I am not sure about that - except that I feel you might be easier if you told this sexton the truth - '

'It isn't only that. It's my last chance. I feel I - can do something there. Besides, I must find out whether there's a gravestone with her name - '

'Really, Mr Huntley, I wouldn't worry about that.'

'I'm not. She's not a ghost. She doesn't frighten me in the same way as a ghost would. She does frighten me - but

258

not in that way. I can't explain. But I must make sure. For all I know, I *may* have seen her name there.'

'Could you not write to the sexton and leave your researches alone? I do feel' - Father Toule seemed quite agitated - 'I cannot help feeling - although I certainly suggested it - that something might happen which you would regret. It hasn't proved a very lucky place for you so far. I am inclined to think you should avoid it.'

'No. I must go. I must go.'

I left the presbytery. I was certain, now, that for better or worse, the last card had to be played in Lusk church and nowhere else. But I hadn't the slightest idea how I was going to play it.

* * *

Alone up in my room, I stared miserably over the street to the warm chimneys of Lessways. How dreary it would be - the house empty, the strains of the harp for ever silenced!

'Murder!' I moaned. 'Murder! That's what it is.' I shuddered. I shivered. I pulled down the blind and turned on the light. I smoked three cigarettes straight off. I shivered. I shuddered.

Mother came in.

'Henry wants you on the phone,' she said.

It was days since I had seen anything of Henry. There'd been a good deal of coolness between us ever since Pat Howard had insulted my father.

'Tell him I'm out,' I said.

'Norman, what *is* the matter with you? You've never quarrelled with Henry before. I don't say much, but I'm very worried. You ate no tea; you hardly ever talk to us; you sit up here alone. I shall really have to get a doctor if you go on like this - '

'Doctor - doctor - !' I screamed suddenly. 'Yes - you all want to lock me up in a lunatic asylum, don't you? Oh, God! Why has this happened to me?'

Mother came up to me. 'Norman - Norman - darling boy - don't go on like this. It's terrible. You're simply breaking our hearts.'

I pushed my way past her. 'All right,' I said. 'I'll speak to him.' I ran downstairs to the telephone.

'Well,' I said, 'what do *you* want?'

'Norman, old boy, I haven't seen much of you lately. Are we on speaking terms, or not?'

'I'm sorry, Henry. I'm about dead. The Dean's just threatened to sack me for insolence to you-know-who.'

'Norman - what a damn shame! Don't take it too much to heart. I'll tell you what I rang up about. That fellow whose house you and Connie spent a night in - did you say he was called Major Wynne?'

'That's right.'

'Well, there's a lot about it in the paper to-day. The place has been robbed. All the silver, jewels - everything. Major Wynne was away in the South of France and has only just returned. It strikes me the fellow who caught you in the orchard must have been the crook. It says the police are following up a valuable clue. Do you think that'd be the bag you said she left behind? If so, I can't help thinking it looks rather black for both of you.'

'Yes,' I echoed, hardly taking it all in, 'it looks - rather black for - both of us.'

'Once they start asking her questions - she'll probably refer them to you, and of course they'll come to you. Well, I don't want to see you doing ten years, old boy. In fact, Uncle Henry's rather worried. We'd better do something about it somehow. Are you there?'

I woke up suddenly.

'Henry, you're quite right. *We've* got to do something about it. This is the very last straw.'

'I'm damned if I know *what* we can do.'

'I do. And I can't do it alone - that's the point. You've got to help me - as you did before.'

'I don't reckon I've helped you very much, old boy. To tell you the truth, I was feeling I'd rather let you down.'

'You helped - in the beginning. Without you I couldn't have created her. Without you I can't - ' I paused. 'Henry - come round to the Happy Union now, will you? I *must* see you.'

'Right-o! Be there in ten minutes. Glad to hear your voice again, Norman. All drinks on me to-night.'

I rang off and went out. Across the road from an open window I heard the strains of 'Dear Little Shamrock' slowly plucked from a harp. My heart ached. A policeman passed. Already I could feel his eyes upon me. I turned quickly up Candole Street, and swung into the private bar.

*   *   *

For over an hour we sat in the Happy Union talking.

'You gave me the solution,' I said, 'when you said " *we've* " got to do something about it. My God, Henry, what a fool I've been. *I can't do anything powerful alone.* That's the point. I couldn't have created her without you. How can I expect to - the whole thing's gone hopelessly wrong because I've been working without your co-operation.'

'Look here, Norman. This business has worried Uncle Henry as much as it's worried you. I've tried to pretend all along that there must be some perfectly natural explanation - '

'There isn't. You must, *must* believe that Miss Hargreaves is utterly and solely *our* creation.'

'I hardly had anything to do with it, you know.'

'Finishing touches. Without you, she'd have been nothing but a shadow. If I'd have gone into the church alone that day, do you suppose Connie could ever have really come to life? No.'

'I suppose you never found out anything about that bath?'

'Never.'

'I wish to God I could get an explanation of that.'

'Oh, damn you and your bath! God alive, Henry - we're on to something - tremendous - something elemental - and you go on harping on baths - '

'Go easy, old boy. I can't bear the idea of Connie harping in her bath.'

He ordered another round of drinks.

'Are you going to help me?' I challenged. 'Or are you afraid?'

'Afraid? What do you mean?'

'Destructive thought destroys. That's what I mean.'

'Enlarge on that, old son.'

I did so for a long time.

'You see,' I ended up, 'this isn't just a joke now. You and I have got to find some formula whereby we can convince ourselves and that fool sexton that Connie Hargreaves does *not* exist - just as we convinced him and us that she *did* exist. We've somehow got to get back to the state of mind we were in before we created her. You and I together, as before.'

'It's no good merely telling that squint chappie the truth,' said Henry suddenly.

'I'm glad you say that,' I said. 'Because I don't think that'd be the slightest bit of good.'

'We've got to know what we *are* going to do, haven't we?'

'Yes. And that's what I don't know - yet.'

Henry slowly drained his glass. He looked at me. He smiled suddenly. 'What fools we are!' he said.

'Why?'

'Plotting and planning - like this. Tell me - did we plot and plan for hours before we created her?'

I saw daylight; I saw it as clear as you see it at four on a summer morning.

'You mean - ' I cried. 'Leave it - to the Spur of the Moment?'

Henry nodded and started to fill his pipe, spilling tobacco all over the table. I could tell he was excited.

'This is what I reckon we must do,' he said. 'It's just an idea. We must go to Lusk church and wait outside it as we did before. Simply that. No planning or plotting at *all*. She didn't come into the world that way, and she mustn't go out of the world that way. We don't even want to *talk* about what we're going to do any more. Just go there and - hope for the best.'

'Or the worst,' I said. But I could see his idea; it was a sound one.

'We'd better go to-morrow,' he said, 'and put up at the hotel at Dungannon.'

'I must see this concert through on Monday night.'

'What the devil for?'

'I don't know. I - well, if it's going to be the last time. I see her, I want to remember it. I can't help it, Henry. Besides, she's so looking forward to this concert. I couldn't bear to spoil it for her.'

'I call it damn dangerous.'

'Perhaps it is. But I'm going to risk it.'

'Tell me this, Norman' - Henry was knocking out the pipe he had just filled. I wondered why he was suddenly so worked up - 'tell me this. Can you remember the first actual moment when Miss Hargreaves came into your mind? Was it when you gave the sexton her name?'

I thought. 'No,' I said. 'I don't think it was. I think she was in the back of my mind when we stood by the lectern and I madly said, "Dear Mr Archer". I didn't *know* she was there, if you get me; but I'm sure she must have been. In reserve, so to speak. The moment the sexton said, "You knew Mr Archer?" I said - do you remember - that *I* didn't know him but that I knew somebody who did - '

'I believe you said you'd heard a lot about him.'

'Yes. Well. I knew then that I might have to create somebody who *had* known Mr Archer. She was in my mind then - only half visualized - but there right enough.'

'Dear Mr Archer!' murmured Henry. 'So that was the dangerous moment?'

'Yes. That was the dangerous moment.'

We were silent for a long time. Henry had completely forgotten his pipe now. I felt that there was something on his mind which he wouldn't tell me.

'My God!' he said presently, 'I don't mind telling you that this business makes my flesh tingle.'

'Round the back of your neck; up your spine. Yes.'

'It's like - murder, almost.'

'It *is* murder.'

'Don't talk so loud, old boy, for God's sake.'

'No good calling it anything else,' I whispered. 'It's murder. But if we don't do it, then I might as well be dead.'

'So might I,' muttered Henry.

'And another thing,' I said. 'This Major Wynne affair. She'll get me locked up over that. But worse than that; she'll ruin me, body and soul. I shan't have one free moment. The situation's reversed, don't you see? And here's another thing you may not have thought of. When she's finished with me, *she'll start on you* - '

Henry spluttered over his beer as though I had hit him on the back.

'What's bitten you?' I asked. He didn't say anything for a moment. Then: 'Norman, old boy. I'll own up. She *has* started on me. That's why I rang up. To tell you God's truth - well, I'm scared.'

'Henry - tell me, what's happened?'

'Nothing much - outwardly. She gets her petrol at our place, you know. Well, there's nothing in that. But just lately, whenever she stops, she asks for me. She won't rest unless I fill up for her. Gedge was starting to give her ten this morning when he comes round to me - I was working on that old Sunbeam of Canon Auty's - and he says to me, "Mr Henry, Lady Hargreaves wants you to fill up her tank".'

'Did you go?'

'Yes. And, do you know, she kept her eyes on me all the time. When I'd finished and was giving the chauffeur the change, she leant out and said to me, "Mr Beddow, I am thinking of buying another car. Will you be good enough to call and see me about it?"'

'Oh - not much in that,' I said.

'Ho - wasn't there! It was the way she said it, my boy; the walk-into-parlour way she said it.'

'You know' - I suddenly remembered it - 'the other night when I was there, she asked for your name. She'd forgotten it.'

'Well, something in her manner got me, Norman. I began to understand a bit of what you must have been through. And I felt a toad - '

'Don't talk about it, Henry. You *were* a bit off-hand. But never mind. I know I've been a damn bore.'

'The trouble is - ' He paused and hesitated. 'Well, I *like* the old witch.'

'That,' I said, '*is* the trouble. We loved her from the start. And we shall go on loving her, whatever happens.'

'But we've got to do this for her own good. That's how I see it.'

Henry walked slowly to the bar and came back with two noggins of rum which he poured into our glasses.

'Do you remember,' he said, 'how we drank her health on the boat coming over?'

'I said "Long may she live". I meant it.'

'Silly of us.'

'Yes,' I agreed. 'If only we had known! And yet - '

We raised our glasses, looked at each other solemnly, and drank in silence.

THE next day, a Sunday, the judge of assize attended Matins in the Cathedral. Anybody who happened to be there that day is not likely to forget the remarkable and queerly touching little ceremony which marked the visit of Mr Justice Hurlstone as different from any other judicial visits.

More people than usual filled the chancel. A little before eleven the choir filed in; the Doctor honoured the occasion with all five Great Open Diapasons; the Dean and the canons lined up on either side of the choir gates, facing each other in two rows by their stalls. The tenor bell tolled eleven. The group of civic dignitaries assembled by the south door stiffened to attention as a car drew up outside. The Doctor, warmly improvising in B major, and warned by his assistant, who kept running along the loft, that Justice was imminent, enriched the firm prose of the Diapasons with the drama of the Full Swell. Everybody in the chancel turned their eyes to the nave. Only one familiar figure was absent. Constance Lady Hargreaves, for some reason, was not in her customary seat.

Walking up the nave very slowly, the Mayor, Aldermen, Sheriffs, Clerks and Magistrates crossed the dais. The Doctor, his eyes glued to the little mirror which gave him a view of what went on below, made a sudden dramatic modulation to C major. The Dean and the canons pulled themselves up sharply, preparing for their ceremonial bow to the Judge. Finally, at the end of the procession, his lordship himself reached the choir gates. He was a small man with a nut-like, acid countenance that bore even less expression than the wig which fell round his shoulders. A slight, a very slight inclination of his head was his acknowledgment of the homage paid to Justice by the low bows of the Dean and Chapter. The next moment he ascended sharply to his seat in the Residentiary Canon's stall. The canons and the Dean found their places; the Precentor hurriedly swallowed a lozenge; the Doctor quickly fell to B major and the choir Lieblich Gedacht. Meakins went to close the gates.

At that sacred moment, Lady Hargreaves appeared upon the dais.

* * *

Limping across the dais she reached the gates as Meakins was on the point of closing them. She did not hurry, neither did she linger; obviously, it never crossed her mind that Meakins might close the gates upon her, as he had been known to do upon many a bishop's wife. A thousand eyes that had, a second before, been fixed upon the Judge, now swivelled to her. It was seen that she was carrying a miniature posy of autumn rosebuds, exquisitely woven together with white silk ribbon. 'Too bad of me - too bad of me!' we heard her murmur to Meakins. For the first time in his life, and I dare say the last, he admitted a person into the Choir at the precise moment when the wicked man, via the

Precentor, was about to turn away from his wickedness and direct his attention to Morning Prayer - and that on a Sunday morning when His Majesty's Justice was present. Never in the history of Cornford Cathedral had tradition been so gracefully violated.

But what did she do with her posy? What thunderbolt descended upon her as, stopping under the Judge's stall, she curtsied slightly and reaching up to the desk placed the rosebuds gently upon the embroidered desk-cushion?

No thunderbolt descended. Not one single eyebrow flickered its displeasure. In other words, she got away with it. The lady who had been accused of conspiring with anarchists had made what all silently interpreted as a declaration of her innocence. Almost imperceptibly, Mr Justice Hurlstone was seen to smile; taking the rosebuds he raised them towards his nose, then laid them down a little to one side of the massive Prayer Book before him. Enough. Justice had smiled; openly, the Dean smiled; the Suffragan Bishop of Maidenhead whispered something to the Archdeacon of Wycombe; both smiled and nodded. The lay-clerks grinned; an unfortunate probationer giggled, and was frowned upon by Baker. The Precentor, instead of turning the wicked man away, dared to bid God not to enter into judgment with His servant. Lady Hargreaves, her mission accomplished, walked peacefully to her stall, pausing for a moment to lift a page of an anthem book which had fluttered down upon King John's tomb. 'Your anthem, I imagine?' she murmured to Baker, at the top of Decani. Baker took the page from her, flushing crimson. 'Thank you, Lady Hargreaves,' he said, making a gallant attempt to show his juniors that he was accustomed to the society of the great ones of the earth.

The Lord Justice, his sallow face again a mask, sank to his knees. Lady Hargreaves took off her gloves, glanced round her, adjusted her horn spectacles, and opened her white ivory Prayer Book. A thousand knees nested on five hundred hassocks. Matins began.

*　　*　　*

I watched her, half proudly, half uneasily, during the singing of Stanford's *Te Deum* in B flat. 'We praise thee, O Hargreaves!' I sang to myself. To-morrow night, after the concert, I proposed to travel to Lusk. Could I hope to do anything? Did I want to do anything? Pride flooded up in me. Who else in the world had been able to create an old lady with the courage to present roses to the Judge on Assize Sunday?

My eyes turned to the wrinkled little Judge. Would he one day apply the black cap for my benefit, supposing that . . .

*　　*　　*

'Well, dear,' said Archie in the vestry afterwards, 'did she ever offer you posies?'

'Serve her bloody well right,' growled Dyack, 'if they turned out to be full of green-fly.'

'She seems to have h-lost all interest in you, Huntley,' said Wadge. 'I hoped we'd hear the banns h-read out by Christmas.'

'Why do judges wear all that false hair?' asked Peaty. 'Bald, or what?'

'Black cap sits better on a wig,' remarked Slesser.

I shivered. 'Suppose,' I asked him suddenly, 'they can't find the body? Can they prosecute you for murder?'

'Why, dear? Are you thinking of cutting your countess up?'

I shivered again and hung up my cassock.

'That chap,' said Dyack, 'could hang a spider on his own web. Who put my bloody 'at up there? I've got enemies 'ere, I know. Things ain't what they was. Roses!'

'Did anybody notice that woman putting something on the Judge's Prayer Book?' purred Pussy Coltsfoot.

'Posy,' hummed Peaty in his ear.

'That's just what I thought,' said Pussy. 'Very nosy. It shouldn't be allowed.'

I walked out into the Close with Archie. By the side door to the Deanery we came upon a little group, chatting amiably. The Dean, Archdeacon Cutler, Lady Hargreaves and Mr Justice Hurlstone.

'You must positively command it *always* to be done,' Lady Hargreaves was saying to the Judge. 'It should, of course, have been presented to you at the moment of your entry into the Cathedral, but a minor domestic catastrophe delayed me, just as I was leaving my house. I trust, I do indeed trust, that I was not importunate?'

The Judge smiled gravely. 'Perhaps you will have established a precedent, Lady Hargreaves. Who knows?'

I paused, with Archie, some yards away, and listened. None of them had seen me yet.

'What's this - ah - catastrophe?' the Archdeacon was asking. 'Nothing serious, I hope?'

'Oh, no! Perhaps you remember that tiresome cockatoo of mine? Yes? I keep him in the kitchen solely to amuse the staff. Well, I am sorry to say that he escaped this morning and, driven by some avian instinct which we are powerless to comprehend, made a quite ferocious attack upon my poor little dog, Sarah.'

'I hope the dog was not badly hurt?' said the Dean.

'On the contrary. Dr Pepusch - that is the fanciful name some stupid friend of mine gave to the bird - perished as a result of the encounter. I cannot say I am at all sorry.'

Here Archie said something to me. Hearing him, Lady Hargreaves turned round, glanced at us for a moment, frowned, and quite deliberately waited until we had passed before she went on with the conversation. As we turned under the Northgate I was able to hear her say, 'Judge, what particular medicine do you reserve for tiresome young men who pester harmless old ladies like myself? Have you - '

I heard no more.

*　　*　　*

'It's no good worrying, mother. I've made up my mind to go away. The Dean said I could.'

'But if you're really ill, why don't you see a doctor?'

'It's a change I want. I'm run down.'

'Well, if doing nothing can run you down, you ought to be dead by now,' said Jim.

'Ireland!' exclaimed mother. 'What on earth do you want to go to Ireland for? I'm absolutely positive this wretched Lady Hargreaves is behind it all.'

'No, mother,' I said. 'I'm behind her.'

Father was struggling with a skewer in the sirloin.

'Can't go till after the concert,' he said. 'Nobody understands my tune like you do.'

'I shan't miss that. We're catching the night train to Heysham to-morrow.'

'We? Who's "we"?' asked Jim.

'Henry. He's coming too.'

Mother planked a roast potato on my plate. She looked at me searchingly, holding a fork in her hand.

'Now, just what monkey-trick are you two up to?' she demanded.

'Wish you'd see to the gravy,' mumbled father. 'I can't be expected to carve and do the gravy, can I? Wonder whether those roses came out of her own garden?'

'I'm just sick to death,' cried mother, 'of this story of the Judge and the roses! If you've told it once you've told it a dozen times since you came in. I'm sick to death of everything to do with Lady Hargreaves! As for you, Cornelius, I'm tired of you. You make no attempt to get the truth out of Norman. What am I going to say to everybody? Norman's gone away - Why? they will ask.'

'Simply say he's gone dotty,' said Jim.

'Yes,' I said. 'That'll do. Pass the horseradish sauce.'

'I'd give anything to see you settle down,' sighed mother.

'Talking about judges,' remarked father, 'I once saw, at the Chelsea Flower Show, Mr Justice Dearest. Bending over some peonies, he was; just bending over them like you or me. A fellow came up and said, "Excuse me, but you mustn't bend over the peonies like that". Well - beans, please - this fellow later came up for murder before Mr Justice What's-his-name, and in summing up he said to the jury, "In considering this case you must, as an old Spanish saying goes, bend over the peonies". Jury returned a verdict of not guilty. Wish Janie would skim the gravy more. One day, 'bout a year later, Mr Justice Whatever-he-is meets the fellow on top of a bus, carrying a large bunch of heleniums. They were going down the Tottenham Court Road, just past the Y.M.C.A.—or is it the Y.M.C.A.? Of course, there's good and bad in these C.A.'s - good and bad. You'd better complain to the butcher, Dorothy; this meat's like leather.'

*   *   *

'Monday, October the 31st. Vigil of the Feast of All the Saints. Is C. H. soon to join them?'

My diary recalls a memorable evening.

Father, wearing a velvet dinner-jacket, prowled up and down the room, impatiently twirling his moustaches and fussing his tie.

'Give me another glass of that claret,' he said, 'and a cigarette. Funny thing, I'm nervous. Why the devil can't we start? I expect Grinling Gibbons used this room to work in. Fine writer!'

'He didn't write,' I said, pouring some claret from a Georgian decanter and straining to hear the chatter of the company from the adjoining room. 'He carved - pews and things.'

'I wonder whether this concert's on the air? I see they've got the telephone here. Find the *Radio Times*.'

'Of course it's not on the air.'

'Everything's on the air, boy. Wish you wouldn't wear those made-up bows; anyone can see you didn't tie it yourself.'

'I wish you'd shut up, father. I did tie it myself, anyway.'

'Well, tie it more carelessly next time. You don't understand these things, my boy. Give me A.' He drew his bow over the A string. 'Suppose that's in tune. Do you think they'd like my story about the spinach? When will that archdeacon stop talking? I've never found an archdeacon yet who could stop talking. Give me one of those cream-cheese things. What have you done with my mute, you devil?'

For some time we had been waiting in a small parlour which Lady Hargreaves used as a writing-room. It had a small upright piano in it. The grand, a Bechstein, was in the adjoining room, the drawing-room. Through the open double doors I could see the guests, some standing, some seated, far at the other end. The Dean, Canon and Mrs Auty, Archdeacon and Mrs Cutler, Colonel Temperley and Miss Linkinghorne. Austen and the Irish maid were offering round drinks and refreshments. A little apart from the others in a high, episcopal-looking oak chair, sat the hostess, her two sticks resting on either arm. Wearing a black silk dress with a high white lace collar and one green-stoned ring on her left hand, it seemed to me that she was at the height of her glory. All the appendages, such as whistle, pencil-on-chain, lorgnettes, with which I had first endowed her, had long ago been discarded. There was something sweetly ascetic about her; I could no longer feel she was my creation. It made me sad.

The Archdeacon was trumpeting on foreign policy. What we needed, according to him, was a firm hand. He declared it was essential.

'No doubt about it, Lady Hargreaves. We English were born to govern. What did Blake say? Build Jerusalem *here*. Well, there's still time.'

'I trust it will not be jerry-built,' said Lady Hargreaves rather sharply. Then she smiled at him graciously, with an air of patronage that completely escaped him. 'But, no doubt,' she said, 'if the archidiaconal trowel is applied to the mortar, we need not fear the city will collapse. Canon - you are not eating anything. Take one of these Strasbourg *pâtés*, I beg you.'

'This is *so* nice,' murmured Miss Linkinghorne. She was wearing white in honour of the saints. '*So* nice. So much more interesting than a mere dinner.'

'Time and place for everything,' remarked the Colonel, doggedly engaging himself with a recalcitrant siphon in a corner by the fire. 'No armchairs in Persia. They sit on the floor.'

'This delightful informality,' continued Miss Linkinghorne, 'puts me in mind of the East, somehow. The Archdeacon mentioning the Holy City brought it all so vividly before me. Have you ever been there, Lady Hargreaves?'

'Probably. I have been *almost* everywhere. Mrs Auty, I can see you are positively stifling. Take this little rush seat here. It comes from Norway and was once the property of Grieg.'

'And you really composed all these verses yourself! Well!' Mrs Auty, moving to the Grieg chair, had pounced on a copy of *Wayside Bundle* lying conveniently at hand on an occasional table.

'*Oh*, dear!' cried Lady Hargreaves. '*How* did you come by that? Where did you find it? These stupid servants! They will *not* put things away.'

'Oh, let me look at it! Do let me look at it. I think poetry is so important.'

Miss Linkinghorne reached out for the volume, but Mrs Auty had already claimed it. She was a very large woman, Mrs Auty, whose great ambition in life was to run Cornford. Mrs Cutler had always been her Waterloo. Canon Auty, it was said, had first met his wife on a mountain in Switzerland, where he found her presiding over an impending avalanche. The choristers called her Excelsior.

But she was not to be allowed to preside over poetry. Firmly, yet gently, Lady Hargreaves took the book from her.

'It should never have been left lying about.' She spoke almost angrily. Then, idly, she opened it. 'Tch-tch!' she murmured. '"Cleft in the narrow gulf of gusty grief..." *What* a line!' She snapped the book to contemptuously and threw it aside on the table, well within Mrs Auty's reach.

'For pure beauty, take Shelley,' said the Colonel. 'Eh, Dean?'

Mrs Cutler, a thin female with eyes that could have drawn the past life out of a paper-weight, snatched the volume a second before Mrs Auty could again take it. Lady Hargreaves, murmuring something to Austen, did not notice.

'Archer - Archer?' Mrs Cutler screwed up her eyes, boring her gimlet nose deep into the pages. 'Archdeacon, didn't we know a clergyman called Archer - Philip Archer?'

'Archer? H'm. Yes. I was up at Cambridge with a Philip Archer. He rowed in the Cambridge boat in '81. Fine athlete.'

Lady Hargreaves, the moment she heard the name, rose and walked slowly towards the Archdeacon.

'You knew Archer?' she cried.

'Think it must be the same man. Years since I saw him, of course. I heard he was married and had five daughters - '

'The same - the same!' Lady Hargreaves returned to her chair, closed her eyes and bent her head into her hands as a person does suddenly overcome by memories of the past. A respectful and slightly embarrassed silence fell over the company. The Archdeacon cocked his head towards the Dean inquiringly. Meanwhile, Mrs Cutler was rushing through *Wayside Bundle* in search of plums from the Archer tree.

'When the *hell* are we going to start this music?' said father, brutally breaking the silence.

All eyes turned on us. Lady Hargreaves, rousing herself from her reverie, sighed deeply and smiled a sad, far-away, reminiscent smile.

'Forgive me, my friends,' she murmured, 'I trust that I am usually in control of my feelings. But I admit that the name Archer still has power to affect me.'

'No good trying to hide feelings,' mumbled the Colonel. 'Never could myself. Don't believe in it.'

'Mr Archer,' continued Lady Hargreaves, 'many years ago - oh, *so* many years ago! - was my dearest friend. I still treasure a hip-bath that he once gave me - Oh, no!' Her hand shot up imperiously as though to check at once any possibility of innuendo. Mrs Cutler worried *Wayside Bundle* from page to page. 'Oh, no! It is *not* a story I can repeat except to the very, very closest friend.'

She glanced at the Dean.

'Oh, quite, quite!' he murmured.

'I knew him,' she went on, 'at the University. Mad young things - wild young things! What days! Do the young people of to-day have so good a time, I wonder!'

'There's a lot of looseness about,' said Mrs Cutler. 'A terrible lot of looseness. Eh, Archdeacon?'

The Archdeacon tightened himself up, worried his coat buttons and nodded irritably.

'Oh, I don't agree,' said Mrs Auty, who would rather die than agree with Mrs Cutler. 'Let young people have a good time, that's what I say. I always had a good time. People ought to have a good time. The Canon agrees, don't you, Edward?'

Canon Auty, who had sat silent most of the evening, stroked his beard reflectively as though there, and only there, could a good time be found. 'A *good* time,' he said. 'Yes. A *good* time. Let people enjoy themselves provided there is no - horseplay.'

'Archer and I,' remarked Lady Hargreaves, 'were precisely of that opinion. As for horseplay, I have never favoured it and I never will. Is not that light a little trying for your eyes, Mrs Cutler? Take this seat, I beg you. My poor little book seems to entertain you. Yes,' she continued in a reminiscent tone, 'they were halcyon days - "halcyon days, wrapped in high summer's indigenous haze..." I quote from one of those youthful and yet perhaps spirited indiscretions in *Wayside Bundle. No*, my good Miss Linkinghorne, put the book down - I positively insist! Yes, dear Archer was my afflatus in those happy days.'

'Really?' said the Colonel, peering over his glass. 'Afflatus, eh?' He suddenly winked at the Dean.

'Halcyon days - !' echoed Miss Linkinghorne. 'How lovely! But how *unusually* lovely! There is something of the eternal abandon of the East in those words.'

'Too much abandon about, eh, Archdeacon?'

'I do think,' remarked the Dean sleepily, 'that our hostess ought to read us some of her verses. We all know she is a far more accomplished poet than her modesty allows her to admit. Come now, Lady Hargreaves!'

'Oh, but I could not - I could not! Oh, no! Do not tempt me. I abominate fuss!'

(Did I imagine it, or was something of the old Miss Hargreaves creeping into her voice?)

'Please - please, Lady Hargreaves,' purred the Linkinghorne. 'I am so very fond of poetry.'

'But this is mere versifying.'

'I shouldn't bother about it - ' began the Colonel. Lady Hargreaves broke in on him quickly.

'Well, well - since you all insist. But you must not laugh at me. Thank you, Mrs Cutler' - (for Mrs Cutler had again got hold of the book, preferring to read than to be read to) - 'Oh, you have spilt a little wine over it! Oh, no, it does not matter at *all*! Wine and poetry are old lovers, are they not? I was merely thinking of your loss. Austen, fill Mrs Cutler's glass - '

'Nice thing if we're on the air,' said father, 'and everybody waiting everywhere.'

'What shall I give you?' Lady Hargreaves turned over the pages, running the ends of her spectacles along the lines. 'Well,' she announced, 'I will give you "Halcyon Days".'

She paused a moment, put on her spectacles, moved a lamp a little closer to her, cleared her throat and began:

'Halcyon days, halcyon days, wrapped in high - '

The Colonel's siphon chose that moment to start working. Lady Hargreaves stopped reading, frowned at him over
her spectacles, and waited. The Archdeacon nudged him.
There was silence. Lady Hargreaves proceeded:

'Halcyon days!
  Halcyon days!
Wrapped in high summer's indigenous haze!
Peacocks and muscovy; jellies and jam;
Flannelled young athletes patrolling the Cam;
Hearts beating high, the barometer up -
Did we know then that there's many a cup
'Twixt the slip and the lip and the tangerine pip?
In those far-away days when a crank was a quip
And never a handle for turning a car -
When Collects on Sunday were read by Papa -
And spice could be found in a parish bazaar -
Oh, where have they gone to, those comfortable, far-away
      Halcyon, halcyon days?'

'Look here,' said father, 'if she doesn't give the order
for this music soon, I shall go out and start on my own.
Come on, Norman. Let's get going on my tune.'
'Oh, shut up!' I snapped. 'Can't you let her enjoy herself?'
(I wanted the evening never to end for her.)
'I *love* that piece about the tangerine,' Miss Linkinghorne
was saying.
'Quite charming,' said the Dean. 'Full of youth's impulse.
You must read us another.'
'Yes - another - another!'
'Well, what shall I choose? Remember, these are all tri-
fles, seeds thrown out at random, ships that have, long ago,

passed into my night. Perhaps you will find a thought here and there; no more. Christina Rossetti was good enough to say this one contained beauty. A strange thing. I wrote it at night on some tower - I cannot now remember where. It is very brief.'

Again she read:

> 'I came, I go, I breathe, I move, I sleep,
> I talk, I eat, I drink, I laugh, I weep,
> I sing, I dance, I think, I dream, I see,
> I fear, I love, I hate, I plot, I be.
>> And yet -
>> And yet -
> I sometimes feel that I am but a thought,
> A piece of thistledown, a thing of naught,
> Rocked in the cradle of a craftsman's story,
> And destined not for high angelic glory.
>> And yet -
>> And yet -
> I came, I go, I move, I breathe, I sleep,
> I talk, I eat, I drink, I laugh, I weep.'

There was a long silence. She had read it slowly, with great feeling. I saw her touch her handkerchief to her eyes and I was terribly moved. Did she understand what she was? One line rang in my ears - 'destined not for high angelic glory'. Not with the saints, then! Oh, Connie - *where?*

'Oh, profound!' murmured the Dean at last. 'You have obviously read your Donne.'

Again I detected the old Miss Hargreaves breaking through the later personality. Slamming the book down on the table, she rose and took off her spectacles.

'I never read a page of Donne in my life!' she snapped.

Father, weary of waiting, suddenly stepped out into the drawing-room and walked up to the party.

*　　*　　*

'Evening, all,' he said genially. 'Bit chilly, isn't it? Hullo, Miss Linkinghorne. How's Jerusalem looking? Ah, Colonel - wondered where the whisky was. Hey there, bring me a glass, will you?'

I watched Lady Hargreaves anxiously. To my astonishment she showed no signs of annoyance; on the contrary, she was obviously amused by father.

'Nice of you all to come and hear my tune,' he said. He took a cigarette from a silver box. 'Got a match on you, Mr Archdeacon? No? I'll make a spill then - '

He took up *Wayside Bundle* as though to tear a page from it. It was a shop habit that he could never get out of.

Miss Linkinghorne let out a horrified scream.

'The poems! The poems!'

'What poems?' said father, pausing rather irritably, the book still in his hands.

I expected Lady Hargreaves to pounce on him. But again she astonished me. Saying nothing, making no effort to rise from her chair, she smiled slowly, shaking her head from side to side. She seemed terribly tired suddenly. And when I realized that, I realized too, with a shock of understanding, that the lassitude of the last few days had gone from me and that I felt full of energy and power.

The Archdeacon had taken the book from father. 'An odd way of lighting a cigarette,' he said.

'Oh, sorry,' murmured father. 'Never can remember. So many books about in the shop, y'know; sort of get used to tearing pages out. I suppose nobody's seen my mute, have they? Some books are much too long, anyhow. Take *The Bible in Spain*. If that were written to-day he'd reduce it to a middle for the *Manchester Guardian*. By th'way - ever tell you the story about Addison?'

I turned away, back into the parlour, and drew the curtains to the window which looked out to the front garden. I felt tense, on edge, full of frightening energy. At ten-fifteen Henry was calling for me in the car and we were driving to London to catch the night train for Heysham; my bag was packed, ready for Henry to collect. If the music didn't start soon, we might miss the train. And if I missed the train I knew with absolute certainty that I should never again be able to bring myself to make that journey to Lusk. Why? Because she was changing - changing back to the Miss Hargreaves I had loved - to the Miss Hargreaves I had flung aside. The day of her independence was spent. I knew it. She was coming back to father and me, back to the people who truly understood what she was, back to the will who had made her and who would be able, yet again, to direct the path that her feet should take. Yes, I wanted her back, under my power. And yet - and yet - could I spend the rest of my life controlling her? It was a whole-time job; many years would have to pass before I could hope to do it perfectly.

'Hurry up,' I moaned. 'Hurry up. Let's get the music over. To Lusk - to Lusk - '

I heard father talking in the drawing-room. He'd quite forgotten about the music now; as usual, he was in the middle of a story.

' - and there he was, this fellow on the bus, and Mr Justice Sweetheart said to him, "You mustn't bend over the salvias like that, you know". Of course, he'd done the murder and Avory knew it.'

Lady Hargreaves rose very slowly, took her sticks and touched father's arm.

'Come, Mr Huntley,' she said, 'let us start the music. Give me your arm to the piano.'

'Take the other arm, Lady Hurley. That arm's never quite the same since I had that accident in the National Gallery. Did I ever tell you about that?'

I came out from the parlour and started arranging music on the piano in a fever of impatience. Lady Hargreaves directed Austen to move her harp nearer to the lamp. She was still resting on father's left arm.

'Come - come, Austen,' she said, 'a little this way. That will do.' She reached the piano and rested one arm upon it, turning and facing the guests. 'Thank you, Mr Huntley. Austen, see to Mr Huntley's violin stand.' While Austen fixed it up, she addressed the others. 'We have planned a quite informal little concert. I had hoped that Schnabel would be able - ' She shrugged her shoulders. '*Naturally*, he has many engagements. However, let that not worry you. We have excellent talent in Cornford. Mr Cornelius Huntley assisted by Mr Norman Huntley and - myself, hope, for a brief space to - '

The siphon hissed again from the Colonel's corner.

Lady Hargreaves glanced sharply over.

'Austen,' she snapped, 'get the Colonel a quieter siphon.'

'By the way,' asked father, 'are we on the air?'

'Air, Mr Huntley?'

'Yes. Air.'

'I do not quite understand, Mr Huntley.'

'Oh, well, never mind. Don't suppose we are, in that case. Pity. Told Mrs Paton at the Happy Union to listen. Hand me my tune, Norman.'

'We are opening our little concert,' announced Lady Hargreaves, 'with an original composition of my own.

A slender link between the human consciousness and the untamed voice of nature. It is entitled a *Canzona* - and I think I am betraying no secrets of composition when I tell you that it was inspired by the song of a willow-wren - '

'Give me A, Norman, you devil. Here, what's this? I said my tune.'

'But she's announced the *Canzona*.'

'I don't care what she's announced. Give me my tune. And give me A, too.'

' - I shall not easily forget that evening in a valley in my native Rutlandshire when from this elfin bird there poured forth notes which, in the words of a poet - I cannot remember whom - "plunged th' incredulous universe to silence". Much of it was written in my diary on the actual spot. Sir Henry Cowen was kind enough to commend it; it had imagery, he said. A *Canzona*, inspired - in F sharp major - by a willow-wren.'

She sat down, not far from the piano, and smiled at father. 'We are ready,' she said. 'Give it *legato*, Mr Huntley. I beg you not to overlook the repeats.'

Father overlooked the whole thing. Without a word he started to play his tune for the G string.

*   *   *

Lady Hargreaves seized her sticks, rose, and made as if she were about to walk towards us. 'Sit down!' I muttered suddenly. She looked at me speechlessly, it was almost an appealing look, and slowly returned to her chair. I went on playing uneasily. I could not understand what was happening, except that I knew power was returning to me, slipping from her into me. I watched her. She was deathly still, her head low on her bosom, as she had been that day in the

Cathedral when I had turned upon her. I was in anguish. Could I ever find the heart to destroy her?

Meanwhile, father soared away, suddenly beginning to improvise a *cadenza* which I was totally unprepared for. Holding a vague chord I waited, knowing that when he felt like it, he would return again to the original theme. So, after a few bars, he did. I don't think I have ever heard him play so well. I felt proud of him. Every now and again I glanced over to Lady Hargreaves; although her eyes were covered by her hands, I knew she was watching father through the slits between her fingers. I wondered what she would say at the end of the piece, what words she would choose in which to tell the guests that we had *not* been playing her *Canzona*.

Richly, father approached the last bar, drawing, it seemed to me, much more than mere music out of the piece of wood held to his shoulder. Bending low, with his ear near to the strings, he sounded the last, long note. It was like a new sound in the world, as though father himself had discovered it and was loath to leave it. When he finally drew his bow from the violin, still holding it just above the strings, there was a long silence in the room, broken finally by the Dean, who murmured, 'Bravo, bravo!'

And still Lady Hargreaves sat inert in her chair.

'Reminded me of Beethoven,' said the Colonel.

'Thanks,' said father. 'Shall we do it again?'

'Again - again!' cried Miss Linkinghorne.

This stirred Lady Hargreaves. 'No. It would be - a great mistake to repeat it.' Every word now seemed an effort to her. I heard her murmur, 'Beautiful, beautiful!'

The Archdeacon laughed. 'You composers are too modest, Lady Hargreaves.'

'You could hear the willow-wren in every bar, couldn't you, Canon?' said Mrs Auty.

'Yes,' he boomed. 'One could certainly detect the voice of nature.'

'When Carless next gives a recital,' said the Dean, 'I shall ask him to get Mr Huntley to play it in the Cathedral. This is a light, Lady Hargreaves, that must not any longer be hidden under a bushel.'

Lady Hargreaves looked at father, smiling almost sadly.

'Here,' I whispered to father, 'do you realize they all think we were playing her *Canzona*?'

'Oh? Well, what does it matter? They seemed to like it, that's all that matters. What're we doing next?'

'You *must* tell them it wasn't her *Canzona*. You - '

But Lady Hargreaves came towards us and interrupted me.

'Thank you, Mr Huntley,' she said, 'for the most moving performance that I have ever heard.'

'But - ' I began. She quickly silenced me, putting her finger on her lips. Turning to the guests, she announced, 'And now, my friends, another original composition. This time by Mr Cornelius Huntley.' She whispered to father and me. 'You will now play my *Canzona*. Yes, yes - I *know* I have announced it as your composition. No matter. I am interested to see how it will be received. Norman dear, find the music.'

She had called me 'Norman'; she had smiled; I was again dear. I put the *Canzona* on the music-stand while father tuned his violin. 'All right, ready,' he said. He closed his eyes dreamily.

Lady Hargreaves, with great deliberation, announced it. 'Mr Huntley, accompanied by his son, will play an original air on the G string.'

'H'm,' muttered the Colonel loudly, 'always fancied that was by Bach.'

'Fool!' I said, half aloud. 'Fool!'

And, at the same moment, Lady Hargreaves uttered aloud, with remarkable vehemence, what I should like to have said. 'Bach, my dear Colonel, did not *invent* the G string.' She beckoned to Austen. 'Austen, take the Colonel another bottle of whisky.'

A deathly silence fell amongst the guests. Nobody looked at anything except the carpet. Even the Cutler eyes could find no other field for investigation.

'Proceed,' commanded Lady Hargreaves, with a wave of her hand. 'Proceed with your air, Mr Huntley.'

For the second time that evening father played his air on the G string. I often wonder whether he ever intended to do anything else.

*   *   *

'No - no - ' I muttered at him.

'Shut up!' he hissed. 'What's the matter with you? She told me to play it again. Get on, you devil!'

Lady Hargreaves was beaten; there was almost a startled look in her eyes. Nothing short of an earthquake would have stopped him; and I'm not sure that he would have taken much notice of that. Already we were six bars into the composition.

I heard the Archdeacon whisper something about 'this modern stuff'. The Colonel struck three matches over his cigar. The Dean jingled money in his pocket. Canon Auty searched in his beard. Mrs Cutler yawned very loudly.

When we had finished there was a chilly silence. Presently the Dean said, 'Very nice. Perhaps a little beyond me.'

The Archdeacon said, 'A little too advanced for us, eh, Mr Dean?'

Miss Linkinghorne said, 'One would need to hear it several times, of course.'

The Colonel said, 'I like tunes, myself.'

Mrs Auty said, 'Funny stuff, wasn't it, Edward?'

Canon Auty said, 'It was certainly very well *played*.'

Mrs Cutler, who at least was honest, said, 'I seem to have heard it before somewhere.'

Suddenly Lady Hargreaves, who all this time had said not a word, rose from her chair, tottered weakly into the little parlour without the use of her sticks, and slammed the double doors upon us all.

*   *   *

Panic seized me. Suppose she had a stroke and suddenly passed out? The thought was too awful.

I didn't care a damn now about anything except her. Connie Hargreaves, my creation, was in that room, perhaps suffering, perhaps at the point of death.

Rushing to the parlour, I hurled open the doors. Austen was striding across the room towards me. I heard the Dean's angry voice:

'Huntley, stop! Come back!'

Rage seized me; a burning sense of the truth possessed me. With my back to the doors I turned and faced them all, the people who would never *believe*.

'You go to hell!' I cried. 'Yes - you, Mr Dean - and all of you. She's mine - *mine*! She wants *me*. She doesn't want any of you. You've - '

Austen took hold of my arm and tried to swing me away from the door.

'Father!' I screamed. 'Help me with this brute. Help!'

Suddenly Lady Hargreaves cried out from the parlour.

'How dare you, Austen! *How* dare you! Norman, come to me. Austen, show them all out - at once. I abominate - ' Her voice broke; she could not finish her sentence.

I ran in. She was half lying on a sofa, her head buried in cushions, her voice choked with sobs. It simply tore my heart out. Oh, yes, call me a hypocrite! Tell me that I'd planned to get rid of her and altogether been unmercifully cruel to her. But I tell you, seeing her there like that simply tore my heart out.

I fell down on my knees beside the sofa.

'Dear Miss Hargreaves - Oh, Miss Hargreaves - Connie, dear - don't cry, please don't cry. I can't bear you to be unhappy.'

Her hand fell and clutched mine. 'Norman - Norman,' she whispered.

'What's the matter? Tell me. Please. I'm your *real* friend.'

'Oh, I know - I *know*! That is why I am so unhappy. I realized it suddenly, during your father's beautiful music - all those stupid, stupid people - only applauding your father's music because they thought it was by me. I am so tired. Call your father - I want him - I want you both. I have been unkind, so very unkind. How will you ever forgive me?'

The Dean was standing in the doorway; in a whispering group behind him, the other guests.

'We must send for a doctor at once.' The Dean stepped forward. 'Huntley, you are doing no good here. Leave us.'

'It's you who have upset her,' I said. 'You and all your gang. Go away all of you!'

'Monstrous impertinence!' snapped the Dean.

'Away! Away!' screamed Lady Hargreaves with amazing venom. 'Out of my house - all of you! Yes, you too, Dean! Away! Away!' She fell back again, exhausted.

Father pushed his way through the others and came in.

'Air!' he cried. 'Give her air! What you want is anodyne. You want anodyne in a case like this. And cotton-wool. Norman, get some cotton-wool. She'll be all right. Cousin

Terence went off like this - cotton-wool and anodyne and in five minutes he was cycling home fit as a fiddle.'

The Dean had backed away almost nervously. Outside I could hear the impatient tooting of a motor-horn; I went to the window and looked out. Over the other side of the road I could see the lights of Henry's car. I went to the doors and closed them deliberately on the bewildered guests.

Lady Hargreaves sat very still on the sofa, looking before her into space, as though she saw something we couldn't see. Her lips moved; I heard her muttering something.

'A joke. He told me once - I am only a - joke - '

Nobody said anything. Father shook his head and looked at me significantly. The front door closed and the house was silent.

*   *   *

'Give her a glass of wine, Norman,' said father presently.

I offered her some claret. She smiled, but refused it. 'Thank you. Thank you. But - no. Mr Huntley, take some wine yourself, I beg you. And you, Norman.'

She rose in a valiant attempt to fill our glasses. But she could not manage to walk far without her sticks.

'You sit down now,' said father. He took her arm, helped her back to the sofa while I arranged cushions behind her. 'Might as well be comfortable,' said father, returning to the claret.

'My dear, dear friends,' she said. 'I have treated you so badly. Can you set it down to this detestable title? I do not know how I came by it; I never asked for it and I feel it was not meant for me. I am no aristocrat. I belong to no class.'

'You know,' said father, his hand on the decanter, 'on the District Railway they used to have *four* classes. Extraordinary!'

'Oh, Cornelius!' She smiled affectionately at him. 'You must let me call you by your first name - '

'Anything you like. Got three Christian names, but never use them nowadays.'

'Cornelius, how I love your drollery! I sometimes think you understand me better than anybody - except, of course, Norman. No one can understand me as Norman does. And now - he sees me for what I really am: a lonely old woman who - '

'Oh, don't!' I muttered. 'Don't!'

Outside, Henry's motor-horn tooted again. The clocks struck ten-fifteen. In an agony of uncertainty I walked to the window, then back to the centre of the room.

'Yes, a lonely old woman,' she went on, 'who broke beyond the bounds prescribed for her by - her maker.' She paused and looked at me. I *knew* then that she knew; I knew, too, that it could never be mentioned openly between us.

'I have no friends,' she said, 'no friends except Norman - and you, Cornelius. And - there is somebody else. Another friend - a young man - a friend of yours, Norman. I cannot quite remember.'

'You mean' - I looked at her - 'Henry Beddow?'

'Yes. Henry Beddow. He, too, understands me - understands something of my terrible limitations.'

I had a sudden idea. 'Father,' I whispered, 'look after her for a minute.'

I ran out and went to the door; down the drive I saw Henry's car. 'Henry!' I called. 'Henry!'

I ran to the car.

'You're late,' he said. 'Don't say you've changed your mind now.'

'No. We must see it through. But - it may be the last time, Henry. I want you to come in. I can't - ' I couldn't speak.

'Do you know,' said Henry, getting out of the car. 'I wanted to come in.'

Slowly we returned to the house.

*　　*　　*

As we came into the room, she looked up, smiled, and rose, walking towards us on father's arm.

'Henry!' she murmured. '*Dear* Henry!'

We all three stood silently looking at her, smiling, unable to find a word to say.

'Oh, my friends!' she cried suddenly. 'Can you believe - will you ever believe - in spite of my unkindness to you recently - that I cannot exist without your friendship - I might almost say, without your co-operation?'

'We know that,' muttered Henry thickly.

'You mustn't rely on Norman,' warned father.

She clasped her hands before her and a strange, far-away light came into her eyes. 'Can I see,' she cried, 'a future stretching away for us? Away! Away - somewhere! How weary I am of this Cathedral society! Sometimes I pine for the open country - for a caravan, a donkey, the benison of friends. The world is so dull. Could not we four polish up the tarnished armour of life and make it glow again? We four - on some far-off horizon where sunward floats the gull? My friends, my friends! Life, if we choose it to be so, lies in the hollow of our hands!'

Father poured himself a second glass of claret and thoughtfully examined the palms of his hands.

'Never again,' she cried, with a burst of old energy, flinging out her arms, then clutching to the sofa for support, 'never again must we four be parted! Never! Our fate - yours too, Cornelius - for, in some way I know not, you are truly one of *us* - '

'That's right,' said father. 'Blame me.'

'Our fates are intertwined,' she said. 'I feel as close to you as - the mistletoe to the oak.'

'Remarkable stuff, mistletoe,' observed father. 'Ever tell you how my Uncle Arly found some growing in an old horseshoe that used to hang over the place where he shaved every morning? Well, really extraordinary - he took that shoe, see? And shod his mare with it - horse called Sorrel it was, and - '

'Father - stop!' I cried. I couldn't bear his talking.

'Sorry,' he said. He really looked hurt.

'Do not stop him,' murmured Lady Hargreaves. 'Never stop him. He must never be stopped.'

I knew I must say something.

'Miss Hargreaves - ' I went closer to her.

'Yes, dear?'

'Connie, I - '

'Yes, dear? What do you require of me? What do you - both require of me?'

'I - I - ' I struggled for words. Never had I so hated myself; never had I so loved her. But she had said she felt as close to us as the mistletoe to the oak. It was too close.

'Norman,' groaned old Henry. He was sweating. 'We can't do it. We - '

'We *can*,' I muttered. I turned again to Miss Hargreaves. 'We're going - away,' I said slowly.

'Away?' Disappointment, fear, clouded her face.

'For a few days. To - Ireland.'

She said nothing. She only looked at me in a long searching gaze which I could not bear to interpret.

'To - Lusk,' I whispered.

'Yes?' she said. 'Yes?' I could barely hear her.

When I could bring myself to look at her I saw there were tears in her eyes. For what seemed a long time we stood there looking at each other, saying nothing. Then she came forward and took both my hands in hers. I knew what had passed in her mind; I knew she had been tempted to make a last stand for her existence.

'Listen.' She spoke to us all. 'Let it be said. I am not - as other people.' She stood in the centre of the room, all three of us gathered round her as though we feared she would collapse. 'For a little while,' she went on, 'I broke into a life which I was never intended to lead. But now - I know what I am. " . . . a thought, a piece of thistledown, a thing of naught, rocked in the cradle of a craftsman's story . . . " Yes. When I read those lines, I remembered - what I was.' She paused. Then. 'Come! It grows late. I am tired. But before you go - oh, I am so very tired! - I want to play you one of my dear Irish airs.'

Slowly we moved to the doors. Stopping for a moment, she laid her hand on Henry's shoulder and smiled at him. 'I did not get to know you well enough,' she said. 'But perhaps there may yet be time. I do not know.'

We all three went into the drawing-room. Sitting on a little stool, she drew her fingers across the strings of her harp. Very slowly and lingeringly she played 'Over the sea to Skye'.

When she had finished, nobody spoke. She walked with us to the door, wrapping a silk shawl round her shoulders. There was a hint of frost. As we opened the door the Cathedral clock chimed the half-hour.

Father coughed. 'Well, sorry we never played your piece, Miss Hargreaves; must do it - another time. Good-bye. Like your cotoneaster here.'

'Good-bye,' said Henry.

'Good-bye,' I said. For a moment I held her hand.

'I have - enjoyed it all, so much,' she said.

We went down the drive. I stopped at the gate and waved. Faint in the misty air, I saw her waving back.

I ran across the road and leapt into Henry's car.

'Quick!' I muttered. 'For God's sake, drive quickly!'

FAR behind us stretched the long road from Dungannon. We tramped on silently through the rain. Lusk had not changed. The chopper still lay in the butcher's window; the oak tree still stood in the middle of the road, its last tattered leaves moping to the ground.

We stopped by the church gate and tried to dry ourselves on our handkerchiefs. We were silent, horribly aware that the moment had come. We still did not know what we were going to do. The wind howled round us; clouds massed, dark and heavy, against a sky already sunless. I opened my mouth to speak; I closed it again. My mind was a blank. I groaned. Had we come all this way for nothing? Should we return to Cornford to find her still there - and could I be sorry if we did? Which was more bearable? I did not know.

Suddenly, Henry caught my arm and looked at me. I couldn't understand his expression. Neither, for the moment, could I understand what he meant when he said in a queer, strained voice:

'Might as well' - and here he paused as though in search of the right words - 'take a look at Lusk church, don't you think?'

What did he mean? Why did he speak in that unnatural way? I stared at him, knowing dimly that he expected a particular answer from me; that he was playing a game which demanded an accomplice - like the game *I* had played here eleven weeks ago when I had demanded his support.

'There might be,' he said slowly, still holding my arm and digging his fingers tightly into it, 'some old brasses worth looking at.'

Immediately, in a flood of understanding, I knew what he was doing. For a moment all thought of Miss Hargreaves slipped from my mind as I said, with an almost sinister promptitude:

'I hate brasses.'

I thought I heard him sigh, as though with relief that I had found my cue. Releasing my arm he said in a tone deliberately casual:

'Well, we can shelter from the rain, anyhow. Come on.'

I followed him up the path. My mind went whirling back through the year; from November to October - from winter to autumn - from autumn to dying summer - to the evening when we had first walked up this path. Vividly the memorable occasion came back to me, the actual words of our conversation becoming clearer and more accurate in my mind. I knew what Henry must say; knew what I must say. Something had inspired him to utter the same words he had spoken that August evening; the words that were responsible for our going into the church; the words that were responsible for -

This was the formula we had wanted, I saw in a flash. And, as in August, Henry had, on an impulse, dragged me into this place, so now, in November, on another impulse, he must do the same. All that we had said then must, as closely as possible, correspond with what we said now. *For how long?* At what precise point must the repetition be varied? At what precise point must the recapitulation find its coda?

I suddenly realized that Henry was rattling the door of the church. As before, it was locked.

'Thank God for that!' I exclaimed, remembering my lines as an actor does when he sees a familiar bit of business on the stage. 'Let's get back to Dungannon and have a last binge at the hotel. I detest Lusk.'

'I'm going to get the key,' said Henry.

But - I was still asking myself - at what point must we steer another course? All depended on that.

Suddenly, I knew. The lectern. The vital words, the three vital words, that, this time, *must not be spoken.*

'It isn't your church,' I said quickly. 'It's Ireland's, it says so on the board.'

'It's everybody's church,' maintained Henry. 'I'm going to find the sexton.'

We were in the porch, sheets of rain blinding the view from us. Violently I struggled to assemble and control my thoughts. It was not, I knew, speech alone that must correspond; it was thought as well. What had my thoughts been that August evening? I had been depressed; I had been annoyed with Henry; I had been almost hauntedly reluctant to go into the church.

'Oh, come on, Henry!' I snarled. 'We don't want to go into this horrible church.'

The sexton (thank God!) was running up the path, a cape over his head. Henry went up to him quickly.

'My friend,' he said grimly, 'is very interested in old churches.'

'Holy God!' cried the sexton. 'On a day like this?'

Here was an unexpected variation. Suppose he wouldn't let us in? Suppose his summer enthusiasm for Mr Archer had waned? Suppose he recognized us?

None of these things happened. Even a vile November afternoon could not cool the one passion of the sexton's life: the beauty of Lusk church.

He produced the key. With almost the same energy as before he unlocked the door, threw himself upon an inner door, dragged aside the curtains and bade us to enter.

'A very fine old church,' he reminded us. 'Built in 1863.'

We followed him. As before, an empty, hollow feeling rose in me. The building was almost in darkness. The pews rose like loose-boxes round us. Pulpit and lectern crouched under their dust-sheets, the same sheets but more dusty.

I sat down. A great weakness was overcoming me. I felt I should not be able to go through with it any longer. The sexton was walking towards the draped lectern, Henry following him, glancing back nervously at me over his shoulder.

'You will please to observe the beautiful lettering on the Choir walls. "I saw the Lord . . ."'

Knowing I must go, I rose and dragged myself up towards the Choir. Henry whispered to me, 'My God! This place is awful!'

The words struck an old chord; struck the melancholy chord out of which I had before developed the theme of the past weeks. My thoughts raced back to August; November was forgotten. I re-experienced the same terrible dreariness of spirit, the same overpowering desire to make the day a memorable one.

I gripped the pew; I closed my eyes.

'Now, I wish you to observe our beautiful lectern.' I could hear the slipping aside of the dust-sheet.

'Unique!' I forced out the word required.

'Remarkable!' echoed Henry.

'Magnificent!'

'Bloody!'

'In a class by itself,' I muttered hurriedly. Hadn't he said 'filthy' before?

'Ah, it is indeed beautiful work!' exclaimed the sexton. 'Given by our people in memory of - '

My heart was beating wildly, my head whirling. Past and present surged together in my mind. Suppose, November tempted me, I were to say again those three vital words? What would happen?

' - in memory of - '

('Create! Create!' said August. 'Destroy! Destroy!' said November.)

' - our late very beloved pastor, Mr Archer.'

The words were burning on my lips; the fatal words that had sent me dizzily on to the topmost peak of the Spur. On my lips, trembling on my tongue, the words, 'Dear Mr Archer!' My mouth was open; my mind was flooded by a sudden vision of an old lady stumbling along a close, dark, narrow plankway - like a tunnel - a place that I knew well but could not then give a name to. Stumbling along, limping with her sticks, crying somebody's name, alone in the darkness - crying a name. And, while I struggled to hold back the words, 'Dear Mr Archer!' - and while that old lady cried my name aloud in her darkness - 'Norman - Norman - Norman - ' the calm, level, almost cold voice of Henry sounded from another world:

'Was the Vicar here for very long?'

My three perilous words fell back into me, slain by Henry's weapon of the commonplace. Immediately, where there had been that old lady was now only a greenish darkness, broken faintly by a dusty light from some great windows. Her voice died away, far away, echoing deep and long into space, vibrant at first, then thinner; fainter, the 'n' like a note struck from a taut string. The silence that was not silence fell round us.

I opened my eyes. I caught Henry's eyes. Very slowly he nodded; so did I. The wind, that had been roaring round the roof, suddenly stopped. Henry and I lowered our heads as if by mutual understanding. We both knew that she had gone from us.

*   *   *

As we walked back to Dungannon in the rain, the darkness of evening falling over us, the chill of winter in our bones, I said to Henry after a long silence:

'Why did you stay behind in the churchyard, Henry?'

I had gone on quickly ahead the moment we had left the church. But Henry had stayed for some minutes.

'I looked - at all the graves,' he said.

'Surely that wasn't necessary?'

'No. It wasn't necessary. Her name was nowhere to be found.'

Neither was her place, I told myself. And suddenly I remembered that to-day was All Souls' Day.

*   *   *

I could not return to Cornford as I had intended. Three days later a letter and a *Cornford Mercury* arrived from my father. This is what the letter said:

'I shouldn't come back yet awhile, boy. Read the paper and you'll see why. People are suspicious of you. Mother keeps fussing, but I can keep her down. Stay where you are for a few weeks. Money enclosed. Told you not to do it, boy; here to-morrow, gone to-day, that's what I say. Wouldn't surprise me if I disappeared at this very moment. What comes first? Figure one, or figure nought? Told you not to do it. By the way, wasn't Tennyson. Poet called Walke wrote those words. People like you and me have got to be careful.

'Ever your loving FATHER.

'PS. - Lessways is gloomy. Miss the harp.'

I searched for the money father had mentioned, but I couldn't find any. Then I fingered the paper nervously. Finally I braced myself to read it.

'Scotland Yard is investigating the extraordinary mystery which surrounds the disappearance of Lady Hargreaves, etc. etc. On Wednesday afternoon, November the 2nd, she left her house and was driven by her chauffeur to the Cathedral. As she entered, Mr Josiah Meakins, the Dean's verger, was showing round a party, then about to proceed up to the nave roof, traverse the whole length of the building and descend by means of the stairway to the Lady Chapel.

'Lady Hargreaves expressed her desire to join them. The party went slowly along the narrow little plankway between the inner and the outer nave roofs, walking in single file, and it was not until they came down to the Lady Chapel that her absence was remarked upon. Mr Meakins went back immediately, but finding no trace of her, he came down, summoned the other vergers and organized a thorough search of the nave roof, bell chambers, triforiums, galleries, tower and - indeed - the entire Cathedral. Meanwhile, the chauffeur drove back to Lessways to see if she might have returned on foot. She had not done so. The search in the Cathedral yielded no sort of evidence and we understand that subsequent searches have proved equally fruitless.

'The police take a somewhat serious view of the matter, but were bound to admit that they have no evidence whatsoever that could point to the possibility of foul play . . . '

In the nave roof - alone - crying 'Norman - Norman - Norman!' And I - in Lusk church - with all my power denying her existence. Even the realization that destructive thought had at last destroyed could not lighten my wretchedness.

*　　*　　*

For many weeks I could not bring myself to go back. Staying alone at Dungannon (I did not revisit Lusk), I wrote most of what you have now read. One day, near Christmas, a letter came from Marjorie which made me realize that somehow life had to be resumed.

'Norman dear [she said], please do come back. Terrible things are being said about you. I can't bear it because I know they can't be true. If you stay away everybody will say you have killed her, even when they can't find the body. I'm sure you wouldn't do that, whatever you would do. Henry has told me everything and I'm simply forcing myself to believe it. Darling, you must come back and face it. I'll help you. I'm sorry we quarrelled. I think you're wonderful, really.'

It touched me. I knew I should have to go. With an aching heart, dreading to face all the talk, I took the boat for Heysham.

I remember moodily gazing at a lot of cows being lowered into the hold and marvelling at their patience. I walked along the deck, attracted by the figure of a nun leaning over the rail and looking at the lights of Belfast. There was something soothing about her quiet, pensive figure, so detached from all the bustle of the ship getting under way.

'Belfast looks lovely at night, doesn't it?' I said to her.

'Ah, it is always lovely to me,' she murmured. 'It was my home. It is twenty years since last I was there.'

'Twenty years! Well!' I did not know what to say. 'But time is nothing,' I added. 'Twenty years might be twenty minutes, really.' And, I was thinking, twelve weeks might be twelve years.

From below, down in one of the saloons, a drunken sailor with a voice that made me grate my teeth started to sing 'Over the sea to Skye'. I sighed heavily, leaning over the rail, far up in the stern of the boat, and looking at the black sea. The engines started; Ireland was sliding away from us; something, for ever, sliding away from me.

For ever?

I murmured her name into the dark sea.

'Miss Hargreaves - Miss Hargreaves - '

Could I hear my own name, or was it only the sighing of the wind?

Again I called.

'Miss Hargreaves - Miss Hargreaves - '

Mevagissey 1939
La Chaise 1940

POSTSCRIPT

MUCH water has passed under the bridge, or down the weirs, or wherever it is water flows in the proverb, since, nearly thirty years ago, I closed my account of the most extraordinary thing that ever happened to me, or (perhaps it could be put this way) the most extraordinary thing I ever happened to. For all I know, Constance might have gone with it, though water, they say, finds its own level, and that is one of the few things Constance never tried to find. However that may be, from the moment when my father, Henry and I said good-bye to her after her party at Lessways we have never seen her again. 'I have enjoyed it all so much.' Those were her last words to us.

Yet there have been more than hints in the passing years that she has never travelled far away from us. For example: when I was married in Cornford Cathedral Dr Carless, who was to have played the Wedding March for us (Mendelssohn, not Wagner), said that he was driven out of the loft by a kind of a warm blast, and that he saw the keys depressed, and saw the stops shoot out, as the Wedding March sounded. (And who will forget with what brilliant timing the tubas were coupled on that occasion!) Then there is my father, Cornelius (who still runs his bookshop in Cornford); many times, he says, he has been aware of a disturbance of the dust on the books in his 'specials' case, where he keeps his Tennyson 'firsts', and other treasures. And then there was the mystery of the 'Bundle': although we had some run off by a local printer and gave most of them away, the original copy was shot 'like an arrow into the air' falling to earth 'I know not where'. In short, it was pinched; and who is to say the Author didn't pinch it? Fortunately, I still had the typed copy which I made from the original; and I cannot end a latter-day edition of a book which has wandered around the globe a good bit since its first publication, without giving some of the verses in full. Lines from some are quoted in the preceding pages (and some misquoted, due to my carelessness); but there are some which are only hinted at, and not included in the text.

And as to these hints of Constance's continued existence - there is also my wife, Marjorie, who swears to this day that our oldest son, Peregrine, has often been heard talking to Constance over the telephone at the Ministry of Dis-establishment, where he has an office. In Cornford Cathedral the shadow of a tall hat has from time to time been seen in the bishop's throne, falling across the pages of the great Prayer Book on its dark blue velvet cushion. Much of the City itself - which I seldom visit nowadays - would be unfamiliar and perhaps not pleasing to Constance: a supermarket where once the old Butter Cross stood (with the Butter Cross itself enshrined in a hideous courtyard within the place); an abominable hotel eaves-dropping right by the north-east corner of the Cathedral; Canticle Alley all offices; 'Lessways' part of the new Town Hall - one would hardly know the place if it weren't for the Cathedral which, fortunately, 'they' dare not touch. What would Constance make of the place now? Even though she might dislike much of it, I have the feeling that she would still be at home there, because although she always celebrated the past she was also essentially a part of the present. I would give very much to see her in command of play in the new skittle-alley, which is built on the site of the old flea-pit cinema. Or bidding her chauffeur drive contrariwise in the oneway traffic of the High Street.

This is not the place for me to say anything about myself - where I live and work - nor what I work at. Suffice it, that it took me a long time to 'settle down' (to use a phrase my dear Mother used); and that now, sometimes, of an evening, when it is quiet about the house, I hear a harp playing 'Over the sea to Skye', and I know there are certain harmonies which can never be lost.

So I leave Constance Hargreaves, not behind, but beside me.

And on those words, I will close, once and for all (knowing that if I go on it will continue, as they say in my village in the West); I will close, leaving the Reader with some of Constance's own thoughts about life, as expressed in 'Wayside Bundle'.

Norman Huntley
July, 1965.

THE LAY OF THE LAST CRICKET

Cleft in the narrow gulf of gusty grief
My soul is like a cricket on a leaf,
Who peering down amongst the autumn grasses
Peevishly wonders where he left his glasses.

Old is the cricket; lame; he cannot hop
As once he did in Old King Willow's shop.
There, often, on the Hearth the Cloister sat,
Young crickets gathered round him on the mat.
Happy the Hearth - the Hearth of his beginnings,
Where first he played his modest maiden innings!

Old is the cricket; blind; he cannot see
That X Y Z must follow A B C.
Old, with a slow, rheumatic, autumn clicking -
Voice harsh, green armour tarnished, knee-joints sticking.
Old, too, the crinkled leaf of sycamore
Where mourns his wife, knowing he'll never kick her more.

He sighs, he sobs, his tear-drops fall to grass,
And over them the mists of autumn pass.
Now, through the falling apple-rusty sun
He sees dead years, and knows that laurels won
On Willow's Hearth can nevermore be flaunted.
What use the chaplet on a brow so haunted?

My soul is like a cricket on a leaf,
Cleft in the narrow gulf of gusty grief.

A SMALL THING

(Written on some tower, I cannot remember where)

I came, I go, I breathe, I move, I sleep,
I talk, I eat, I drink, I laugh, I weep,
I sing, I dance, I think, I dream, I see,
I fear, I love, I hate, I plot, I be.
        And yet -
        And yet -
I sometimes feel that I am but a thought,
A piece of thistledown, a thing of naught;
Rocked in the cradle of a craftsman's story
And destined not for high Angelic glory.
And yet -
And yet -
I came, I go, I breathe, I move, I sleep,
I talk, I eat, I drink, I laugh, I weep . . .

THE FERRY

What various hindrances we meet
  Before we cross the Bar!
The path is choked with weeds, the weeds
  Most fascinating are.
We linger in the undergrowth,
  We loiter 'midst the sedges;
Full many a country lane conceals
  Poison in its hedges.
We pick up this, we pick up that,
When given tit, we offer tat,
Till suddenly we find we're at
  The dark and dismal Ferry.
Though to step forward we are loth
  The past we have to bury.
    Reluctant as we are
    We have to cross the Bar.

EVENSONG IN ADVENT

Lo, He comes with clouds descending . . .
Helmsley rings its clarion call!
In the Close the elms are bending
'Neath the wild December squall.
Candles in the Choir-stalls flicker,
Aisles are dark and nave is dim,
Where some lonely country Vicar
Listens to his favourite hymn.

Hark, a thrilling voice is sounding . . .
(Zion waits to greet the Star).
Mr Dean in tone astounding
Wrecks the anthem bar by bar.
Next to him a mild Archdeacon
(Eighty-three, completely deaf),
Wishes he were not so weak on
Reading in the alto clef.

These are days to be remembered,
(Purcell, in the Lord rejoice!)
When the year is being Decembered,
(Wisdom, answer Doctor Boyce!)
When the wind in transept cries,
And Thomas bears the shortest day,
Warm the heart who knows that sighs
And sorrowings shall flee away.

A FRIEND FOR TEA

'Muffins for tea!' he used to cry,
    And fall into my chair.
Above the soda-cake, tobacco
    Smoke lay on the air.
Exhausted after Evening Prayer
He'd play himself at Solitaire,
Toy vaguely with his third éclair -
    Happy young hostess I!

Now when I light my lamp and drain
    My cup beside the fire,
I see the ghost of him I lack. Oh
    Memory retire!
Muffins for tea ... My thoughts conspire
To conjure up King's College Choir
And happy days in Cambridgeshire
    That will not come again.

SONNET TO MY BATH

Belovéd Bath, wherein my tiréd feet
Have oft-time plunged before the peaceful hour
When sleep descends, within you blooms the flower
Of rosy youth. Across the years I greet
Him who to me bequeath'd thee. Ever plastic,
His figure to thy cracked enamel clings.
I see him now, a bariton at King's,
A little sharp, but so enthusiastic!

Belovéd Bath, when my last sleep shall claim me,
You will remain, a silent witness to
The foolish things that Undergradu'tes do.
And though the word might judge, you will not blame me.
You will remember and you will not speak
The lines he wrote in you to me in Greek.

DOCTOR PEPUSCH

Doctor P, my cockatoo
Despises birds who bill and coo.
Long he's set his heart upon a
Duet with a prima-donna.
Some composers he dislikes,
Such as Grieg and Doctor Dykes.
Very fond is he of Handel.
Sometimes from the Bechstein grand'll
Float a hollow laugh from Carmen.
(Once he tried the Dresden Amen . . .)

What a bird! O what a bird!
Once in May I swear I heard
Fragments from die Fledermaus
Ringing wildly through the house.
'Over the hills and far away'
Is, of course, his favourite lay;
This he sings with perfect ease,
Con brio, and in many keys.
'Rallentando! Rallentando!'
Once I cried, when Elgar's 'Land o'
Hope and Glory' he was singing,
Quavers into crotchets flinging.
I taught him all the simpler airs —
'It is enough . . . 'A chant by Nares;
'Comfort ye . . .' and 'Daisy, Daisy . . .'
A Gloria by Pergolesi.

Doctor Pepusch most detests
The ignorant, facetious pests
Who call him 'Pretty Polly'. Once
He nipped a Rural Dean from Hunts

Who thus addressed him. (Cockatoos'
Contempt for parrots never lose).
Green he is; and underneath
Shades of pumice, puce and heath.
Black his bill and blue his crest,
Splendid creature, grandly dressed!

Doctor P! Doctor P!
How you worked for your degree!
Sleep now, birdie; done the day . . .
'Over the hills and far away . . . '
There beyond the last horizon
One day you shall feast your eyes on
Groves of orange, where the beams
Of sun exotic flush the streams.
Only you could ever cope
With Yellowshank and Phalarope,
With Hoopoe, Knot and Sanderling,
And other fowls that cannot sing.
Yes, dear birdie, you shall be
Choirmaster to the company
Of all the birds on every tree -
Doctor P! Doctor P!

TRIOLET: EARLY TO ELY

Constantia, he called me in those days -
The far-off days when friendship flower'd freely,
Unchoked by weeds. The name in memory stays . . .
Constantia. He called me in those days
When wonder filled our hearts with songs of praise
To rise at dawn and bicycle to Ely.
Constantia, he called me in those days
The far-off days when friendship flower'd freely.

The Bloomsbury Group: a new library of books from
the early twentieth-century

ALSO AVAILABLE IN THE SERIES

WOLF MANKOWITZ

A KID FOR TWO FARTHINGS

A six-year-old boy in the British immigrant community of Whitechapel believes he
has discovered a unicorn for sale at the market. Though it looks to most people
like a white goat with a bump on its head, young Joe is certain it will make the
dreams of his friends and neighbors come true—a reunion with his father in Africa,
a steam press for a tailor shop, a ring for a girlfriend. Others may be skeptical of the
unicorn's magic, but with enough effort, Joe believes he can make it all real.

*

"Wolf Mankowitz possesed the now largely vanished gift of being able to write
about romance and sentiment without being ever sentimental."
—DENNIS NORDEN

"A small miracle. He writes of the teeming streets round the Whitechapel Road
with such glowing warmth and love that they come triumphantly alive. Wolf
Mankowitz, you are not a star. You are a planet."
—*DAILY EXPRESS* (UK)

*

ISBN: 978-1-60819-048-5 · PAPERBACK · U.S. $14.00

BLOOMSBURY

The History of Bloomsbury Publishing

Bloomsbury Publishing was founded in 1986 to publish books of excellence and originality. Its authors include Margaret Atwood, John Berger, William Boyd, David Guterson, Khaled Hosseini, John Irving, Anne Michaels, Michael Ondaatje, J.K. Rowling, Donna Tartt and Barbara Trapido. Its logo is Diana, the Roman Goddess of Hunting.

In 1994 Bloomsbury floated on the London Stock Exchange and added both a paperback and a children's list. Bloomsbury is based in Soho Square in London and expanded to New York in 1998 and Berlin in 2003. In 2000 Bloomsbury acquired A&C Black and now publishes *Who's Who*, *Whitaker's Almanack*, *Wisden Cricketers' Almanack* and the *Writers' & Artists' Yearbook*. Many books, bestsellers and literary awards later, Bloomsbury is one of the world's leading independent publishing houses.

Launched in 2009, The Bloomsbury Group continues the company's tradition of publishing books with perennial, word-of-mouth appeal. This series celebrates lost classics written by both men and women from the early twentieth century, books recommended by readers for readers. Literary bloggers, authors, friends and colleagues have shared their suggestions of cherished books worthy of revival. To send in your recommendation, please write to:

The Bloomsbury Group
Bloomsbury USA
175 Fifth Ave
New York, NY 10010
Or e-mail: info@bloomsburyusa.com

For more information on all titles in The Bloomsbury Group series and to submit your recommendations online please visit www.bloomsbury.com/thebloomsburygroup

For more information on all Bloomsbury authors and for all the latest news please visit www.bloomsburyusa.com